PECULIAR PRIVILEGE

The Field is a most agreeable coffee-house, and there is more real society to be met with there than in any other situation of life. It links all classes together, from the Peer to the Peasant. It is the Englishman's peculiar privilege. It is not to be found in any other part of the globe, but in England's true land of liberty – and may it flourish to the end of time!!

John Hawkes, *The Meynellian Science*, 1808

PECULIAR PRIVILEGE

A Social History of English Foxhunting, 1753–1885

DAVID C. ITZKOWITZ

Emeritus Professor of History, Macalester College, Saint Paul, Minnesota

EER
Edward Everett Root Publishers. Brighton. 2016.

EER

Edward Everett Root, Publishers, Co. Ltd.,
30 New Road, Brighton, Sussex, BN1 1BN, England.
www.eerpublishing.com

edwardeverettroot@yahoo.co.uk

David C. Itzkowitz
Peculiar Privilege
A Social History of English Foxhunting, 1753-1885

Classics in Social and Economic History Series, no.5.

First published in Great Britain 1977. This edition first published, with new Introduction by the author, 2016.

ISBN 978-1-911204-27-5 Paperback.
ISBN 978-1-911204-28-2 Hardback.

© David C. Itzkowitz 1977, 2016.

David C. Itzkowitz has asserted his right to be identified as the author of this Work in accordance with the Copyright, Designs and Patents Act 1998 as the owner of this work.

All rights reserved. No part of this publication may be reproduced, stored in a retrieval system or transmitted, in any form or by any means, electronic, mechanical, photocopying, recording or otherwise, without the prior permission of the copyright owner.

Cover designed by Pageset Limited, High Wycombe, Buckinghamshire.
Printed in Great Britain by Lightning Source UK, Milton Keynes, UK.

Contents

Acknowledgements vii
Abbreviations. viii
New Introduction to 2016 Edition ix
Introduction to 1977 Edition 1

Part I: A Beginning

1 Hugo Meynell and Nimrod 6
2 Myth and Ideal 17

Part II: The View from Within

3 Hunting People Before the Railways. 31
4 The Railway Revolution 50
5 Hunt Countries. 67
6 Masters and Servants 81

Part III: The View from Without

7 Hunting and Rural Life 99
8 Foxhunters and Farmers. 113
9 The Opposition. 135

Part IV: An End

10 The Depression 152
Conclusion 176
A Short Glossary of Hunting Terms. 180
Selected Bibliography 182
Notes to text 198
Index 241

For K.S.I., L.E.I., and V.S.I.

Acknowledgements

I am indebted to many people for their assistance in the writing of this book.
 I would like to thank the Rt. Hon. The Earl St Aldwyn, K.B.E., T.D., Mr G. A. Cowen, Apperley Dene, Stocksfield, Northumberland, and the Masters and Committees of the Braes of Derwent, Burton, Cotley, Hampshire, Heythrop, New Forest, North Cotswold, and Taunton Vale Hunts for the permission to examine papers in their possession.
 Darley archives, reference ZDA (previous reference Dar 77) are deposited in the North Yorkshire County Record Office at Northallerton, and are quoted here by kind permission of the Trustees of the Darley estate and of G. W. Darley Esq. The Ridley MSS in the Northumberland County Record Office are quoted by kind permission of the Rt. Hon. Viscount Ridley T.D., D.L.
 I would especially like to thank Major J. F. Ballard, Middle Barton, Oxon; Mr G. A. Cowen, Apperley Dene, Stocksfield, Northumberland; Mrs P. DuPre, Minstead, Hants; Lt. Col. R. F. P. Eames, Cotley, Somerset; Mr P. R. H. Elliott, T. D., Ropley, Hants; Dr Robert Fountain, Lincoln; Mr M. A. McCanlis, Laverton, Broadway, Worcs.; and Major J. P. R. Power, Wellington, Somerset, for their kindness and hospitality while I was conducting my research.
 The staff of the British Museum, the New York Public Library and the Columbia University Libraries were uniformly helpful as were the staffs of the local record offices listed in the bibliography.

I would like to thank Mr C. W. Kellaway of the Institute for Historical Research, London for many professional and personal kindnesses.

Mr M. W. Farr kindly let me see a copy of his article, 'Sir Edward Littleton's Fox-Hunting Diary, 1774-89' prior to its publication in *Essays in Staffordshire History*. Brian Harrison and F. M. L. Thompson took the time to answer queries from an unknown American.

Several scholars have read early versions of the manuscript. For their comments and suggestions, I would like to thank Bernard Barber, L. L. Cornell, David Spring, and Trygve Tholfsen. Special debts of gratitude are due Stephen Koss and, most especially, R. K. Webb, whose extensive criticism contributed so much to whatever is of value in the pages that follow. I am, of course, responsible for whatever shortcomings remain.

Finally, I would like to thank my wife, Vicki Itzkowitz. She has participated in all stages of the making of this book from the early research to the preparation of the final manuscript. Without her, it, and I, would be much less.

Macalester College   D.C.I.
July 1976

Abbreviations used in Footnotes

Baily's Mag.	*Baily's Monthly Magazine of Sports and Pastimes, and Racing Register*
Bell's Life	*Bell's Life in London, and Sporting Chronicle*
DNB	*The Dictionary of National Biography*
Field	*The Field, or, Country Gentleman's Newspaper*
HMC	Historical Manuscripts Commission Reports
Sp. Mag.	*The Sporting Magazine: or Monthly Calendar of the Transactions of the Turf, the Chase and Every Other Diversion Interesting to the Man of Pleasure and Enterprize*
VCH	*Victoria County History*

New Introduction to the 2016 Edition

Every historian secretly hopes that his or her work will be so definitive that it will become the last word on the subject. That wish is always in vain. Still, it is striking that for a number of years following the publication of *Peculiar Privilege* and books by Raymond Carr and Roger Longrigg in the mid 1970s historians did not devote a great deal of attention to foxhunting. Perhaps that is because, although the three books differed in approach and detail, our basic conclusions were largely in agreement, and for a while, it seemed that there was little more to say.

This is not to say that the subject went entirely unnoticed. Historians of landscape and enclosure, for example, offered some new insights into the implications of hunting for the reshaping of the English landscape in the late eighteenth and early nineteenth century.[1] The new interest in cultural history that was emerging just as *Peculiar Privilege* was being published saw in foxhunting an opportunity to explore such topics as the cultural construction of gender and the deep meaning of the relationship between humans and animals.[2] And in a pair of articles, Iris Middleton took me to task for ignoring the early history of foxhunting, pointing out that foxes had been the quarry of English sportsmen at a much earlier date than I had assumed.[3] Jane Ridley and Emma Griffin, the authors of the two most recent histories of foxhunting, have also argued in favor of an earlier date for the transformation of hunting than I do.[4] They may be right, but whether the advances in hound breeding and the changes in technique that remade hunting in the early nineteenth century were solely, partially, or not at all the work of Hugo Meynell is ultimately not particularly relevant to my basic argument about the place of hunting, both symbolic and real, in English rural life and in English society more generally.

By the beginning of the nineteenth century, foxhunting, which had in the past been a sport of merely local interest, had come to be seen as a national institution, as an integral part of country society, and as a bond among neighbours, irrespective of their social class. Hunting was, therefore, looked upon as a conservative force, which, by binding landlord, tenant, and labourer together and giving them a sense of belonging to the same community, acted as a counterweight to the forces of radicalism, urbanization, and industrialization that threatened the stability of that community.

In the hunting field, the old England of squires and tenants, of mutual dependence and deference lived on unchanged, unmindful of the growth of cities and the establishment of new relationships. But, paradoxically, hunting was also seen as an entrée into that world for the newly rich urban foxhunters who could ride the new railways into the country to hunt. The agricultural depression of the 1880s challenged that vision. The society whose values hunting had mirrored was changing irrevocably, and hunting people had no choice but to follow suit.

Scholarly interest in hunting has now been revived, and the impetus for that revival was undoubtedly the new attack on the sport that culminated in the banning of hunting with dogs in 2004. Twentieth- and twenty-first-century attitudes toward hunting were, of course, not the subject of *Peculiar Privilege*, which ends with the coming of the agricultural depression of the 1880s, and it could be argued that they really should have no place in this introduction. But it is impossible to resist at least a short discussion on some aspects of the controversy surrounding the ban because so much of that controversy echoes aspects of the nineteenth-century discourse of hunting, though now in a new guise reflective of the culture and society of Britain in the late twentieth and early twenty-first century as opposed to the nineteenth.

Allyson May, who has written the best study of the controversy

New Introduction to the 2016 Edition

over hunting, argued that the opposition to hunting has largely been organized around two major issues, cruelty to animals and class. Between 1781 and 2004, the years covered by her study, she writes, "neither the class nor the cruelty concerns ever totally disappeared, but the relative importance accorded to one or the other would vary over time."[5] During the period covered by *Peculiar Privilege*, neither of these two concerns was able to mobilize sufficient support to pose any serious threat to hunting. I treat the reasons for this at some length over the course of this book but a few words may be in order here.

As I argued, foxhunters were more than just aware of the class implications of hunting. To the contrary, they constructed a vision of their sport that celebrated the openness of the hunting field to all classes and they explicitly contrasted hunting with shooting and angling, which they portrayed as the selfish and exclusionary pastimes of the upper class and of the wealthy. The extent to which that vision of hunting was accurate or not is irrelevant in this context; what is relevant is the fact that they managed to convince a large enough segment of the population of its truth. As a result, even those urban radicals who by the 1870s were beginning to concentrate their attack on the privilege of the great landowners and who often linked their attack on royal and aristocratic privilege with an attention to the treatment of animals chose, on the whole, to focus their attention on other field sports rather than on hunting.[6]

The great paradox of hunting, of course, was that it managed simultaneously to be seen as open to all and as the sport of the traditional upper classes. The very openness of the hunting field, even if it was never as open as foxhunters claimed, allowed urban middle-class foxhunters to see the hunting field as an entrée to the world of traditional landed society, which was one source of hunting's new popularity. As the *Guardian* journalist, George Monbiot, no friend to hunting, wrote in 2004 on the eve of the hunting ban, "the residual power of the landed class arises from other people's aspirations."[7] In the nineteenth century, that power was hardly residual, but the aspiration of "other people" to join that elite could already be seen and hunting was a path for them to do it.

Eighteenth- and nineteenth-century people were not insensitive to the issue of cruelty either. As early as 1785, the poet William Cowper had railed against the "detested sport/That owes its pleasure to another's pain."⁸ What is striking, however, is that, by and large, even those who were sensitive to the issue of cruelty, including many foxhunters, never considered foxhunting to be particularly cruel. In this belief they were strangely allied with George Monbiot, who wrote that "as an animal welfare issue, foxhunting comes in at about number 155," far below many worse crimes against animal welfare.⁹ It is notable that as late as 1958, the RSPCA considered foxhunting to be the least cruel method of controlling the population of foxes.¹⁰

To consider the questions of class and cruelty separately, however, seems to me to miss the point somewhat. It is the particular amalgam of the two that was to become so powerful in the late twentieth century and was, in the end, to doom hunting, at least in the form that had developed by the early nineteenth century.

Allyson May reminds us that perceptions of cruelty can be "shaped by and imbued with contemporary class prejudices."¹¹ Early nineteenth-century anti-cruelty activists, for example, were often convinced that the lower classes were, by nature, crueler and less sympathetic to the plight of animals than were their "betters," and thus focused their attention on working-class pastimes like dog-fighting and ratting. The conflation of class and cruelty could, of course, also be focused on the upper classes. In an article published in 2004, on urban radical attacks on monarchy and aristocracy, Antony Taylor writes that "for critics of the throne, the image of a barbarous and uncaring hunt was a distillation of the corruptions and privilege of royal life that proved corrosive of the liberties of the 'freeborn Englishman.'"¹² Although, in fact, the urban radicals that Taylor describes seemed, by his account, to be much more concerned with driven shooting and staghunting than with foxes, he has identified a key point. What was to make the attack on foxhunting so powerful was neither the contention that foxhunting was a symbol of the power of the upper classes nor the contention that it was a form of cruelty that could no longer be tolerated, but that both contentions could be conflated into one contention; it was that the two great sins of foxhunters were, in fact, one sin.

It is striking to note how quickly the tide seemed to turn against hunting. As late as 1986, *The Politics of Hunting*, a study by Richard H. Thomas, sought to discover why opponents of hunting were so unsuccessful in getting the sport banned despite the fact that polling revealed that by 1958, if not earlier, about half of those polled would support such a ban.[13] Four years later in 1990, Jane Ridley closed her history of hunting by commenting that the sport remained viable, in part because hunting supporters had managed to portray themselves as conservationists. "There are signs," she wrote, "that in the conservation-conscious 1990s the debate is going hunting's way.... By cloaking themselves in green, fox hunters may well have outwitted the antis—for now."[14] The reprieve lasted only another seven years.

In the first history of foxhunting to be published since the ban was enacted, Emma Griffin has, I think, perfectly captured what had changed since 1990. "The fuss," she wrote,

> "is not about animals, so much as it is about us. If we recall the anxiety that early nineteenth-century reformers expressed about bull-baiting and cockfighting the parallels between that campaign and that of our own time emerge clearly. That a society still heavily involved in the slave trade and lacking the most rudimentary legislation governing the employment of children in factories and mines should have focused its gaze on cocks and bulls appears inexplicable if it is not fully understood that the reformers were motivated by a concern about the people taking part and not the animals themselves. Nineteenth-century reformers were striving to create a more civilized, a more humane, a more enlightened society, and abolishing blood sports was a small but integral element of this project. At the end of the twentieth century, blood sports once more became the vocabulary for a public discussion about the society in which we wish to live—an opportunity to define Britishness for the new millennium."[15]

In *Peculiar Privilege* I tried to describe a vocabulary that served as part of a public discussion about a society in which people of the past wished to live—an opportunity to define Englishness (if not Britishness) for a past millennium. I hope the readers of today will still find that useful.

Saint Paul, Minnesota
May 2016

Notes

[1] See, for example, Jane Bevan, "Agricultural Change and the Development of Foxhunting in the Eighteenth Century," *Agricultural History Review*, Vol. 58, No. 1 (2010), pp. 49-75.

[2] See, for example, Keith Thomas, *Man and the Natural World*, Pantheon Books, New York, 1983; Harriet Ritvo, *The Animal Estate: The English and Other Creatures*, Harvard University Press, Cambridge, Mass, 1987; Rob Bodice, "Manliness and the 'Morality of Field Sports': E. A. Freeman and Anthony Trollope, 1869-71," *The Historian*, Vol. 70, No. 1, 2008, pp. 1-29.

[3] Iris Middleton, "Fox Hunting Traditions: Fact or Fantasy?" *Sport History Review*, 28 (1997), pp. 19-32 and "The Origins of English Fox Hunting and the Myth of Hugo Meynell and the Quorn," *Sport in History*, Vol. 25, No. 1 (2005), pp. 1-16.

[4] Jane Ridley, *Fox Hunting*, Collins, London, 1990; Emma Griffin, *Blood Sport: Hunting in Britain Since 1066*, Yale University Press, New Haven and London, 2007.

[5] Allyson N. May, *The Fox-Hunting Controversy, 1781-2004: Class and Cruelty*, Ashgate, Farnham, Surrey and Burlington, Vermont, 2013, p. 2.

[6] See Antony Taylor, "'Pig-Sticking Princes': Royal Hunting, Moral Outrage, and the Republican Opposition to Animal Abuse in Nineteenth- and Early Twentieth-Century Britain," History, Vol. 89, No. 1 (2004), pp. 30-48.

[7] Quoted in May, *Fox-Hunting Controversy*, p. 36.

[8] See below, p. 139.

[9] Quoted in May, *Fox-Hunting Controversy*, p. 150.

[10] Richard H. Thomas, *The Politics of Hunting*, Gower, Aldershot, Hants, 1983, p. 69.

[11] May, *Fox-Hunting Controversy*, p. 64.

[12] Taylor, "'Pig-Sticking Princes'," p. 31.

[13] Thomas, *Politics*, p. 69.

[14] Ridley, *Fox Hunting*, p. 180.

[15] Griffin, *Blood Sport*, pp. 231-232.

INTRODUCTION

Few things seem more English or more aristocratic than foxhunting. As the almost obligatory hunting prints on the oak or pseudo-oak panelled walls of countless restaurants, clubs, and hotels testify, the power of the sport to evoke images of a particular way of life is very strong. This power is hardly new. From the days of Joseph Addison to our own, the hunting squire has been a recognizable literary type, the best known of which was created two hundred years ago by Henry Fielding.

But it was in the years between Fielding and the agricultural depression of the late nineteenth century that foxhunting took on the form and assumed the role that transformed it from the private, informal recreation of a few country squires to a highly organized, extremely influential public institution. Though it never ceased to be viewed as a sport, and preeminently as the sport of the gentry and aristocracy – though, paradoxically, as a sport of the people as well – it became imbued with a significance out of all proportion to its role as mere sport. Hunting became, in the minds of hunting and non-hunting people alike, a full, legitimate feature of rural society, which could affect the lives of all members of that society. It came to be looked upon as one of the chief promoters within a country district of unity, stability, harmony, and devotion to traditional, deferential values. This role was used to justify not only the enormous amounts of time, energy, and money expended on the sport, but also the extraordinary demands that hunting made on all those who lived within the boundaries of a hunting country, which is to say virtually everyone in rural England.

By studying hunting and its role in society during those years, therefore, we may come to a clearer understanding of the way in which that society functioned, of the assumptions that governed it, of the place within it of seemingly unimportant local institutions and personalities, of the role of the traditional, deferential relationships upon which hunting depended, and of the strength with which these older pre-industrial assumptions and relationships were able to withstand the changes taking place in English life during the course of the nineteenth century. Such a study also enables us to see the extent to which survivals of pre-industrial society were able to exert a hold on the imaginations not only of country people but city people as well, many of whom turned to hunting in increasing numbers in emulation of the older upper classes. Finally, it illuminates the way in which the agricultural depression of the late nineteenth century put an end to this traditional way of life, not simply by ending the economic domination of the landed classes, but also by eliminating the emotional and theoretical underpinnings of deferential society.

Before we can understand the way in which foxhunting functioned in society it is necessary to have some understanding of what foxhunting is and how it is done.[1]

'Hunting', as the term is used in England, refers to the pursuit of an animal by hounds, who, though they are under the control of a huntsman, do all the work of finding, chasing, and killing their quarry. For the ordinary participant the sport consists of following the hounds, sometimes on horseback, sometimes on foot, and in recent years in automobiles, and watching them do their work. The enjoyment results from a combination of the pure exhilaration of the chase and the study of the wiles of both the quarry and the hounds.

A foxhunting establishment consists most basically, therefore, of a pack of foxhounds, the number of which may vary, but which rarely falls below forty or fifty hounds, always counted by twos or 'couples'. Twenty hounds, for example, are referred to as 'ten couple', twenty-one hounds as 'ten and one-half couple'. One hound, however, is referred to simply as 'one hound', rather than as 'half a couple'.

Presiding over the establishment is the Master of Foxhounds, or M.F.H., a position that carries great social prestige. Next to the master, the most important man in a hunting establishment is the huntsman, the man who actually performs the work of caring for, training, and 'hunting' the hounds. The position of huntsman may be filled by the master or some member of the hunt, in which case, he is said to be an amateur, or 'gentleman' huntsman, or it may be filled by a professional huntsman, hired for the job.

The huntsman is assisted by one or more whippers-in, whose job, as their title indicates, is to keep the pack together in the field, and to 'whip-in' any straying hounds. The hunt may also employ other men to care for the kennels or stables or to perform any of the other odd-jobs that may be necessary from time to time. All the paid members of the hunt staff were, and still are, referred to as 'hunt servants', and their social position was precisely that of a servant.

The basic technique of foxhunting as it had evolved by around 1820 has changed very little since. Foxes are nocturnal hunters, generally returning to their burrows, or 'earths', by daylight. In order to ensure that a fox will be found, the earths are 'stopped' before dawn. That is, the entrances to the earths in the neighbourhood in which the hunt will meet that day are temporarily blocked. This serves several purposes. It ensures that some foxes will be above ground to be hunted, it prevents hunted foxes from taking refuge during the course of the hunt, and, by preventing those foxes which are in the earths already from coming out, it lessens the possibility that the hounds will switch to a fresh fox in the course of a run when they are already tired themselves.

The foxes that find themselves stopped out of their earths look for somewhere else to lie up during the day, and generally choose patches of gorse or woodland if they are available, piles of sticks, fields of kale, or any similar undergrowth. These are referred to as 'coverts' – pronounced and often spelled 'covers'. The type, extent, and quality of coverts vary from place to place, and can, in part, determine the quality of hunting.

After the hounds and the sportsmen, the latter referred to collectively as 'the field', have met, usually around eleven o'clock in the morning, they proceed to a nearby covert where experience has shown that foxes are likely to lie. Precautions can be taken to ensure that a fox will be there, but these are never spoken of publicly. While the field waits to one side, the huntsman and whippers-in send the hounds into the covert, or, 'throw them into covert', at one end, and the hounds move slowly through the covert sniffing for a fox. This is known as 'drawing a covert'. Should a fox be there, it is hoped that on the approach of the hounds he will break from the covert and run away for safety. If he does not, and the hounds catch and kill him in the covert, this is known as 'chopping a fox in covert', and is considered an unfortunate waste, for the fox has provided no sport. Assuming, however, that the fox does what is expected of him and breaks from the covert, anyone who sees him go draws the attention of the huntsman to the spot, generally by shouting or 'holloaing', – pronounced 'hollering'. Sometimes what is shouted is 'Tally-Ho!' but just as often as not, it is a loud meaningless scream. On hearing the holloa, the huntsman and whippers-in collect the hounds and bring them to the spot where the fox broke covert, where they find his scent and take off in pursuit. The field follows. The hounds chase the fox until they have caught him or until they lose the scent, in which case the huntsman collects them together and 'casts' them, that is, moves them around in a way that is likely to help them regain the scent. It is here that much of the skill of the huntsman comes into play.

Should the fox be killed, the huntsman rescues the carcass from the hounds, cuts off the tail, or 'brush', head, or 'mask', and feet, or 'pads'. These can be awarded to some member of the field as a trophy, and the rest of the carcass is generally thrown to the hounds, who 'tear him and eat him'. In the early nineteenth century, the first member of the field up at the kill had the right to claim the brush, but it was found that this caused reckless riding, and the awarding of the trophies was left to the discretion of the master. [2]

In the medieval traditions of hunting, a special call, the *mort*, was blown on the hunting horn at the death of the prey. This was replaced in foxhunting with the cry of 'whoo-whoop', as the hounds tore the carcass to bits, and the expression 'the whoo-whoop' came to mean the end of anything, one of a number of expressions taken into upper class slang from foxhunting.

The custom of 'blooding' children on the death of their first fox, that is, smearing them with the blood of the fox, another survival of medieval hunting tradition, fell into disrepute under Victoria, but never completely died out, and survives to this day. [3]

Sometimes the fox makes good his escape, sometimes not. Depending upon the length of the run and the time of day, the master may decide to draw for a second or third fox, and the procedure begins once again. By dusk, which comes early in the English winter, the hounds are taken back to the kennels, and the day's sport is at an end.

PART I

A BEGINNING

CHAPTER 1

HUGO MEYNELL AND NIMROD

Foxhunting is not an ancient sport. Precisely when it began is a matter of some dispute among foxhunters, but there is no doubt that it was generally unknown until the end of the seventeenth century. Before then, foxes had been considered vermin – an Elizabethan law required the churchwardens of each parish to pay a bounty for the heads of dead foxes [1] – and Oliver St John's attack on Lord Strafford in 1641 clearly indicates the attitudes of his contemporaries:

> We give law to hares and deer, because they are beasts of chase; it was never accounted either cruelty or foul play to knock foxes and wolves on the head as they can be found, because they are beasts of prey. [2]

The traditional 'beasts of chase', as St John indicated, had been the deer and the hare, and they were to continue as the quarry of hounds for many years to come. The diminishing number of wild deer in all but the most desolate parts of the country, however, made wild-deer hunting rare by the eighteenth century, and hare hunting, though it remained popular, could never provide the excitement that made staghunting and was to make foxhunting the sports they were.

Sometime around the turn of the eighteenth century, however, sportsmen began to discover that the hitherto despised fox, even though it could not be eaten, nevertheless provided good sport, and it is from about this time that foxhunting dates. [3] The earliest foxhunting, however, was very different from the sport whose nineteenth-century devotees were to consider it among the prime supports of the English nation [4]and which more than anything else, according to a modern historian, 'gave vitality, cohesion, and stability to country society'. [5]In those early years, hounds met as early in the morning as light would permit, [6]and, to modern tastes, foxhunting was a tedious sport. The first foxhunters did not breed hounds especially for foxhunting, but took to chasing the fox with whatever hounds they had, generally harriers. It was this that gave the sport its early character, for the fox is a very different type of prey from the hare. Where the hare, despite its reputation for swiftness, depends on artifice and trickery to escape her pursuers, generally running in rings and doubling back to throw them off the trail, the fox, despite its reputation for guile, depends almost entirely on speed. The hounds of the eighteenth century, bred for hare hunting, were slow animals with highly developed scenting powers; once laid on the trail of the hare they could follow it relentlessly, despite all its tricks, but, given ordinary conditions, they could not catch a fox. By meeting early, foxhunters hoped to find the fox with a full belly and tired from the exertions of a night's hunting. Instead of drawing for him, as later became the practice, they hoped to hit upon his scent by chance and then follow it, or 'drag up to him', until they killed him. This involved long, slow hunts lasting many hours; in mid-winter the fox often escaped in the dark of early evening. [7]

This old-style hunting continued until well toward the end of the eighteenth century and in some places, even later. Peter Beckford, writing in 1781, for example, recommended meeting early in the day, though he admitted that he did not always do so himself. [8]In 1795, a writer in the *Sporting Magazine* who signed himself 'Acastus' and who, in fact, lifted much of his material directly from Beckford, advised 'never attempt to find a fox after one o'clock; you had better return home, and hunt again on the next day.' [9]Thirty years after 'Acastus', however, Colonel John Cook was able to write:

> In modern times, hunting early is *unnecessary*; the breed of hounds, the feeding, and the whole system is so much improved, that the majority of foxes are found and killed in the afternoon, (I mean after twelve o'clock). [10]

In fact, the changes that were to revolutionize foxhunting were already well underway when 'Acastus' wrote.

In 1753, a wealthy eighteen-year-old country gentleman named Hugo Meynell — which rhymes with 'kennel', to the great delight of the writers of many hunting songs – who had recently inherited the family property, rented Quorn, or Quorndon Hall near the village of the same name in North Leicestershire, and began to hunt foxes. [11]It was Meynell who first realized the possibilities for sport in breeding hounds fast enough to keep up with a fox, [12] and this apparently small innovation so revolutionized foxhunting that Meynell fully deserves the title 'father of foxhunting', that hunting tradition has bestowed upon him. The new speed of Meynell's hounds was perfectly suited to the large expanses of grass which made Leicestershire then, as now, the best hunting-ground in England. By 1750 around one half of Leicestershire had already been converted from arable land to pasture, and by 1800 much of the rest of it was as well. [13]It was this great expanse of grass land, more than anything else, that made it worthwhile to breed hounds with the speed and endurance necessary to hunt the fox in the way Meynell wished. The grass carried a scent well and was suited for hounds and horses to run after foxes. Although technically most of the land was 'enclosed', that is to say, had come under one or another enclosure award, much of it was still unfenced during Meynell's time. This suited Meynell himself very well. He was never greatly interested in jumping fences, but rather in watching his hounds work. [14]

The speed of his hounds made foxhunting a far more exciting sport than it had been before, and this increased its appeal. In addition, by making it possible for hounds to meet later in the day, at ten or eleven in the morning rather than at dawn, Meynell was instrumental in spreading the appeal of foxhunting to fashionable young men who could not be bothered to rise before dawn to go hunting.

Meynell was no backwoods Squire Western. His political and social connections in London helped to give him and his hunt a prestige that a more obscure local hunt would not have. It also helped him, though he owned no property in Leicestershire at the time he started hunting there (he did buy Quorn Hall several years later), to establish the right of his pack to hunt in the county, for the local landowners considered him a notable addition to the neighbourhood. [15]

Meynell's success at Quorn was rapid and striking, and he became known beyond the bounds of Leicestershire. Alex Hume-Campbell, later Lord Polwarth, wrote to his wife in 1775 that 'no less a man than Mr. Meynell himself' wished to come out for a day with his hounds, and that, while flattered, he was a little nervous at the prospect of having his hounds visited by so august a judge of hunting. [16]

As Meynell's fame grew, sportsmen from other parts of the country travelled to Leicestershire to see for themselves what the excitement was all about, and in doing so, started a new fashion. At first when the number of outsiders was relatively small, Meynell accommodated as many of them as he could in Quorn Hall itself, though they seem to have paid for their own food. [17]
By the 1780s, however, even the local inns were filled to capacity, and sportsmen began looking for empty houses to rent for the season. The need for these accommodations continued to grow. Most of those who came to Leicestershire to hunt came for most if not the whole of the season. Given the state of transportation in Leicestershire in the eighteenth century, these long visits were the result of necessity as well as hunting enthusiasm, for the effort involved in getting there in the winter made short stays impractical. When the neighbourhood of Quorn itself became too crowded, the sportsmen looked around for other places to stay. The vicinity of Leicester itself attracted some, while Loughborough, in the middle of the country most frequently hunted by Meynell, was the chief social centre of those who came to hunt. [18] But even with crowds of hunting men, Loughborough was a dull place to live. Meynell hunted three days a week, of which only two at most were in the grass country, the others being in the woody and rocky parts of the country, leaving his followers with long stretches of time with little to do. They began to look for other amusement and found it nearby, for Meynell's was not the only pack established in the grass countries of the Midlands. The Duke of Rutland's Belvoir Hounds and Sir William Lowther's Cottesmore Hounds were, by the 1780s and 1790s, establishing reputations for showing as good sport as Meynell's own hounds and enthusiastic hunting men began to look for somewhere to live where they could take advantage of all three packs. The place that was hit upon and that was to become famous as the hunting metropolis of all England was the small town of Melton Mowbray, Leicestershire. In 1792, a Melton freehold was advertised in the *Leicester Journal* as being 'in the centre of the hunts of the Duke of Rutland, Sir W. Lowther, and Hugo Meynell', and the opening of the Wreak Canal in 1794 increased Melton's appeal by making the town more accessible to coal and bricks. [19] Though it took several more years for Melton to gain general acceptance, [20] by 1800 the Meltonians – those who hunted regularly from Melton – already were beginning to look at themselves as the elite of the hunting world. [21] By the 1820s, Melton's position was so secure as to have added the term 'Meltonian' to

the language.

What drew these men to the shires [22] above all else was the opportunity afforded for hard and exhilarating riding. Though Meynell himself had bred his hounds for speed and undoubtedly rode harder and faster than had any of his predecessors, his main interest was, nevertheless, his hounds. He rode to hunt, as the saying was, riding as hard and as fast as was necessary to keep up with his hounds so as to watch their work. Many of those who came to hunt with his hounds had far less interest in the hounds than in their own horsemanship; they hunted to ride, and by 1800, the end of Meynell's reign at Quorn, the hard riders, led by Lords Forester and Jersey, were by far the most prominent horsemen in the field. [23]

By the 1790s, the Meltonians began to acquire the celebrity that was to place them in a position almost analogous to that of participants in spectator sports. The fledgling sporting press, consisting in the eighteenth century primarily of the *Sporting Magazine*, began to spread the fame of the Meltonians beyond the boundaries of their own world:

> Meynell's hunt is a species of sport at present so truly refined to a degree of perfection, by the speed of the hounds, the excellence of the horses, and the emulative and determined resolution of the riders, that the scene has certainly never before been equalled in the Kingdom. [24]

By the time Meynell retired from the mastership of his hounds in 1800, Leicestershire and the Quorn Hunt were firmly established as the most prestigious hunt country in England. But Meynell and those who came to hunt with him had done more than simply transform Leicestershire into a playground for rich young daredevils. Meynell's successes in Leicestershire transformed foxhunting all over the country, and by so doing, he indirectly helped to mould the pattern of English social life for a century after his time.

The later years of Meynell's mastership saw not only his fame but his methods spread all over England. Sportsmen who had only heard of Meynell and Quorn, and others who had experienced the exhilaration at first hand but who could not, for one reason or another, remain in Leicestershire themselves, set out to find a way to enjoy the new excitement closer to home. From about 1780, we begin to see the great growth of interest in hunting that was to continue into the 1820s and 1830s. [25]

As we have seen, foxhunting had been carried on long before Meynell.

Even given the comparatively slow speed of early foxhounds, they were often more exciting than harriers. Nevertheless, foxhunting was at best only one of a number of similar pursuits that could be followed by a country resident, and not necessarily the best of them. As one hunting man of the mid-eighteenth century put it, 'twenty in the field after a Hare... find more delight and sincere enjoyment than one in twenty in a Fox-chase.'[26]

But as the new style of hunting became better known in the closing decades of the eighteenth century, many harrier men were converted to the new rage. More and more packs of harriers turned to taking an occasional run after a fox, a wild one if they could find it, a bagged one (generally called 'bag foxes' or 'bagmen') if not.[27] Others abandoned hares altogether. General Barnett of the Cambridgeshire hounds for example, turned his pack into foxhounds around 1787, the Hurworth in Yorkshire switched from hare to fox in 1791, as did the Vine in Hampshire. [28]At the prompting of the Duke of Bedford, William Lee Antonie changed his hounds from harriers to foxhounds in 1796, establishing the Oakley Hounds. 'I can not think but Mr. Lee [Antonie]'s changing his Hare-hounds into Fox-hounds will give general satisfaction, & be highly approved of by all his neighbours,' wrote one sportsman to the duke.[29]

By the 1790s, foxhounds were not only popular in England, but were taken abroad by English colonialists and soldiers, as the sporting press reported:

> Foxhounds are now kept by the British Nabobs in India, in a greater stile than any of our packs in England.[30]

> If the British Cavalry should continue on the Continent, they are to have another pack of fox hounds sent over for their winter's amusement.[31]

To account for this increase in popularity, several factors must be noted. The first, as we have already seen, must be Meynell. By making hunting more exciting it could appeal to a far greater range of people than ever before, and especially to the young. From Meynell's time on, hunting was first of all a young man's sport. [32]Hard riding became the fashion not only in the shires, but among the provincial packs as well, and the spread of enclosure added still more to the excitement. 'Most of those who ride a-hunting', wrote a master of hounds in 1780, consider hard running as the criterion of goodness so mad flying spurt has gain'd my pack ten times more credit than the finest steady hunting chase.... I expect a monstrous rush tomorrow, & to have several hounds rode over.'[33]

A second factor was the increased social prestige given to hunting by Meynell and his field. Hunting could no longer be looked upon as simply the sport of ignorant backwoods squires, but, as Peter Beckford wrote in 1781: 'Fox-hunting is now become the amusement of gentlemen: nor need any gentleman be ashamed of it.'[34] Hunting had attracted the attention of the fashionable. Where heretofore the man of fashion could look at hunting as beneath him,[35] this was no longer the case. The Prince of Wales himself gave his patronage to the sport,[36] and by 1797 the *Sporting Magazine* could refer to 'the competition for superiority in taste and neatness, at the commencement of the season' amongst the followers of the different fashionable or would-be fashionable packs.[37] From this time on, foxhunting was to have a fashionable and social *cachet* it was never to lose.

Complementing this were several other factors which added to the appeal of the newly rediscovered sport. Hunting and other field sports had always served an important purpose in the countryside during the long cold winter months — that of providing entertainment and an opportunity to meet one's neighbours.[38] But in its earlier, duller form, it appealed primarily to older men, whose business would have kept them in the country anyway. Now it showed that there was place for the young man in the countryside as well.

It did so at a time when there was a great need for such an incentive to country living, for the war against Revolutionary and Napoleonic France, which lasted from 1793 to 1815, had circumscribed the leisure of the young gentleman of fashion. Hunting gave him a mode of amusement other than travel, and one that could easily be followed by his less wealthy and less fashionable contemporary. Moreover, the primarily country-dwelling gentleman suddenly found that by enjoying an amusement that had always been open to him but that had never had more than strictly local significance, he was also engaging in an activity that was being adopted by the highest in the land.

It would be a mistake, however, to look for too much too soon. Although Meynell accomplished a great deal and set much of the future pattern of hunting by the time he retired in 1800, Leicestershire was always years ahead of the rest of the country. But in the years following his retirement, a pattern was established all over England, as even more harrier packs turned to hunting foxes, to the great disgust of some old harrier men.[39] The harriers he hunted with in Kent, complained one of them, had taken to chasing bag foxes,

> and for what? – to gratify a few gentlemen, who think it more manly to ride after a poor animal turned out of a sack, because they can go home, and say they have been foxhunting, than to find a hare well, and hunt her well, and kill her well, though much more congenial to the feeling of themselves and horses; and I am convinced these same gentlemen, if they will speak the truth, like hare-hunting best, laying aside the name, the noble sound of fox-hunting.[40]

By the 1820s the harrier men were unquestionably on the defensive. Even those who continued to hunt hare gave in to the new fashion for speed and bred hounds that were more like dwarf foxhounds than like the old breed of harriers.[41] Not only did the harrier men have to contend with the defections from their own ranks, but they were also faced with pressures from the increasing number of packs of foxhounds whose followers claimed priority in hunting. In 1828 a master of harriers complained to the *Sporting Magazine* that the local M.F.H. was making it impossible to continue.[42] By mid-century and even before, foxhunters were claiming the right to organize all hunting in a neighbourhood so as not to conflict with the schedule of foxhunting.[43]

Packs were beginning to appear in countries physically as unlike Leicestershire as can be imagined.[44] A controversy over whether it was worth keeping hounds in Kent, for example, flared briefly in 1823, and the great authority 'Nimrod' encouraged the Kentish sportsmen, though he admitted that money spent on hounds in such countries was largely thrown away.[45]

The growth of the popularity of hunting was accompanied by a corresponding growth in sporting journalism, which first reflected that popularity, but soon was influential in stimulating it still further. Until the very end of the eighteenth century, foxhunters had no place to read of the exploits of their fellows. The first book devoted to the sport – Peter Beckford's *Thoughts on Hunting*, published in 1781 – remained alone in the field until Colonel Cook's *Observations on Fox-Hunting* appeared in 1826, and both were directed toward prospective masters of hounds rather than ordinary foxhunters.

In 1792, the *Sporting Magazine*, the first of the great sporting journals that were to proliferate in the nineteenth century, made its appearance, and for the first time hunting men in all parts of the country were able to read about the doings at Melton Mowbray and in other hunting countries. But in its early years, even the *Sporting Magazine* was hardly satisfying reading to most foxhunters. Started by John Wheble, who as printer of the *Middlesex Journal* had been involved with John Wilkes and Horne Tooke in the controversy over printing Parliamentary Debates, [46]the magazine in its early years reflected the proprietor's essentially urban and non-sporting background. Most of the articles were on decidedly non-sporting topics, such as the theatre, gambling, and London gossip, or were anecdotes with such titles as 'Remarkable Instance of Sagacity in a Dog'. What articles there were on sport were largely devoted to horse racing, boxing, and cock-fighting. There was some material on the game laws and shooting, but very little on hunting, and much of that was sketchy and inaccurate. The magazine seems to have depended for hunting material on whatever was sent to it by interested sportsmen, or on wholesale borrowing from other sources, notably Peter Beckford. [47] Though it published accounts of good runs almost from its earliest issues, most of these were dull and of little interest to anyone. A typical example ran:

> Lord Talbot's hounds ran a fox from Brockton Coppice, near Stafford, over the finest parts of Cannock-hills... into the low country and back to Sir Edward Littleton's, a long and desperate chase, where they killed; the whole pack in view; time, two hours and twenty-five minutes. [48]

Despite its shortcomings, the *Sporting Magazine* remained the sole source of sporting news, aside from articles of purely local interest in the local press, for the first two decades of the nineteenth century, [49]and during that time its coverage of hunting improved.

In January, 1822, however, sporting journalism and hunting were transformed when the magazine announced:

> Our present Number contains the First of a Series of interesting Letters, descriptive of the most celebrated Hunts in the Midland Counties, beginning with Leicestershire in the time of the late Mr. *Meynell* and the Earl of *Sefton*; written by a Practical sportsman, an eye witness of the scenes described. [50]

The 'letter', 'Fox-hunting in Leicestershire', was the first contribution to the magazine by Charles James Apperley, who was to achieve almost instantaneous fame under his pseudonym, 'Nimrod'. [51]

Apperley, who came from an old Herefordshire family, was born in 1778 and educated at Rugby. [52]When farming experiments brought him financial trouble he hit upon the scheme of writing a sporting book to make money but was convinced by a friend to write instead for the *Sporting Magazine*, despite his original objections that it was 'a mere Cockney concern' for which no gentleman wrote. [53]

The success of Apperley's articles was immediate and profound. Within two years, the circulation of the *Sporting Magazine* doubled, despite a rise in the price from two shillings to two shillings and sixpence, and the proprietors began issuing two double issues each year at double the price to meet the demand for space. [54]The great secret of Nimrod's success was that he was the first to realize that what sportsmen really wanted to read about was themselves. Between 1822 and 1828 he toured the country during the hunting season, hunting with one pack after another, and sending back accounts of the sport he saw, and more especially of the sportsmen he met. As Surtees' Mr. Jorrocks observed, 'It's soapin' chaps cleverly wot makes a run read', [55]and Nimrod knew how to 'soap'. Hunting people vied with one another to be noticed in his articles, knowing that they would be read by sportsmen in all parts of the country. [56]He travelled in great style, taking with him six hunters and a covert hack (a horse used to ride to the meet where one mounted one's hunter, which had been brought by a groom at a more leisurely pace), all of which were paid for by the magazine, and which, together with his usual fee of one guinea per page, amounted in six years to an expenditure by the magazine of £9000. [57]

Such was his fame that he was approached by the Society for the Propagation of Christian Knowledge to write a piece for them, combining sport and morality, [58]and after leaving the *Sporting Magazine* in 1829 as the result of a quarrel over money, he was approached by J.G. Lockhart, editor of the *Quarterly Review*. In 1832 and 1833 he contributed three articles to the *Quarterly*, one each on hunting, coaching, and horse racing – the first articles on sport to appear in a 'serious' journal. [59]Though Nimrod's extravagent tastes led him to live his later years in poverty in Calais, his influence was great. It was through his writing and that of his many imitators [60]that many people were first introduced to the sport, and he thus completed the work that had been begun by Meynell.

Between 1800 and 1830, hunting began to emerge as a great national sport. Its importance was reflected not only in the number of people who took part, but in the vastly increased strength of feeling on the part of many hunting men. The sport took on a significance in the minds of hunting people that it had not had previously and that no other sport could match. Other sports had their devotees, many of whom devoted disproportionate amounts of time to their pursuit. Hunting alone developed a mystique that raised it to the level of a national institution that, to the minds of more than just hunting men, could be trifled with only at the risk of wide-ranging social consequences. It is to this mystique that we must turn in order to grasp the peculiar significance of foxhunting, and it is against this background that we must examine the history of foxhunting in the nineteenth century.

CHAPTER 2

MYTH AND IDEAL

From its earliest days, foxhunting developed an idealized conception of itself that amounted almost to a mythology. Hunting and non-hunting men alike came to look on hunting as an institution in national and rural life, rather than as a mere sport. This idealized picture was used by hunting people to justify much of what they did, and when the justification was accepted, it passed from the realm of myth to that of reality. People behaved as though the myth were true and so, in effect, it was. The mythology of hunting was a significant factor in its own time. From the point of view of the modern observer, it possesses additional significance because it presents in microcosm many of the attitudes and ideals shared not only by a large segment of the middle and upper classes, but by all classes of country people. That these clearly stated ideals were often contradicted by the actions of hunting people should come as no surprise. But this too is of value, not because we need to be reminded that people often do not live up to their ideals, but because by comparing myth and reality, we are led to a clearer understanding of the meaning of the idealized concepts in the minds of nineteenth-century people.

The idealized view of hunting developed rapidly in the closing years of the eighteenth and the opening years of the nineteenth centuries, that is, at the time when the popularity of the sport was undergoing its first great increase. By around 1820 it was firmly established and was to remain virtually unchanged for the next sixty years, even though the conditions in which it was born had changed.

Through most of the eighteenth century, hunting men wasted little thought on their sport. They hunted because they liked to, and that was all that mattered. Some few of them, to be sure, saw some element of greater purpose in what they did, but these men were rare. 'The Old Squire', a hare hunter who wrote a short book on his sport in 1733, for example, grudgingly admitted that foxhunters did a service to the surrounding farmers by preserving their lambs and geese from the depredation of foxes.[1] At the time he wrote, there was some truth to the contention, for hunting men had not yet turned to preserving foxes for sport. Hunting men continued to claim that they provided such a service into the first decade of the nineteenth century. In 1786 their contention was upheld by the courts,[2] but even by 1786, few really believed that pest-control was the basic motivation for hunting.

The real development of the idealized view of hunting dates from the 1780s, when the first hunting writers and journalists made their appearance. In reaction to the prevailing view of intellectuals and men of culture that hunting was the pastime solely of boorish backwoodsmen, they were the first to present hunting as more than a simple amusement.

'Rural diversions', wrote William Blane in 1781,

> when followed in a liberal manner (for I do not wish to renew the almost extinguished breed of mere hunting 'squires,) are particularly useful in this island, where from the nature of our government, no man can be of consequence without spending a large portion of his time in the country, and every additional inducement to this mode of life is an additional security to our freedom and independence.[3]

Peter Beckford, writing in the same year, was more convinced of the intrinsic benefits of country life for the countryman himself. He wrote:

> A rural life, I think, is better suited to this country than to any other; because the country in England affords pleasures and amusements unknown in other countries; and because its rival, our English town (or ton) life, perhaps is a less pleasant one than may be found elsewhere.[4]

To Blane, hunting was valuable insofar as it offered inducements to the country gentleman to live upon his estates rather than in the city. As such, it deserved to be supported, but of course it had rivals. Other types of sport would serve the same purpose, and Blane, in fact, was interested in hare, not foxhunting. Beckford, a foxhunter through and through, went further, and singled out hunting as 'the soul of a country life; it gives health to the body and content to the mind, and is one of the few pleasures we can enjoy in society, without prejudice either to ourselves or our friends.[5]

In the ideas of these two men writing in the same year, we see the beginnings of two of the major strands that were to be woven into the mythology of hunting. Hunting was valuable in itself because it was healthy, invigorating exercise which did good for the hunting man at the same time as serving a social purpose, that of keeping gentlemen resident in the country where they could carry out their duties to their tenantry and to the country at large.

These arguments, in the context of the time, were, in fact, valid. Hunting was a healthful exercise, though one may perhaps question its impact on the mind, and the government and economy benefited from the residence of gentlemen on their estates. That they had to be offered some inducements to stay there, was also a valid point; the countryside in the winter could be a deadly place to live without diversions. The growing popularity of London was seen as a threat to the orderly functioning of rural society, for given the relatively poor state of transportation over much of the country, especially in the dead of winter, few could divide their time in short visits to both town and country. The choice had to be made between one and the other, and more and more people were being tempted by the luxuries of the metropolis.[6] 'All authorities agreed that sport was one of the best remedies for the growing tendency to choose town life. The future Lord Torrington, touring County Durham in 1792, for example, noted the establishment of a pack of hounds by Lord Darlington and his son, 'who by thus following hunting, become country residents; (which now none else are) and, by that means, of infinite service to this poor neighbourhood.'[7] Hunting, as Beckford noted, had the added advantage of being a social sport, one in which one met one's neighbours, thus making rural life all the more pleasant. As Sir Christopher Sykes, himself not an ardent supporter of the sport, wrote in 1792:

> When the pleasures of the chase can be made the means of calling the gentlemen of the country together, they become really useful and beneficial to society. They give opportunities of wearing off shynesses, dispelling temporary differences, forming new friendships and cementing old, and draw the gentlemen of the country into one closer bond of society.[8]

The technological improvements that were making country life more pleasant even in the early nineteenth century, coupled with the rapid growth of cities, changed and lent new significance to the concern for country living. There was increasing emphasis on the value of country life for the country dweller himself, and comparatively less on the social need for keeping gentlemen resident there. In 1841, when the railway boom was already remaking the lives of the English people, Robert Vyner began his hunting classic, *Notitia Venatica*, with a hymn to the value of rural life. 'Who, I ask', he wrote,

> is the most likely to enjoy and be benefited by such reflections [on nature]? the man whose early life has passed away pent up in cities, and whose mind and taste have been weakened and vitiated by every kind of refined luxury and excitement; or whose early days have tranquilly rolled on, soothed as it were by the various rural pursuits and acquirements which have so preeminently distinguished Englishmen upon all occasions of competition? [9]

Country life thus became associated with the hardy virtues, as contrasted with the softer, effeminate life of the city. Though these sentiments reached their peak in the mid-nineteenth century, they have their roots in the eighteenth.

Blane had contrasted the sports of the field to the 'softer amusements of the assembly and card-table,' [10] and the French war had served to raise the prestige of robust physical activities. Foxhunting was held to be especially praiseworthy because it was believed to be excellent training for war. As James Yorke wrote to the Countess de Grey in 1802:

> I need not enlarge upon the political advantages of encouraging a sport which propagates a fine breed of horses, and prevents our young men from growing quite effeminate in Bond St., nor upon the high reputation of the English horse abroad, which are perhaps the only cavalry that ever won whole battles against a very superior force of horse and foot... [11]

The glorification of hunting as training for war persisted unchallenged up to the First World War. Hunting was credited with producing every English victory, and even gallant defeat, from Waterloo through the Crimea and the innumerable colonial wars. 'This winter belongs to history as the terrible one spent by our Army in the Crimea', wrote Will Goodall, the Belvoir hunstman, in 1854, 'and the magnificent patience and courage with which our men bore their hardships spoke volumes for the training given them by English sports.' [12]Fifty years later, another hunting man had similar thoughts:

> How many of that first batch of gallant yeomen who sprang to arms five years ago in the hours of their country's difficulty, and who did such splendid service for their native land in South Africa, were trained in the hunting field! [13]

Army officers were encouraged to hunt, though few of them needed any great encouragement, and most of them could generally get long leaves during the hunting season for that purpose. [14]Officers quartered within the boundaries of a hunt were usually welcome to follow the pack without paying a subscription because it was believed that the hunt was thereby aiding the country, as well as repaying the officers for their gallant service. When Lord Lonsdale, master of the Quorn, was told during World War I that hunting was not necessary to the war effort he was shocked. What, he wanted to know, would officers home on leave from the front do if they could not hunt? It was totally beyond his comprehension that there could be officers in Britain's wartime army who had never hunted in their lives. [15]No one seemed to find it odd that some of the foremost hunting officers of the Victorian years found hunting such valuable training that when their regiments were sent to fight, they transferred to others so as not to miss the hunting. [16]

Ironically, not only was hunting not the good training that its proponents claimed, it may have even been harmful. Though it undoubtedly inculcated reckless courage in many young officers, it taught neither prudence nor good sense; the hard riding and reckless, devil-may-care bravery that made Lord Cardigan one of the most prominent Meltonians of his day also contributed to the charge at Balaclava. Cardigan, a hero to most of the population, was an even greater hero to foxhunters, who quickly pointed out that both Cardigan and Captain Nolan were staunch foxhunters and that several packs of hounds were kept by British officers in the Crimea. [17]

Throughout the nineteenth century hunting continued to be justified on the grounds that it was conducive to manliness. Manliness was taken to mean more than simple physical courage. It included such virtues as hardiness, temperance, coolness, and clearheadedness. It was considered as much a mental as a physical trait. [18]Hunting was held to strengthen the mind, intellectually and morally, as well as the body. Delabere Blaine, who wrote a treatise on field sports in 1840, for example, included a chapter entitled, 'The beneficial Effects of Field Sports on the Mind'. [19] The Rev. Charles Kingsley, Canon of Chester and Westminster, Chaplain to Queen Victoria, and Professor of Modern History at Cambridge, 1860-69, was another ardent sportsman. [20] He advocated hunting for clergymen on the grounds that the moral qualities it fostered were needed by clergymen as much as, or even more than, laymen. [21]

Foxhunters were also quick to seize upon the fact that, though other nations had their own forms of hunting, foxhunting existed nowhere else. It was uniquely British. [22] They therefore treated it as being both the product and the moulder of a uniquely British character. They were proud of the fact that few foreigners seemed capable of understanding its traditions. Stories abound in sporting literature of foolish mistakes made by foreigners in the hunting field. Their point was generally not that foreigners were themselves laughable or contemptible, but that, by its very nature, hunting was incomprehensible to them. A typical example was this story told by a Berkshire foxhunter in 1851:

> I recollect once having met a foreigner at a foxhunt. The horses and dogs were in the best of spirits, the sky was everything that it ought to be, and everything looked promisingly, and augured a good day's sport; but there occurred one of those untoward accidents which it is impossible to forsee or provide against, and the fox was chopped in cover. My friend the foreigner thereupon turned to the Master of Hounds... and exclaimed: 'Oh, my lord Duke, I congratulate you on having killed that animal so soon, and with so little trouble!' [23]

Many more examples might be chosen. Anthony Trollope based the plot of a novel, *The American Senator,* on the inability of an American to understand the conventions of foxhunting.

Manliness and Britishness were generally treated as two facets of the same trait and were associated with country living and especially with foxhunting, which was looked upon as the symbol of the uniquely British manliness that enabled the nation to maintain its world prestige in peace and war. The manly British foxhunter, living in the physically and morally healthful and invigorating countryside could, therefore, be compared to the city-dwelling, effeminate foreigner. If hunting were to be stopped, wrote a sportsman in 1826,

> the gentlemen would turn into a degenerate race of *petits-maitres*, deeply imbued with the vices of foreign countries or with a squeamish hypocritical morality

and the lower classes would turn from honest boxing to the stiletto. [24]

Patriotism was yet another virtue that was said to be strengthened by hunting. Though no direct link could be found between hunting and patriotism, the connection was nevertheless made by association. The people to whom the manly virtues, supposedly inculcated by hunting, most appealed, of course, were precisely the people to whom patriotism was most important. Patriotism in this context included not only support of one's country in time of foreign threat, but also a devotion to the established system. When Chartism, Reform, and the growing spectre of urbanization and industrialization were threatening the established social order, hunting was eagerly looked to to help swing the balance the other way. Though, in fact, hunting numbered amongst its adherents such critics of the established order as Henry Hunt, William Cobbett, and Sir Francis Burdett, hunting was nevertheless held to be a bulwark against internal subversion and sedition, which was associated in the minds of conservatives then, as now, with effeminacy and moral degeneracy. Nimrod, therefore, could refer to foxhunting in 1828 as one of the 'lion-supporters' of the crown, [25] and a hunt chairman in 1864 could go further and refer to hunting as a part of the constitution. [26]

In addition to breeding good men, hunting was also held responsible for breeding good horses. Farmers, the theory was, would be encouraged to breed horses both for their own sport and to sell to others. This would benefit the nation as well, because it would provide a stud that could be drawn upon for cavalry and general transporation. [27] The need to provide for the breeding of horses was a real one. England was the most horse-mad country in Europe in the nineteenth century – a 'sort of island of the Houyhnhnms' was the verdict of one foreign visitor [28] – but was incapable of producing the horses it needed. [29]

Though each of the justifications for hunting already considered was important in the eyes of hunting and non-hunting men alike, they could not have been responsible for the mystique hunting enjoyed, and were, in fact, used to justify other field sports as well. What set hunting apart from all the rest was the way in which hunting men were able to ascribe selfish motives to the followers of these other sports, while presenting themselves as open and generous. They were enabled to do so by the fact that there were no legal barriers to prevent anyone from entering the hunting field, and that, traditionally, farmers and other non-gentry had followed hounds. From this it was but a short step to the idea that since hunting was open to all, it benefited all. Every fox killed by hounds, therefore, became a national benefactor, and every man who hunted conferred a blessing upon the community by so doing. Every enemy to hunting was an enemy to the national welfare.

The high moral tone was set early in the nineteenth century by John Hawkes, a friend of Meynell's, who, around 1808, wrote, printed, and distributed to his friends a small pamphlet describing Meynell's hunting techniques. In it he wrote:

> The Field is a most agreeable coffee-house, and there is more real society to be met with there than in any other situation of life. It links all classes together, from the Peer to the Peasant. It is the Englishman's peculiar privilege. It is not to be found in any other part of the globe, but in England's true land of liberty – and may it flourish to the end of time!! [30]

Hawkes was among the first to give expression to the ideal that hunting unified all classes. By the 1820s, however, it had begun to appear with increasing frequency, and from that time it remained the foremost argument in the hunting man's arsenal. 'Hunting', wrote a correspondent in the *Sporting Magazine* in 1821,

> is considered by many to be no unimportant advantage to the country in which it is fostered; because it is a social sport – it brings men in various situations of life together, and unites them in the pursuit of the same object. [31]

Hunting people delighted in listing the men in 'humble' positions who loved to hunt. The chimney-sweep who hunted with the Duke of Beaufort in the 1830s was raised to the level of a national celebrity by an article about him in *Bell's Life*, [32] and from then on foxhunters could say, as did the master of the Old Berkshire in 1851, that 'no other country but England knows anything of a sport which allows a chimney-sweep or the lowest man of the community to ride by the side of a duke'. [33] As late as 1886, G.F. Underhill, a leading hunting journalist, could write:

> I even do not hesitate to assert that so long as foxhunting endures, so long will all the classes of English society be safe together: the high from the blights of envy and the spoliation of rapacity, the low from the iron hand of oppression and the insolent spurn of contempt. [34]

The argument, as we can see, remained virtually unchanged in the eighty years between Hawkes and Underhill.

The great attractiveness of this ideal lay in the fact that, though it was simple and straightforward on the surface, it was sufficiently ambiguous to be used to justify a wide range of opinions and practices. It enabled hunting to maintain an image at one and the same time as the most aristocratic and the most egalitarian of English institutions. It enabled what was never more than a small minority of the population to expect that everyone else in the countryside would order his interests so as to foster the amusement of that minority. What is more remarkable is that this expectation was fulfilled.

That the hunting field was open to all no one can deny. This was the result of three factors. The original status of foxes as vermin, which all were encouraged to destroy, meant that they were unprotected by any game law. Even had they been protected, the hounds killed the prey, and so only the owner of the hounds would have had to be qualified to kill game, since the followers were mere spectators. Second, since the hounds killed the fox, there could be no conflict among sportsmen for the prey. Unlike the shooter who was deprived of a bird himself every time one was shot by someone else, it made no difference to the master of hounds whether five or five hundred watched his hounds kill a fox, so long as they did not interfere. It was this lack of possessiveness that endeared foxhunting to so noted a man of the people as William Cobbett, even though he hated shooters and their game laws. [35] Finally, the fact that hunting could only exist if hunting people were allowed to cross the lands of others made it, in the words of one sportsman, 'an amusement of sufferance, and, being so constituted, open to all the world.' [36]

No one, however, could claim that England was a socially egalitarian society in the nineteenth century, and least of all the foxhunters. From the very beginning, the ideal recognized that the social contacts of the hunting field were governed by certain restraints. The very nature of the sport could separate the elements of fraternization and equality. In the course of a hard run all were equal, at least to the extent that differences of riding skill and quality of horses allowed. The dustman was welcome to ride beside the duke, or ahead of him, if he could. But in the course of such a run, fraternization was impossible. Each was too preoccupied with his own riding to be aware of the existence of the other as anything more than a moving obstacle in the field. At the meet of the hounds, on the other hand, when conversation was possible, and when, in fact, there were contacts between members of different classes, these contacts were limited to definite, recognized forms. The sporting farmer or local tradesman, it is true, often exchanged words with members of the local gentry or aristocracy, and these meetings were, in fact, one of the major sources of contact among the various classes, but the relative differences in social station were never forgotten.

The chimney-sweep who hunted with the Duke of Beaufort is an interesting case in point. Though he obviously enjoyed hunting and went well in the run, he seems, at the meet, to have been almost a licensed entertainer. He rode in his chimney-cleaning clothes, carried a chimney brush instead of a whip, and, after being greeted by the duke, saluted him with his brush, leapt up on his saddle, and rode around the crowd on one leg, posing 'like a flying Mercury... amid the waving of handkerchiefs, and to the infinite amusement of all present.' [37]

Farmers, of course, occupied a higher social position, but what the hunting man hated above all else, in a member of any class, was pretension. So long as the farmer or tradesman made no pretence to gentility but was content to appear no more than he was, he was welcomed. At the various social events associated with hunting, such as balls, dinners, and races, the social differences were maintained all the more sharply. It was this which led *The Times* in 1858 to describe the idea of hunting as a bond of society as 'a delusion and snare. It is an excuse for associating with men whom you do not associate with off the field or at the hunting breakfast, and some of whom you could not possibly associate with.' [38] But while *The Times* was correct as far as it went, it had, in fact, fallen into a snare itself. The hunting ideal had never claimed that hunting was a social leveller or even that one associated freely with all who hunted. The sporting writer 'Scrutator' was quite right to take *The Times* to task on that point: 'A gentleman may, I suppose, speak to a horse dealer or a coltbreaker in the field, or have a long chat with a neighbouring farmer on agriculture without sitting down at table or exchanging visiting cards with either the one or the other.' [39]

The ideal of the hunting field as a meeting place for all classes dates, as we have seen, from the pre-railway age, when, with the exception of the shires and the packs in the immediate vicinity of large towns, the hunting field was made up entirely of local men. Every member of the local community had his known and accepted place in that community, and the unquestioned acceptance of that local social order made social intercourse between members of different classes simple, for no threat to the order could be seen in it.

While hunting people boasted of the openness of the hunting field, there is no question that the values the field fostered were conservative and aristocratic, and it was considered to be one of the great benefits of the openness that even the lower classes could be thus embued with gentlemanly ideals. One of the foremost of these was that of largesse and hospitality. It had long been a tenet of the country gentleman that the ability to dispense largesse and hospitality raised one's social status. The great difficulty was that hunting offered less opportunity in this line than did other sports. Shooters, generally despised by hunting men as selfish since one shooter required hundreds of jealously preserved birds for his amusement while one fox could provide amusement for hundreds of foxhunters, were in a better position, since the dead birds could be given away. Gifts of game had long been one of the traditional means of dispensing largesse. Foxhunters, on the other hand, had nothing that they could give away.

There were only two ways in which the foxhunter could show generosity. The first was to provide hospitality for other hunting men. Though few could afford to welcome the entire hunt at a lawn meet in front of their houses, providing a hunt breakfast to hundreds of sportsmen and onlookers, hunting people were constantly urged to provide such hospitality in other ways, such as by having food and drink on hand to welcome passing foxhunters on their way home after a long day. [40]Farmers who provided bread and cheese and 'good October ale' to all foxhunters that passed their doors were regularly singled out in the sporting press as representatives of 'the good old sort', perhaps the highest praise in a foxhunter's vocabulary. [41]

The other way in which largesse could be dispensed was by contributing to the welfare of hunting in the neighbourhood. This went beyond a mere subscription to the pack, which was regarded as the obligation of all those who regularly hunted. It could take the form of gifts to the hunt or extra efforts in the preservation of foxes. The greatest praise was reserved for those who, though they did not hunt themselves, contributed to the pack in one way or another. Sir Theophilus Biddulph, for example, who did not hunt but provided the coverts and preserved foxes was singled out in this Warwickshire hunting song of the 1830s:

> May merry Old England then nourish
> Her pristine affection for sport
> For Foxhunting ever shall flourish,
> While our Squires lend their ready support.
> Here's a health, then, to all the true lovers

> Of the Chase, while the wine goes the rounds
> To Sir BIDDULPH, who gave us the covers,—
> To THORNHILL himself, and the hounds. [42]

If the non-hunter was a shooter, who thus had special reason for not wanting foxes in his coverts, but had them preserved anyway, he was considered as meriting even extra praise, which was freely given. If, however, the shooter did not preserve foxes, he was singled out for great criticism. It is in this sort of case that the moral tone adopted by foxhunters was most evident. Since hunting was enjoyed by all the community, the man who did not preserve foxes was guilty of the selfish act of spoiling the sport of all his neighbours. When, for example, in 1859 the master of the Rufford Hounds was prohibited from drawing certain coverts until after they had been shot through, *The Field* declaimed:

> When all the generous, manly ties of rural life, all the rights and privileges appertaining to the more noble and far more important sport of fox-hunting, when the duties which connect the mutual interests of landlords and tenants are sacrificed to a morbid taste for the preservation of an immense profusion of game, it becomes a social evil, against which every man has a right to express his condemnation. [43]

The rural ties were held to be strengthened not only by the fact that all classes hunted, but also by the fact that all classes participated in the preservation of foxes and the support of the hunt. The farmer, by allowing his land to be ridden over, was himself dispensing a kind of largesse, and this was held not only to increase his social status, but also to make him feel more a part of the unified community since he too was contributing to the general welfare. 'Hunting and field sports', wrote 'Harry Hieover',

> bring on a kind of good understanding between the gentry, the farmer, and the peasant. The gentleman is civil to the farmer because he allows him to ride over his lands; the farmer is civil in return, because he supplies the gentleman with hay, oats, and straw; but much more so because the farmer occasionally joining in the chase (or if not), by preserving foxes, abstaining from improper destruction of game, and permitting his cover to be drawn, he feels he has the power to oblige, and thus has a right to expect as his due a proper courtesy from his more aristocratic neighbour, or even his lordly one. It gives him a justifiable feeling of independence, and in moving his hat to his superior he does it to show his sense of their different grades, and feels certain of the compliment being properly acknowledged. [44]

Hunting people never quite resolved the conflict between the image of hunting as a sport of gentlemen and as a sport open to all the people. Sometimes one aspect was stressed, sometimes another. The problem was compounded by the fact that the duality existed. Hunting was open to all, and members of all classes participated, but, on the other hand, the upper classes predominated in all but a few packs. Thus, in 1862, during a dispute over the advantages of hunting versus shooting, *The Field* could, in the same editorial, praise hunting because it amused all classes and yet call it 'essentially the pastime of the country gentlemen of Great Britain'. [45]

That hunting people never tried hard to resolve the dilemma may be interpreted as merely a case of self-serving, but it can also be taken as a sign of a real ambivalence on the part of many. Foxhunting was, in fact, a unique institution, carrying the greatest social *cachet* and looked to by many merely in search of social advancement, and at the same time was an essentially popular sport in many rural districts. Similarly, foxhunting did, in fact, illustrate quite well the possibility of close social contact based on the acceptance of inequality. The power of the sport to promote this contact despite the changing social conditions of the nineteenth century will be seen presently.

PART II

THE VIEW FROM WITHIN

CHAPTER 3

HUNTING PEOPLE BEFORE THE RAILWAYS

In the pre-railway age, the hunting field, with a few notable exceptions, was the province of the local man. The early meetings of hounds in the days before Meynell and the relatively poor state of transportation even afterward, made hunting difficult to come by for all but those who lived in the vicinity, as did the relative privacy with which many meetings of hounds were arranged. Local men were not restricted to only one class, but, hardly surprisingly, the class that predominated in the hunting field was the rural gentry. The reasons are obvious. Regular hunting, even on a relatively unpretentious scale, required time and money. It was the gentleman more than any other country dweller who had both.

The amount of time and money needed, however, could vary greatly. The Meltonian who hunted six days per week had time for little else for the duration of the season. The farmer or professional man who hunted once per week, or even once per fortnight, on the other hand, found that his other pursuits were not greatly affected. In order to hunt of course, it was necessary to own, or at least have the use of, a horse; the more hunting one did, the more horses were necessary. To hunt six days per week at Melton required at least seven or eight horses. [1] Four days per week in a provincial country were possible with three horses. [2] Many occasional hunting men, however, managed with only one.

Though Meltonians were known to pay as much as one thousand guineas for a hunter, [3] few other hunting men were so extravagant. A hunter could cost anything from twenty-five pounds and up during most of the nineteenth century, depending upon its age, condition, breeding, the weight it had to carry, and the reputation it might have acquired in the hands of a previous owner. During most of the century, an average hunter cost around £75 to £150, and £300 to £400 was generally considered a high price. ⁴The expense of keeping a horse also varied. At mid-century, for example, a farmer could keep a horse for twenty-five pounds per year. ⁵ A Londoner, on the other hand, forced to board his horse at a livery stable, might expect to pay up to one pound per week, or even somewhat more by the 1870s and 80s. ⁶In addition, the regular hunting man had the expense of a subscription to the local hounds, which could amount to anything from one pound to eight hundred, but which, for most country gentlemen, generally amounted to ten to twenty-five pounds per year. ⁷In 1876, a writer in the *Saturday Review* estimated that the cheapest rate, including subscriptions and all other expenses, at which a man who weighed thirteen stone (182 lbs.) could hunt 'with comfort' was about £100 per year. ⁸This, however, only applied to the man who kept a horse solely for hunting, which was not the case with many rural foxhunters. It was also calculated on the basis of horses costing 150 guineas.

These expenses effectively kept the great majority of the population out of the hunting field. Agricultural labourers, domestic servants, small shopkeepers and craftsmen, and factory operatives did not hunt. On the other hand, any man who ordinarily kept or could borrow a horse of any kind could occasionally turn out with hounds, at no extra expense to himself. He was not expected to subscribe or to wear special clothing, and, if he could not hope to keep up with the rider of a £200 hunter, he nevertheless was able to mingle with his friends at the meet and to get some fresh air and exercise.

According to Nimrod, an average field in the vicinity of Oxford around 1790 consisted of about fifty gentlemen and half a dozen farmers. ⁹ Nimrod's figures would not be much out of line in most provincial countries through the 1820s and 1830s. The country gentlemen and the farmers composed the two largest hunting groups.

Though most of them did not hunt, farmers, like country gentlemen, were considered 'natural' hunting men and were to be found in the hunting field from the earliest days of the sport. Because of the restrictions of the game laws, hunting was the only field sport that many farmers could conveniently enjoy, and this, coupled with the fact that the hunting season fell at the time of year when farmers had the most leisure time, made hunting popular in their eyes. In the eighteenth century, many farmers not only followed hounds, but kept them. In some of the more remote sections of the country, especially in Yorkshire, farmers were, in fact, the backbone of the hunting community. Some of the packs of the North Riding, such as the Sinnington and Bilsdale, were started by farmers sometime in the eighteenth century, and have continued to be managed by them ever since. In other packs, farmers predominated, though they might not have had control. Though the Brocklesby, in Lincolnshire, for example, had been hunted by the Earls of Yarborough from its foundation, most of its followers were prosperous farmers until the depression. [10]

Two factors combined to bring farmers into the field in increasing numbers at around the turn of the nineteenth century. The high agricultural prices generated by the war years had the double effect of enabling more farmers to afford the sport and of giving many a taste of luxury and a hunger for social advancement at precisely the time when hunting was beginning to acquire more social prestige. The increasing practice of meeting later in the day enabled farmers to rise early, put in a fair amount of work, and still meet hounds at mid-day. By the turn of the nineteenth century, farmers began to appear more and more regularly in hunt reports. 'The only people at the end were Mr. Forester, Mr. Craven and another gentleman with whose name we are unacquainted; also two farmers', [11] ran an account of a day with the Belvoir in 1805. Those in at the death with Sir Mark Sykes' hounds in the East Riding one day in 1806 were 'Will Carter, the huntsman, Sir F. Boynton, Messrs. Treacher, Hawke, Best, Lascelles, and Mr. Batty the farmer'. [12]

The fact that the writers of these reports saw fit to single the farmers out as such, alerts us to the fact that farmers occupied a special place in the hunting field. They were always welcomed, partly because the field afforded gentlemen a pleasant opportunity to meet their tenants, and partly because farmers held it in their power to interfere significantly with hunting, if not to put an end to it altogether. Meynell, it was said, would always wait at covert side for twenty minutes for an absent farmer, while ten minutes was all he would allow a duke. [13] Meynell and other masters arranged their meetings so as not to conflict with market day in order that farmers might hunt, and this practice became common in the nineteenth century. [14] But as the hunt reports quoted above show, farmers, welcome as they were, were always a class apart. Both the extremely snobbish Nimrod and the generally more tolerant Surtees felt that it was in poor taste for a farmer to hunt in scarlet, and though not everyone agreed, most farmers, in fact, did not wear red. Those who did were either the most prominent farmers in the district or were generally considered ostentatious. [15]There were, of course, those moralists, like the writer in the *Morning Herald*, [16] who disapproved of all sporting farmers and spoke contemptuously of them as 'the doubtful gender', neither gentleman nor farmer, created by the high prices of the war years. Members of the sporting community, however, generally disagreed.

The term 'hunting farmer' could of course encompass a wide variety of types. On one extreme there were men like Monk, a tenant of Lord Spencer in Bedfordshire, who hunted regularly with the Oakley for thirty years, wore a red coat, and called S.C. Whitbread 'Sam'. [17]At the other extreme, there were men who followed hounds infrequently or irregularly, sometimes even falling in with them accidentally, like the Essex farmer who noted in his diary in 1800: 'Mr. Sach's hounds hunted a baig [bag] fox past my house. I mounted my horse and joined them against Donyland Church, where they were at a check.' [18]

The number of farmers who hunted with any pack at a given time generally depended on economic conditions. The high prices of the war years, as we have already seen, acted as a spur to farmers to join the hunting field, and in times of poor prices, their numbers naturally thinned. [19]Local custom, too, influenced the number of farmers in the field. Yorkshire farmers were especially well known as avid sportsmen, as were the Leicestershire graziers who followed the Quorn and were known as the 'Blue Coats' for the costume they wore. In other parts of the country – Sussex, for example – farmers generally did not hunt. [20]

For the farmer who hunted irregularly, and even for those who were regular followers, hunting did not have to cost a great deal. Only the more well-to-do farmers went to the expense of keeping specially bred hunters. Most made do with farm horses of one sort or another, and the horse that carried the farmer after hounds one day would have to take its turn pulling the plough or wagon, or simply carrying its owner around the farm, the next.[21] Some farmers, primarily in Lincolnshire, Yorkshire, and Leicestershire, [22] managed to combine business and pleasure by raising a few hunters each year and by riding them out hunting in the hopes that they would catch the eye of a prospective buyer. The more daring a rider the farmer was, of course, the greater the possibility that the horse would fetch a good price. This was one of the reasons that many farmers acquired a reputation for dare-devil riding. The precise number of farmers who actually rode to show off hunters is hard to establish. They always figure prominently in the anecdotes and stories of fox-hunters, but these exaggerate their importance. Though the actual number of farmers who raised horses was probably quite small, it is undoubtedly true that the most successful horse breeders among the farmers were those who were best able to show off their wares in the hunting field. At any event, even if they did not make much money from horse breeding, the sportsmen among them could generally at least break even, hunting on a better horse than they might ordinarily get to ride.

Farmers, unlike gentlemen, were not expected to subscribe to the pack within whose country they lived, and with whom they generally hunted. It was felt that by allowing his land to be ridden over, the farmer contributed enough to the welfare of the pack. The opposite side of the coin, of course, was that, with a few exceptions, farmers had little say in the management of the pack until the end of the nineteenth century. They rarely belonged to the hunt club, were not considered members of the hunt, were often segregated at hunt breakfasts and lawn meets, and they were not invited to the hunt ball. In 1824, Nimrod visited the hunt races of the Hampshire Hunt to see the race for the farmer's cup:

> Your readers may imagine that I did not ride those twenty miles to see a race ridden by Farmers, or to dine with them afterwards; but my object was, to present to the sporting world the fair example set by Mr. Villebois on this day; and I think they will agree with me, that it is one well worthy of imitation. He not only gives them, out of his own pocket, a handsome cup for the best, and a whip for the second-best horse; but, at the expence of the Hunt fund... about two hundred of them sit down afterwards to an excellent dinner with the master of the hounds — supported by some of the members of his Hunt — in the chair. [23]

The implications are clear. The farmer was to be treated well, but he was not, nor could he hope to be, a member of the hunt.

Though the gentry and farmers between them made up most of the fields that turned out with the provincial packs in the pre-railway era, there were others who could be found there. These, too, were predominantly local men, and were a mixed bag of tradesmen, professionals, and others who, though they did not live on the land, were part of the agricultural community of rural England.

At the top of the social ladder among these were the clergy. The hunting parson was a familiar figure in the fields of the pre-railway age.

The country clergy of the period were traditionally allied socially with the landed gentry, and many of them, in fact, were younger sons of gentry families. It is not surprising, therefore, to find that many of them shared the gentry's sporting tastes.

The clergyman with a taste for sport was in a perfect situation to indulge his taste. Eve a conscientious country parson was likely to find himself with long periods of idleness. If he united his love of sport with a taste for literary production, which many did, he was likely to find himself becoming the poet-laureate of his hunt. 'The Billesdon Coplow Run' of 1800, one of the earliest and most famous of the innumerable hunting poems written to commemorate a great run, was written by the Rev. Robert Lowth, [24] and many other hunting parsons, often the best educated members of their hunts, followed his example. [25] The Rev. William Daniel (1753-1833) indulged his literary tastes on a more ambitious scale and published *Rural Sports* (1801), one of the earliest treatises on field sports.

Perhaps the most famous clerical foxhunter of the nineteenth century was the Rev. John Russell of Iddesleigh, Devon, known to all as Jack Russell, [26] but he was by no means unique. The first two masters of the Old Berkshire Hounds, for example, were clergymen. For some reason, clergymen who kept their own hounds were especially common in Devon and Dorset. It was estimated that in the 1830s approximately twenty clergymen in the diocese of Exeter kept hounds, to the great annoyance of the Bishop, Henry Phillpotts, who tried with varying degrees of success to stamp out the pastime. [27] There is a story that shortly after having been consecrated, and before he learned of the sporting habits of the clergy of his diocese, Phillpotts was passing through North Devon, and, seeing a pack of hounds in full cry, followed by a large number of sportsmen in black coats, remarked: 'Alas! this neighbourhood must have been visited by some fearful epidemic! I never saw so many men in mourning before.' [28]

Although the hunting clergyman was, as might be expected, accepted by the hunting squires and farmers as a particularly 'good sort', Phillpotts' efforts alert us to the fact that there were other opinions. The very existence of clerical foxhunters was deemed enough of a curiosity to warrant special attention by a foreign visitor like Prince Pückler-Muskau, who toured England in the 1820s. 'They told me', he wrote,

> of a famous clerical foxhunter who always caried a tame fox in his pocket, that if they did not happen to find one, they might be sure of a run. The animal was so well trained that he amused the hounds for a

time; and when he was tired of running, took refuge in his inviolable retreat — which was no other than the altar of the parish church. There was a hole broken for him in the church wall, and a comfortable bed made under the steps. This is right English religion....[29]

Even among the English, however, there were those who, while willing to accept hunting as a sport for laymen, saw it as an unfit occupation for the clergy. When an advertisement for Daniel's *Rural Sports* appeared in the *Gentleman's Magazine* in 1802, it provoked an attack by one correspondent who questioned 'the consistency between being a fisher of men and a hunter of beasts'.[30] William Jones, vicar of Broxbourne, Hertfordshire, complained of clerical 'Jimmy-Jessamies' who, having purchased the presentation to valuable livings, devoted their time to sport while their overworked curates did all the work of the parish.[31] There certainly were hunting clergymen who neglected their parochial duties because of their love of sport. The Rev. Griff Lloyd, who hunted constantly with Sir Thomas Mostyn's hounds in Oxfordshire in the 1820s, was a prime example. He scheduled marriages and burials to suit the meetings of hounds and never wrote a sermon, but relied on printed ones, which he read verbatim in the pulpit without preparation. It was said that he once preached a Christmas-day sermon in February without realizing it.[32]

Though there could be no argument about the impropriety of a clergyman neglecting his duty in order to hunt, or do anything else for that matter, there were those who went further and argued that hunting was an unfit amusement for clergymen even if it did not interfere with their parochial duties. William Gilpin (1724-1804), prebendary of Salisbury, and author of *On the Amusements of Clergymen* (1792), would have barred the clergyman from the field because hunting was both 'riotous' and 'cruel'.[33] He objected to clergymen taking part in any amusement that involved the shedding of blood,[34] but was perhaps even more disturbed at the prospect of a clergyman making the acquaintance of men in the hunting field 'to whom, for your character's sake, you would not wish to be known'.[35] Gilpin was not alone in his dislike of the hunting parson, though the depth of his feelings may well have been stronger than most.

On the whole, attitudes toward the clerical hunting man of the early nineteenth century were somewhat ambivalent. There was a feeling among many that there was something 'not quite right' about the spectacle of a clergyman hunting, though few could actually put their finger on just what was not right about it. Somehow hunting was not serious enough for the members of a calling that was supposed to concern itself with the most serious of issues. Yet, with few exceptions, there was no real attack on the hunting clergyman. Many hunted, and those who did seem, on the whole, to have been admired by those of their parishioners who expressed any opinion, rather than the reverse. So long as he was not ostentatious about it – 'did not holloa' as one man put it [36]– the clergyman with a taste for hunting could pursue his pastime with little danger of censure. If, however, he devoted too much time to the pursuit, he risked being stigmatized as a wastrel or worse by many, though he might find himself all the more popular as a guest at the squire's table. [37]

It would serve little purpose to devote too much time to listing other local men who took an occasional day with hounds, though the hunting man's delight in pointing them out has provided us with a long list of them. People of all types above the rank of agricultural labourer were to be found at the meeting place of hounds, mounted on every description of horse. Their presence was taken as perfectly natural. [38]

Some occupations seem to have contributed far more than their share of hunting people, but all contributed some. Horse-dealers, of course, hunted to show off their wares, and if they were not themselves sufficiently good riders to show off their horses to the best advantage, hired roughriders like the famous Dick Christian to do it for them.[39] Innkeepers were yet another group who seemed especially prominent in the field. Innkeepers have traditionally been sporting men, and inns, centres of gambling and sporting discussion. Surtees singled out 'Peter Pigskin', a sporting innkeeper, as one of the stock types to be met in the hunting field. [40]

Wealthy local men, who did not quite qualify as gentry, also turned out regularly. For the rest, the field was made up of a random collection of lawyers, doctors, and prosperous tradesmen, together with a few oddities like the retired coachman who hunted in Hampshire in the 1820s, [41]and the chimney-sweep who hunted with the Duke of Beaufort in the 1830s. [42] These men always formed a minority of those out on a given day, and few of them were more than occasional followers, but when they turned out they were not made to feel unwelcome. Whatever their social status, that status was known, and their place in the community was known, and that place ensured them a welcome in the field.

There were two prominent exceptions to the general pattern of predominantly local men in the field, and, if the packs already described represent the ordinary state of hunting, the exceptions may be seen as the sublime and the ridiculous, though one might question which was which. The two exceptions were the elite, who hunted where they wished – primarily in the shires – and the Londoners, who hunted where they could. Even before the craze for foxhunting began to take hold, it was not unknown for the city man to follow hounds. There was a pack of hounds kept by the Lord Mayor of London in the eighteenth century,[43] and civic hunts did not entirely disappear in the nineteenth.[44] We must not forget, after all, the rural setting of English towns. Even London, so much bigger than all the rest, had not yet spilled into the countryside, creating a vast indeterminate suburban area. The Londoner could follow hounds of some sort within ten miles of St Paul's Cathedral. In 1792, the *Sporting Magazine*, under the title 'A rich Field Circle', published a list of eleven packs of hounds that hunted within a circle of twenty miles diameter centred on the city.[45] The list included four packs of foxhounds, six of harriers, and one of staghounds. This list did not exhaust the number of packs with which the Londoner could hunt within a short distance of the city. Hounds met at Wimbledon, Hounslow, Twickenham, Southgate, Finchley, Streatham, and Dulwich in the early nineteenth century.[46]

The city man with a taste for sport found an increasing attraction in hunting by the 1790s as other forms of sport, notably shooting, became increasingly difficult to come by because of increased taxes on dogs and game and the general scarcity of game as well.[47] But for many Londoners, particularly businessmen who could only spare a day or even part of a day, foxhunting was not the ideal field sport. Far more suitable was the chase of the carted deer, which he could enjoy with the Royal hounds, those of Lord Derby, and, later in the nineteenth century, the hounds of Baron Rothschild in the Vale of Aylesbury. The hunting of deer had for centuries been the premier sport of royalty and aristocracy. By the eighteenth century, however, wild deer had disappeared from virtually the whole of the country, and they could only be hunted in a few remote places like Exmoor and Dartmoor. The successor to wild-deer hunting was the hunting of the carted deer, in which a semi-tame animal was brought to the place of meeting in a cart, turned loose, and given a set amount of time to get a start before the hounds were turned loose on its trail. At the end of the hunt, the huntsmen could generally stop the hounds before they did the deer any harm, and the same animal could thus be used many times over.

In fact, many of the deer that were used frequently were well known by name to the followers of the hounds. [48] This tye of hunting, though generally held in contempt by avid foxhunters who called it 'calf hunting' and mocked the idea of hunting a tame animal, had certain advantages for the city sportsman. The deer generally provided as fast and lively a run as a fox without the waste of time inherent in finding a fox or the risk of wasting a day without finding one at all. The follower of staghounds could appear at the meet, secure in the knowledge that he could have a morning's sport, and then return to town in time to do some business in the late afternoon.

Deer hunting continued to attract large numbers, not merely of Londoners, but of other sportsmen who cared mainly for the ride and convenience and were not too concerned with the niceties of finding and killing game. But the craze for foxhunting that was affecting sportsmen in the more rural areas spread in London as well, and more and more city men who could afford it turned to following the foxhounds in the vicinity of the metropolis, especially since going foxhunting could advertise that the sportsman did not care if the day was wasted. Surrey was the primary hunting field of the Londoner, and by the 1820s, Croydon, from which one could easily reach three packs of foxhounds plus an equal number of harrier packs and Lord Derby's staghounds, was known as the Melton of the South. [49] By the end of the eighteenth century, the *Sporting Magazine* was printing information on the London packs, and the new sporting journals founded at the beginning of the nineteenth, primarily *Bell's Life in London*, followed suit.

The appearance of the city man in the hunting field did not go unnoticed by his rural contemporaries. To the countryman, the Londoner was a figure of fun. The very word 'cockney', used by the countryman to refer to any citizen of London, was said to have its origin in the city man's supposed ignorance of country life. A city man, the story runs, was visiting the country and heard a horse neigh. 'Oh', he said, 'listen to the horse sing'. 'A horse doesn't sing', replied the countryman, 'he neighs'. Some time later the city man heard a cock crow. 'Oh', he said., 'listen to the cock neigh'.

Though many city men were undoubtedly good sportsmen, the citizen was unquestionably in an alien environment. Much notice was taken of his different clothing and ways, and this was extended to make of him a general figure of fun. A new figure, the Cockney sportsman, was added to English low comedy, and though he was to appear in many incarnations, he remained a stock character throughout the nineteenth century. R.S. Surtees' Mr Jorrocks is, of course, the best known, but differs from most by virtue of his real love and knowledge of hunting. Though the *Sporting Magazine* and its imitators were always ready to point out that the packs of hounds in the vicinity of London offered good sport, and that the followers of them, city men though they often were, were good sportsmen for all that, the countryman was not wholly convinced and relished the Cockney sportsman jokes that the magazines continued to print. [50]

Even those who did not give much credence to the wild stories of Cockney sportsmen could nevertheless find the popularity of hunting among city men alarming. Though the number of city men who hunted was always a small minority of hunting men in general, there were enough of them to swell the fields of the packs that were easily accessible to them, and this could lead to friction with the surrounding farmers, many of whom were market gardeners, who resented having their crops trampled by the crowds. Some of the hunts in the neighbourhood of London tried to keep the crowds down by not advertising their fixtures, [51] but this rarely succeeded. In 1808, the landowners and farmers of Harrow, Pinner, Watford, and Stanmore organized to keep the Old Berkeley from hunting over their lands, and their actions led to *Essex v. Capel*, the case that established the right of landowners to bar hounds from their land. [52] The Essex Hunt, which always numbered London men among its members and which was generally glad to have them, was worried about crowds of London riffraff in the 1820s, and in 1826, H.J. Conyers, the Essex master, wrote to assure his London subscribers, whose money he could not afford to lose, that he could differentiate between them and the other type of Londoner. [53]

The hunting Londoner was likely to find obstacles in his path not only from the countryman, but from his non-hunting compatriots who saw him as putting on airs. Surtees' picture of Jorrocks before the lunacy commissioners in *Handley Cross* may be an exaggeration, but his description of Mr Jorrocks' reception from the Cockney street urchins as he rode through London in full hunting costume on his way to a meet of the Surrey, [54] is probably no exaggeration at all.

Nevertheless, despite the obstacles placed in their paths, hardy city sportsmen hunted in increasing numbers. Facilities for the city hunting man sprang up to meet his needs. Riding schools to teach the would-be sportsman how to ride to hounds made their appearance in the metropolis by the 1830s to fill a need that the country-bred sportsman could generally satisfy in a more informal way. [55]

For the man who did not choose to own a horse, there were facilities for hiring them. John Tilbury of New Road became famous among both city and country sportsmen for providing good hunters. He would provide hunters by the day for one pound, or the sportsman could hire them for longer periods of time. His price for one hunter was twelve guineas per month or fifty for the season, with the hirer paying all other expenses. For forty guineas per month, he would provide two hunters and a groom, plus all keep and expenses. [56]Though this was expensive for the man who hunted from home, it was reasonable for the man who, like the Londoner, often had to board his horse at an inn or livery stable, and if anything happened to the horse, Tilbury would supply another. [57]

The impact of the Londoner upon the hunting world in general was minimal so long as the state of transportation limited him to hunting only with the packs in the immediate vicinity of the city. Most sporting men knew of him only through Cockney sportsman stories, though even so fastidious a critic as Nimrod declared the Surrey Subscription Hunt, most of whose subscribers were Londoners, to be a worthy pack. [58]It was not until later in the century that the city sportsman was to become anything more than a curiosity for most of the country, but in the vicinity of London, at least, he had already established himself as a legitimate member of the hunting community by the third decade of the nineteenth century. He was, in effect, the counterpart of the local sportsman of the rural districts, and, by overcoming the difficulties inherent in hunting from London, he often proved to be the most ardent sportsman of all.

At the opposite end of the spectrum from the Cockney sportsman rode the Meltonian. The period of Hugo Meynell's mastership had seen the beginning of the annual pilgrimage of the wealthy and fashionable to the fields of the shires. The years between his retirement and the coming of the railways saw the flowering and demise of a hunting society that was never to be reborn. Though the 'golden age' of foxhunting for most of the country was roughly the period between 1840 and 1870, the golden age of Melton was the period between 1800 and the mid-1830s, and more especially the twenties and thirties. [59] It was in those years, before the railways threw the Midlands open to a wider circle of sportsmen, that the real Meltonian of the type portrayed by Nimrod, Surtees, and 'The Druid' flourished. It was in this period that the inhabitants of Melton became nationally known figures whose exploits were devoured in country houses – and city ones as well – all over the country.

The Meltonians of this period form a sort of middle group between the hunting squires of the eighteenth century, who hunted for the enjoyment of watching hounds work and meeting their neighbours, and the hunting people of the later nineteenth century, many of whom hunted because it was the fashionable thing to do. The Meltonians of the middle period, whose dare-devil exploits have come down to us, hunted mainly for the pure exhilaration of the chase, and for the thrill of fast and hard riding over the best country in England.

The seeds of what Leicestershire – and above all, Melton Mowbray – was to become had been planted during Meynell's mastership. The young bloods who gravitated there were already acquiring a reputation for extravagant living, extravagant riding, and extravagant spending. 'The Leicestershire Hunt', according to an account of 1797, 'which has already (with all its *mad* collaterals) *ruined* so *many*, has been very near its own annihilation by the preponderance of *extravagancies*, with which it abounds. [60] But though the seeds were planted in Meynell's time, it was in the years following his retirement that the Melton of hunting legend flourished. Meynell was succeeded as master of the Quorn by Lord Sefton, and it was during his mastership (1800-1805) that the pattern of Melton life for the ensuing thirty years was set. Under Sefton, the passion for hard riding, already developing under Meynell, really took hold. Sefton, who weighed around 280 pounds, is said to have been the first to introduce the second horse system, in which each hunting man took out more than one horse, the spare one ridden by a lightweight groom, to enable him to have frequent changes of horse. The system was soon taken up even by lightweights who had no real need for a second horse, but who were enabled to ride all the harder for having one. [61]

The primary occupation of life at Melton was hunting, or, more properly for many of the Meltonians, riding. As we have seen, the main attraction of the town lay in its situation at the junction of three hunts, the Quorn, Cottesmore, and Belvoir, and a residence in the town or its vicinity, in the days when the only way to get to a meeting of hounds was to ride there on horseback, gave the avid sportsman the opportunity to hunt with one or another of these three packs six days a week. In the days of Meynell and his immediate successors, there was little else to do in Melton, and only those who were interested in taking advantage of this rare opportunity ever took the trouble to come there. [62] There were those who came for a week or two just to have a few hunts with the Quorn, but the real Meltonians stayed for the season.

The daily life of the Meltonians of those days has been described in great detail in numerous anecdotes and stories by the great sporting writers of the time, [63] and we probably know more about t(e essential quality of that life than we do about Melton at any subsequent date. It was a life devoted to the pursuit of foxes and pleasure. The Meltonian would rise, breakfast, and mount his covert hack to ride off to the meeting of whatever pack was most convenient, meeting friends and often taking the time for an impromptu steeplechase along the way. [64] During the course of the day's sport, hard riding was the rule, and the object for most Meltonians generally was to outride one another, rather than simply follow hounds. [65] The opportunity for hard and daring riding had increased since the days of Meynell. As we have seen, much of his country, though technically enclosed, was, in fact, unfenced, but during the first thirty years of the nineteenth century, real enclosure proceeded at a fairly rapid rate, and the new fences made riding all the more hazardous and exciting. [66]

The evenings could present a problem. There was little in the way of diversion in Melton, and the Meltonians had to create their own. During the reign of Lord Sefton, the passion for horses was at its height, and a great deal of time was spent in examining one another's studs and trading horses. The price of horses reached its peak in the first ten years or so of the nineteenth century. Nimrod claimed [67] that 500 to 800 guineas was a common price under Sefton, at a time when the army paid no more than £25 for a troop horse. [68] Lord Plymouth gave 1,000 guineas each for two horses, while Lord Jersey went so far as to hunt a Derby winner. [69] A favourite pastime in the evening was auctioning off one another's horses. Any Meltonian could name the horse of another, which was then bid upon. The horse's owner had only one bid, which was written on a piece of paper and placed under the candlestick. If any bids were higher, the horse was sold. Since the bidders were often drunk at the time, the prices paid were unusually high, and a Meltonian might awake the next morning to find that he had bought or sold a horse and had no recollection of it. [70] As the supply of good hunters increased and the Meltonians came to realize that the high prices were no guarantee of quality, the prices gradually came down, but 100 guineas was still a moderate price for a Leicestershire hunter. [71]

Drinking was yet another pastime of the Meltonians, though this was kept in check by the knowledge that the next day's riding required a clearer head than an all-night drinking session would produce. Gambling, cockfighting, and dogfighting were yet other amusements favoured by some. [72]

In the early years of the century, Melton was almost exclusively a masculine society. Many Meltonians were unmarried, and many of those who had wives left them at home. The memoirs of George Osbaldeston testify to the presence of prostitutes in the town, and Harriette Wilson, the noted courtesan, visited Melton around 1812, writing in her memoirs of 'a few wretched squalid prostitutes' who used to tap at the windows of foxhunting men in the evening. [73]

The rowdiness, drunkenness, gambling, and open whoring reached its peak in Melton in the mid-1820s. After that, we begin to hear of Meltonians being accompanied by their wives, who were perhaps getting worried about the reports they had heard. [74] By 1832, the *Sporting Magazine* was praising the Meltonians for 'making the place agreeable to the Ladies, who now go down as regularly as their Lords; and add by their presence a grace and a charm which was the only thing wanting to Melton to make it perfect.' [75]

The increasingly common presence of women in Melton by the 1830s is a sign of the fact that shire hunting was becoming the sport of the upper classes, and not just of one segment of them. It is also in the early 1830s that we first begin to hear of people being attracted to the shires for the 'swagger' of it, rather than for the riding. [76]

The hunting in the shires was unlike that of any other country, and a prime cause of the differences was the Meltonians themselves. The Meltonians were different from ordinary hunting men in three ways. They were wealthier, spent far more time hunting, and were not local people. They were probably younger as well, since only young men had the stamina and time to devote to Leicestershire hunting. [77]

These characteristics were, of course, closely related. The Meltonian had to be wealthy, for to hunt at Melton was an expensive proposition. The greatest investment a Meltonian had to make was for horses. Though with five good hunters, a prudent man could manage to see quite a lot of hunting even in Leicestershire, the 'grandees' at Melton generally had from seven to twelve horses, and some had as many as twenty-three. [78] Even if most of these horses were not purchased at exorbitant prices, a Meltonian typically spent upwards of £2000 on horses, some of which he might expect to recoup by selling them at the end of the season. Beyond the price of buying the horse was the price of keeping him. Nimrod estimated that to keep twelve hunters and two hacks at Melton cost from £1000 to £1200 for a year. [79] Nimrod's tastes were always expensive, but so were those of the Meltonians. As we have seen, Nimrod himself was allowed £1500 per year by the *Sporting Magazine* for the maintenance of six horses, from 1824 to 1828, but his expenses were unusually high owing to the need to travel. In 1826, a horse could be boarded at the George Inn, Melton, for twenty-six shillings per week including all provisions, [80] which for a stud of twelve works out to something of the order of £300 to £350 for the season, much lower than Nimrod's estimate, unless that estimate is actually for a full twelve months, rather than the 'hunting year'.

The Meltonian also had all his personal expenses to consider. They dressed, ate, and drank well and had to pay for expensive lodgings. For a small house in the centre of Melton, having only one room on a floor and no yard, a rental of 250 guineas was asked in 1824, and an offer of 200 guineas refused. [81] Expense was one reason why so many of the Meltonians shared lodgings, especially in the days before it was customary to bring women to Melton.

For virtually all Meltonians, the expenses of a hunting establishment were in addition to those of maintaining a permanent home elsewhere, for, as has been indicated, few of the Meltonians were local men. The Rev. J. Empson, a Leicestershire hunting parson, compiled a list of the forty-five best riders at Melton around 1820. Only eight were local landowners, and of these, five belonged to only two families. [82] The great number of outsiders, though welcomed by the local tradesmen to whom they brought business, were often resented by the local gentlemen, few of whom hunted with the Quorn or Cottesmore, and who split the Quorn in the 1830s and 40s so as to establish their own hunt. [83] The outsiders were also a problem to the master, especially since only a handful of them spent more than a few seasons at Melton before age or responsibility made them give up. [84] George Osbaldeston complained in his autobiography that it was almost impossible to give any satisfaction to the Meltonians 'who are only birds of passage.' [85]

C. D. B. Ellis, the historian of the Quorn, has pointed out that many of the most prominent Meltonian peers held titles less than fifty years old and indicates that many of them had probably inherited wealth from a recent ancestor. [86] This is hardly surprising. Melton life required ready cash, as we have seen, and the oldest families were not always the most plentifully supplied with it. The Meltonians were not, however, self-made men. Though Nimrod, in his *Quarterly* article, described a stranger — himself — being accepted by Melton society after just a few days, primarily on the strength of his riding, it was unlikely that many were so accepted.

The 'grandees' of Melton were no democrats. Even Nimrod who had claimed that the stranger who rode well might be invited to dine after five days, was careful to add that this would only be done after 'inquiries' were made into the newcomer's background. [87]Melton society was not open to all, even if the hunting field was.

It is something of a paradox that the ideal of hunting was Melton, at a time when one of the chief justifications of foxhunting was that it induced the country gentleman to live at home, but there was always a certain amount of hardly concealed ill-will and jealousy held by many provincial sportsmen toward the Meltonians. A Craven Hunt song of 1823 compared their hunt, under the famous John Warde, with the Quorn:

> Here is health to John Warde, and success to his hounds:
> Your Quornites may swish at the rasper so clever,
> And skim ridge and furrow, and charge an ox fence;
> But will riding alone make a sportsman? No, never!
> So I think we'd just send them some tutors from hence. [88]

Many looked at Melton merely as a place where a young man might let off a bit of steam and complete his education in the ways of the world before returning home to take up responsibilities. In his famous *Quarterly Review* article, Nimrod took up this very question:

> We must not, however, leave the subject without expressing our regret that resorting, *year after year,* to this metropolis of the chase should seem at all likely to become a *fashion* with persons whose hereditary possessions lie far from its allurements. It is all very well to go through the training of the acknowledged *school* of 'the craft'; but the country gentleman, who understands his duties, and in what the real permanent pleasure of life exists will never settle down into a regular Meltonian. He will feel that his first concern is with his own proper district, and seek the recreations of the chase, if his taste for them outlives the first heyday of youth, among the scenes, however, comparatively rude, in which his natural place has been appointed. [89]

Though the local landowners did not hunt with the shire packs, the same was not true of other local people. There was a regular contingent of Leicestershire graziers in the Quorn field from the days of Meynell. The graziers who rode with the Quorn could be distinguished by the blue coats they wore, and many of them were among the most daring men in the field. [90]They were also among the few farmers who could manage to turn a profit raising hunters because of the ready market available in the vicinity. So widespread did this business become that the old breed of heavy black horses for which Leicestershire had been famous disappeared almost overnight at the beginning of the nineteenth century. [91]

The Melton of Nimrod began to disappear in the 1830s. Many of the old Meltonians had died or retired, and money was becoming harder to come by. Agriculture was depressed, and those who had made money in other fields had yet to start coming to Melton. [92] But coincidentally a new development was coming which would raise the fortunes of the Midlands, the railway boom.

Others besides the Meltonians also hunted in a country not their own. Individual packs in various parts of the country attracted outsiders as early as the 1780s. John Byng described the Cotswold country around Broadway, Worcestershire, for example, as 'a fine fox and hare-hunting country, to which many gentlemen resort in winter...', [93] but these travelling sportsmen did not have the impact on their adopted countries that the Meltonians had. There were rarely more than a comparative handful in any one country and generally were greatly over-shadowed by the local gentlemen. Only in the great resort areas and near the universities was the presence of outsiders felt. Brighton, Bath, Leamington, and Cheltenham all had nearby packs patronized by visitors, but the great age of the spa as a hunting centre did not arrive until after the railways. [94]

Not surprisingly, hunting also had a great attraction for the young scions of the upper classes who attended the universities as a fashionable finishing school. Many of them had hunted from boyhood, and those who had not were introduced to the sport by their friends, especially at the more fashionable colleges like Christ Church. From about 1800, undergraduates began to appear in increasing numbers with neighbouring packs, often to the great annoyance of the master, the local followers, and the neighbouring farmers, all of whom resented the crowds of often irresponsible young men out for a gallop with no regard to crops, hounds, or foxes. [95] There were undergraduates who devoted great amounts of time to hunting. George Osbaldeston, when at Brasenose around 1800, kept two hunters and hunted three days a week. [96] Many others followed his example, though few matched the enthusiasm of Henry Chaplin, who, as an undergraduate at Christ Church in the 1860s, hunted six days a week throughout the season. [97]

One more thing may be said about hunting people of the pre-railway age. Whatever class they came from, they were almost exclusively male. Women, and especially women of good family, did not ride to hounds in any numbers until well after the middle of the nineteenth century.

There were exceptions of course. The greatest exception was the Marchioness of Salisbury, who, after the death of her husband, acted as master of the Hatfield Hunt from 1793. [98]Lady Salisbury's hunt always had a reputation for extreme exclusiveness, [99]perhaps because as a lady she had to be protected from meeting riffraff; but more likely because of the proximity of the hunt to London. One can only guess what her reaction would have been to the great transformations brought about by the railways.

CHAPTER 4

THE RAILWAY REVOLUTION

In 1827, two years after the opening of the Stockton and Darlington Railway, Nimrod passed through that part of the North on one of his hunting tours. 'The distance from Darlington (which I passed through) to Yarm,' he wrote,

> is five miles, for which I allowed myself somewhat about half an hour, the road being none of the best, but I did not reach it under an hour. The delay arose from my meeting something, which I could only compare to *a moving hell*. [1]

It was a steam locomotive, which so frightened Nimrod's horse that he was forced to get the animal into the ditch at the side of the road to quiet him.

This was the first recorded introduction of the hunting community to the railways. The reaction that followed was hardly more favourable. Foxhunters saw the new development as a double menace. First, the railways, they felt, would split the country and form an uncrossable barrier for foxes and hounds. [2] This fear was hardly novel. Eighteenth-century hunting people had opposed canal construction for precisely the same reason. [3] Secondly, it was believed that the railways would make it too easy for people to get to London, and the country gentlemen would no longer want to live in the country, though this was a reversal of the earlier claim that it was hunting that kept people in the country. Surtees went so far as to predict, in 1834, that 'in a few years hunting will be a matter of history' [5] 'as a result of the railways.

In fact, neither of these worries proved to be serious. Although the railway lines did, in fact, cut across hunting countries, adding one more hazard to the sport, the hazard was a relatively minor one. [6]As for the second fear, that the railways would drain the country of sportsmen, it, too, proved illusory. It was to take longer for hunting people to perceive that the real danger threatened from precisely the opposite direction.

Despite their early fears, hunting people were not slow to take advantage of the new development. Masters soon saw that horses and hounds could be sent to distant meets by train, thus saving time, the expense of extra kennels, and wear and tear on the animals. The Holderness Hunt first made use of trains for this purpose in 1846; by the 1860s it was common practice. [7]By far the greater impact, however, was on the followers of hounds. As early as 1841, when the fears about railways outnumbered the hopes, the *Sporting Magazine* published a map and list of meeting places of the Quorn, with their distances from Leicester, where 'there is a railway station'. [8]By the middle of the forties, the railways were fast becoming accepted as a convenience. Local sportsmen began using what Mr Jorrocks called the 'best covert hacks in the world' to reach distant meets of their hounds so regularly, that the real covert hack largely disappeared from the stables of most of them. [9]Even more striking was the discovery that the railway made it easier to visit other countries than it had been to hack to a distant meet in one's own. In 1853, the editor of the newly founded *Field* turned his back on old tradition and wrote:

> It may seem strange for us to make discouraging observations on a sport we profess to espouse, but the fact is, we believe gentlemen in bad countries will find it more to their account to avail themselves of the facilities of railways for getting to good countries, than in poking about home with the indifferent sport generally shown by inferior packs. [10]

For the first time, the ordinary hunting man was no longer forced to choose between hunting in his home country, or going to the great bother and expense of relocating himself and his horses for the length of the hunting season. He could now live at home, or at most take a week or two, and sample the sport with any pack in the country. Articles and guides began appearing in the sporting press advising the sportsman on the best ways to take advantage of the railways, telling him where to go and what to expect when he got there. [11]Itinerant sportsmen, who owed loyalty to no pack, but made short visits to many, bcame common by the 1860s.[12]

The most dramatic and most highly visible result of the railways was the facility they offered for the city dweller. It was not simply that the old packs that had catered to the city man were now more convenient. He could now find it easy and cheap to hunt further afield than ever before. By the fifties, the shires themselves were within reach of the Londoner, who could, leaving Euston Square at 6.30 in the morning, hunt with the Pytchley or the Quorn and still return the same night. [13]Warwickshire, Northamptonshire, Hampshire, Oxfordshire, Wiltshire, and Gloucestershire could all be hunted over, and the Londoner could hunt six days a week if he so chose. In 1854, 'Cecil' listed twenty-four packs of foxhounds that could be reached in a day's outing, not to mention staghounds and harriers. [14]Not only was the choice a wide one, the expense of hunting was cut to a fraction of what it had been. Gone was the need to send one's horse on the day before, or the need to sleep at a hotel oneself. In general, the rail fares from London in the 1850s, for transport of a horse and his rider, were £1.1s to £1.5s. for thirty miles and £1.7s. to £1.10s. for forty miles. [15]

The railway companies themselves were quick to realize that hunting meant business for them, and many of the companies went out of their way to promote that business. The London, Brighton, and South Coast Railway, for example, subscribed twenty-five pounds to the South Down Hunt, many of whose followers it carried to the meets. [16]Almost all of the companies provided special reduced-fare hunting tickets for the length of the season. Six-month hunting tickets from London to Leighton, Tring, and Aylesbury were issued beginning in the 1850s. [17]The railways also found it worthwhile to run special trains for the convenience of foxhunters, or to arrange for regular trains to make extra stops to pick up or drop off hunting men. [18]

There were even those like Henry Chaplin, who, when master of the Burton, from 1864 to 1871, used to attend late sittings of the House of Commons, and then hire a special train to take him to Lincolnshire, where, on a remote cutting near the meet, he would be met by his groom with a hack. [19]Chaplin was richer than most, and his devotion to hunting was greater than most, but he is a fine example of the way in which hunting people came to terms with railways. Though they were feared and resented upon their first introduction, they became a necessity to the hunting man within a very short time.

The result of this new ease of travel was that hunting became more popular than ever, first among the upper classes, and then among some members of the middle classes as well. Between 1845 and 1875 the number of people who hunted increased remarkably, often to the astonishment of contemporary observers who saw the numbers growing almost daily.[20] Even in so relatively unfashionable a country as the Holderness, in the East Riding of Yorkshire, the number of people who hunted was estimated to have increased tenfold in the thirty years between 1843 and 1873.[21] The number of packs of hounds continued to grow. The sporting press listed 99 in 1850, 115 in 1867, and 137 in 1877.[22] Since virtually the whole country had been apportioned into hunt territories by 1850, this growth does not reflect an increase in the amount of country hunted. Instead, each acre was hunted over more frequently — a development that, as we shall see, was to cause much trouble in later years.

The railways were changing the pattern of upper class life. The old distinctions between town and country were breaking down. In 1846, Surtees mourned the passing of the 'real country gentleman',[23] the man who lived in the country all the year round. Many of his contemporaries, as we have seen, foresaw the doom of country life as the young, having tasted the delights of city luxury, would desert the countryside.[24] What they failed to realize was that, no longer forced to choose between town and country, the upper classes were able to enjoy both. Modern improvements had made country life far more comfortable than it had been in the days when rural privations were the subject of songs, and people who could afford to live where they liked, chose to spend much of their time in the country because it was a pleasant place to be. While the railway made it easier for the country dweller to take advantage of the city, the young man attracted by the joys of fashionable London, or forced to earn his living there, no longer had to turn his back on the country. Hunting and other country sports were turned to increasingly by this new country-house society.

From the mid-1840s, hunting was becoming 'the thing to do',[25] and by the 1860s there was no question of its position as the height of fashion. By 1869, *Baily's Magazine* could call hunting 'the most fashionable of all winter recreations and pastimes',[26] and in 1876, the *Saturday Review* called the sport 'one of the leading features of English life among the monied 27 This prestige was not new, of course. We have already seen how the sport had begun to acquire *cachet* in Meynell's day, and how it continued to grow in the years following his retirement. Nimrod and his imitators had done much in the 1820s and 30s to attract national attention to foxhunting, and had portrayed foxhunters as the social elite of the countryside. But the relative hardships still associated with the sport, even in Nimrod's time, had the tendency to set hunting people aside as a group of their own within the upper classes. Hunting was now becoming so much more convenient, that the old distinction between hunting and non-hunting men was breaking down. Many of those who turned to the sport, did so in the same way they shot grouse or went to Cowes, as a social event, and no longer devoted themselves exclusively to hunting. [28]

'I am afraid hunting is going downhill', lamented the narrator of *Market Harborough,* George Whyte Melville's popular hunting novel of 1861.

> I think there are few specimens left of the old hunting sort, who devoted themselves exclusively to their favourite pursuit and could not even bear to hear it mentioned with anything like levity or disrespect. [29]

But there were many more who welcomed the change, which, they claimed, set them apart from the ignorant, besotted squires of the eighteenth century and the three-bottle bucks of the early nineteenth.

Hunting novels like *The Master of Hounds* [30] began to utilize the hunting field as a symbol of upper-class life, and the sporting aspects were played down. Similarly, hunting journalism, which in the past had stressed the daredevil exploits of the Meltonians, began to turn to reporting Melton weddings and divorces. [31]

It is highly significant that the second half of the nineteenth century produced no legendary hunting figures to rank with the early Meltonians. Though there were those, like Lord Willoughby de Broke and Henry Chaplin, who devoted much of their time to the sport, and whose names were probably recognizable to far more of their contemporaries than had been the names of their illustrious predecessors to theirs, they did not catch the imagination in the way that the old daredevils had done. In fact, it became vulgar to boast of one's riding prowess. Even in the shires, the hard-riding thrusters no longer rode against one another as they had in the days of Osbaldeston and Assheton Smith. The shires, to say nothing of the provincial countries, were attracting many who did not wish to ride hard at all, but who merely went there each year for the company, the sake of fashion, and moderate exercise. As one man put it in 1863:

> The ride from cover to cover is always cheerful and over grass; the gates are accommodating; society first-class; and as long as they are

well got-up about the breeches and boots nobody cares one sixpence whether they have jumped one fence or twenty. [32]

To deal with the stout cut-and-laid fences which had become almost universal in Leicestershire by 1850, an extensive system of hunting gates had been installed, which made it possible to follow hounds without having to do much jumping at all, though a good start was advisable if one did not wish to wait one's turn as two hundred riders tried to pass through a gate. [33]

There were even those who wintered in the shires and never hunted at all. They would appear at the meets, but never follow hounds, and were always sure of pleasant company at dinner and a game of cards afterwards. [34] By 1861, the onset of a frost that stopped hunting no longer sent Meltonians scurrying off to London, though it was certainly easier to get there than ever before. Instead, they remained in the town, enjoying the society and skating on the frozen river. [35] That same year we read of their entertaining themselves in the evening with amateur theatricals. [36] George Osbaldeston would have had little sympathy for either amusement. He would probably have been totally mystified by the man who wrote to *The Field* in 1881, asking for help in finding a pleasant town near the south coast with a good club and society, and which offered three or four days of hunting a week and a good golf course. [37]

For many people whose tastes did not run to Melton, but who fancied a trip away from home, the railways gave rise to a new group of hunting centres. Cheltenham and Leamington Spas became mini-Meltons, and some of the men who hunted from them, especially Leamington, acquired reputations among 'serious' sportsmen as unsavoury as those of some of the daredevil Meltonians of an earlier day. [38] Rugby, which had the double advantage of being a railway centre and being conveniently located for the shires and some of the top provincial packs, continued to attract large numbers of hunting visitors throughout the sixties, seventies, and eighties. [39]

One sign of the new social aspect of hunting was the increasing presence of women in the field. As we have already seen, it was rare to find women, especially women of good family, in the hunting field in the first half of the nineteenth century. From about midcentury, however, their numbers began to increase. The propriety of women hunting was the great controversy of the 1850s. An American 'bloomer' who appeared with Lord Elcho's hounds in 1851, had been the subject of humour in

Bell's Life, [40]but as more and more women found the sport to their liking, the old-fashioned hunting men who looked upon hunting as a masculine preserve, turned to more weighty arguments to keep women out. Quite apart from the danger, they argued, hunting was unsuitable for the gentler sex who were likely to hear language not fit for their ears, to be jostled by all sorts of low types, or to have their clothing torn. Besides, the argument ran, gentlemen far preferred to be able to have the society of ladies in the evening, when they could be polite to them, which was plainly impossible in the rough-and-tumble of a hunting run. Left unspoken was the fear of being outridden by a woman, a very real possibility, according to observers like Trollope and Surtees, since most women who hunted had generally taken the precaution of taking lessons first, something which many men never admitted a need to do. [41]

When, in 1855, a correspondent asked the editors of *The Field* for advice on what women should wear when hunting, they replied that it was best for them not to hunt at all, [42]but the efforts to keep women from hunting were of little avail. Women took up hunting in increasing numbers throughout the fifties and sixties, led by women of such unquestioned social prominence as the Countess of Yarborough, Lady Grey de Wilton, and the Dowager Marchioness of Westminster and her daughter, Lady Theodora Grosvenor. [43]In 1868, *Baily's Magazine* printed its first short story with a hunting heroine, [44]and by 1870, *The Field* had completely reversed itself on the propriety of women hunting, dismissing most of the arguments it had endorsed twelve years earlier. [45]By the time the Empress of Austria came over to hunt in the shires in 1878, placing the final seal of respectability upon the woman hunter, and swelling the Pytchley fields to monstrous size with those who came out to see her, [46]her influence was hardly necessary. In 1878, 'Brooksby' (Captain E. Pennell-Elmhirst), who in the seventies and eighties occupied the high position in the sporting world once held by Nimrod, estimated that ten per cent of the approximately three hundred who turned out each day in Leicestershire were women. [47]

The involvement of ladies in the sport demanded that it be untouched by the slightest breath of scandal. Gone were the wicked days of Melton when one hunting man could joke about another's unsatisfactory performance with a prostitute. [48]The 'Cheshire Difficulty' of 1857-58, in which the master of the Cheshire Hounds was forced to resign when an 'indiscreet' letter he had written to a married woman became public, demonstrates that hunting no longer belonged to the world it had inhabited forty years earlier.[49] Shortly after the Cheshire Difficulty, however, the public morality of the hunting field was brought into conflict with the cherished belief in its openness, and what followed indicated that the latter still had the power to sway public opinion.

Catherine Walters, better known as 'Skittles', was one of the most notable of the Victorian courtesans. She had also been a circus equestrienne and was, therefore, an excellent horsewoman. She had a taste for hunting, which she occasionally indulged with a number of Midland packs, including the Quorn. Unfortunately, Lady Stamford, wife of the Quorn master, had also begun life as a circus equestrienne, and, having gone to great lengths to escape the stigma of her past, she took the presence of one who had not achieved her respectability as a personal affront.[50] She prevailed upon her husband to bar 'Skittles' from the field, which he did, apparently reluctantly. Whereupon 'Skittles', with the aid of a number of Quorn followers, managed to get in a fair bit of hunting without bothering to come to the meets. She later switched her allegiance to the hounds of W.W. Tailby, who hunted the Billesdon, or South Quorn country.

The 'Skittles' affair aroused a great deal of interest in sporting and fashionable circles and prompted a great debate in the sporting press on the right of a master to bar from the field anyone who did not interfere with the working of the hounds.[51] 'Scrutator' set himself up as the defender of morality in this case, and taking the Cheshire Difficulty as one of his guides, asserted that the master had a duty to prevent the hunting field from being turned into a 'bear-garden'.[52] Most people, however, agreed with *The Field's* leading article, which, while lamenting the fact that 'the laws of society have been greatly relaxed in reference to the treatment of such persons in public places', nevertheless asserted as a matter of principle:

> Hunting has been supported, even to the great annoyance of the pheasant-preserver, and, in some instances, of the farmer also, chiefly because it has been made a means of encouraging social intercourse among all classes; and to give a master the power of forbidding the presence of anyone at the covert-side, is a dangerous innovation upon established usage.[53]

Tailby refused to follow Stamford's example, though he was threatened by 'a certain nobleman' that if he allowed 'Skittles' out with his hounds he would find some coverts closed to him. 'I took my stand', he wrote in his diary, on the broad principles that 'The hunting field is open to all the world', that 'I am not the censor of the morality of the hunting field,' that I have 'no right to disappoint others to gratify the prejudices of an individual,' — and that, in short, nothing could induce me to take the hounds home merely because 'Skittles' is out. I am encouraged to this the more that I never hear any complaints of her conduct in the hunting field, or that she is in any way objectionable to the ladies who come out. On this I take my stand, let the result be what it may. [54]

The great difference between the Cheshire case and that of 'Skittles' was that the former case concerned the master of hounds, the latter a simple member of the field. The master of foxhounds was expected to be above all reproach. The hunting field, however, was a public place, and those who frequented public places could not be as strictly controlled.

But while 'the hunting field', in its abstract meaning, had always been a public place, in the sense that it was open to all, in its more literal meaning — the field in which hunting was taking place — it was far from a public place. Custom had dictated that it be open, but that custom was rooted, in part, in the premise that most of those who rode were the neighbours of the man over whose land they rode. In many countries, however, this was no longer the case.

The great social prestige that hunting had attained was not lost on growing numbers of the newly enriched urban middle classes. When the railways made it possible for them to hunt without having to bear the stigma of the regular followers of 'cockney' packs like the Surrey, many of them turned to hunting because of its position as the sport of landed society, and because shooting, its only serious competition, was often much harder to come by. Not only was hunting the sport of the gentry, it was also the sport that boasted of its openness. Having read Nimrod's account of riding himself into society at Melton, and encouraged by the glowing reports of the people to be met with in the field, many turned to the hunting field for the opportunity to rub elbows with the 'swells'.

In one sense, the man who sought social advancement through hunting was not a new phenomenon, as we have seen. But the involvement in hunting, in pre-railway days, almost always had been accompanied by the purchase of land, and was an attempt to gain acceptance as a local landowner in the society of other local landowners. The railways, by changing the exclusively local character of hunting, eliminated the need for the would-be social climber to acquire land before making his first foray into the hunting field.

Members of the older hunting community very quickly became aware of the newcomers in their midst, and they reacted with a mixture of amusement, shock, welcome, and dismay, often out of proportion to the actual number of outsiders who appeared. On the one hand, they could not help feeling gratification that the sport they loved was extending its appeal to yet another element of the population, but on the other, the prospect of a horde of strangely mannered city men descending on the field could not help but be alarming.

By this time, of course, 'city man' no longer referred exclusively to Londoners. The growth of the cities of the Midlands and North had produced a new set of urban sportsmen, eager to escape the towns for a day of sport in the country. Men from Liverpool and Manchester generally hunted in Cheshire. [55]Those from Birmingham and Coventry had the whole of the Midlands open to them, and those who did not fancy turning out with the Quorn or Pytchley, generally favoured the Warwickshire and North Warwickshire. [56]A Birmingham Hunt Club was founded in the fifties, made up of men who hunted from that city, and the club sent donations to several hunts near the town. [57]Leeds men had the choice of several packs in Yorkshire, and many favoured the Bramham Moor. [58] The 'cockney sportsman' found himself being crowded out of humourous stories by the 'cotton lord' of Manchester, who had the double disadvantage of being a city man and of being associated with anti-agricultural elements. [59]

In the early days of the invasion, at least, the sporting press, eager for the larger circulation that an increasing interest in sport would bring them, espoused the cause of the newcomers. Proclaiming that, thanks to the march of progress, the townsman was no longer the 'cruel cockney' of former days, they rushed to guide him into the world of hunting. Articles appeared congratulating the new sportsman on his taste and offering advice on where and how to hunt. [60]A change came over hunting books as well. From the days of Peter Beckford, they had been aimed at the young squire who wanted his own pack, and hence, treated almost exclusively the skills of kennel management and the 'science' of hunting. The new set of books was aimed at the man who had not the slightest interest in such matters, but who sorely needed advice on how to ride to hounds. [61]The established sporting journals, the weekly *Bell's Life in London* and the monthly *Sporting Magazine*, which had, between them, monopolized the field, were faced with new competitors, founded to take advantage of the rising interest in sport. *The Field* began publication in 1853, and is still publishing weekly. One of the influences behind its founding was R. S. Surtees, who saw the opportunity to capture the weekly market that had been monopolized by *Bell's Life*, which was tainted by its old position as the organ of the prize ring. [62] *Baily's Magazine*, a monthly, began publication in 1860.

No less an authority than George Whyte Melville, the favourite hunting poet and novelist of the fifties and sixties, set the stamp of his approval on the sporting pretensions of the middle classes. 'You', he told them,

> are the true sportsmen, after all, – the *pater familias*, the respectable householder, the responsible vestryman, churchwarden or other parish magnate, loving the Diana whom you worship with an ardour all the more glowing in proportion to the rarity of her favours... Like your excellent prototype, Mr. Jorrocks... your enjoyment of field sports is a stolen pleasure, a forbidden fruit, of which the flavour is as exquisite as it is costly. [63]

In many countries, the newcomers, particularly if they subscribed handsomely and made every effort to conform to custom, were welcomed. Though the old days of the Surrey had passed, there were still packs in which businessmen predominated. The North Staffordshire, for example, was followed by more businessmen than landowners, and the historian of that pack boasted, in 1902, that it was that fact that gave the hunt much of its 'geniality and good-fellowship'. [64]

But from the very beginning, there were also signs that, for many, the newcomers were unpopular. There was the simple problem of larger crowds, which made riding less pleasant, and which antagonized farmers because of the greater damage they caused. Secondly, there was the fact that many of the newcomers, and not all of them middle-class men, either, depended upon their anonymity to hunt without paying. [65] Finally, in many countries, this anonymity did away with the old easygoing social atmosphere that had prevailed in the days when everyone knew everyone else.

There was little remedy for the first of these problems. If there was anything about which hunting men were most proud, it was their boast that no one who was willing to behave himself and not deliberately spoil the sport of others could be excluded. Attempts were sometimes made by neighbouring packs to arrange their meetings to compete with one another, so as to keep the crowds at each small, [66] but, aside from grumbling, little else was done.

The second problem was equally vexing. The predominant method of financing a hunt had developed in the days when all who hunted knew one another. Though it was expected that those who hunted regularly would subscribe to the hunt fund, that subscription had always been entirely voluntary, and most hunts depended on a sense of obligation on the part of their followers to pay as much as they were able. [67] The aristocratic ideal of largesse was reinforced by the egalitarian one of the openness of the hunting field. Though those who followed only occasionally might be expected to tip the huntsman or make a contribution to the damage fund, [68] there was no regular provision for collecting money from them. In the early years of the sport, when these occasional followers were few and far between, it was tacitly assumed that any stranger who came out was a subscriber to another pack of hounds in his home country, and was, therefore, treated as a guest, with the understanding that the favour would be reciprocated. [69] But many of those who now rode the railways had no home country of their own. These included not only merchants and manufacturers out for an occasional day with hounds, but idle young men with time and money on their hands, who enjoyed sampling the hunting with as many packs as they could. They had, in fact, been encouraged in this life by the countless articles in the sporting press giving advice on how best to use the railways for getting to hounds.

The problem facing the hunt secretaries and treasurers was that to ask the interlopers for a contribution would have flown in the face of hunting tradition, so again, though there was some grumbling, little more was done. Though there were few, if any, hunts that could not have used more money, the generally prosperous times that kept the farmers from complaining too loudly about the damages done by the larger fields also made it possible for the country gentlemen, who were still the backbone of most hunts, to dig into their pockets for whatever money was needed.

The third problem was in many ways the most fundamental. The great pride that hunting men took in the role of the hunting field as the unifier of all classes was based, as we have seen, on the fact that the hunting community existed within the framework of the local rural community, and was possible only because of this framework. As people hunted in larger numbers, and as hunting people began to be drawn from outside the local residents, the hunting community ceased, in fact, to be a community. In the old days the complete stranger who turned up with any pack outside the shires or the immediate vicinity of the large towns was

extremely rare, and because of this, was generally taken at face value.
As late as midcentury, 'Harry Hieover' could claim that

> a kind of freemasonry actuates hunting men. In provincial hunts, a man well mounted and spoken to by a M.F.H., is virtually introduced to the hunt, even if a stranger.... He is a hunting man, his look and bearing are those of a gentleman, and as a stranger, every man — at least every gentleman — is willing to show him a civility. [70]

But to the extent that this was true, it could only be true because the occasional stranger offered no threat to the harmony of the existing community. Because he was a rare occurrence, it made no great difference even if he was not what he appeared to be. He had come, and would soon go and be forgotten.

It was the possibility of pretence that most frightened the conservative soul of the foxhunter. That is why he was perfectly willing to welcome 'humble' followers, so long as they remained 'humble'. That is why so normally tolerant and unpretentious a man as Surtees was so insistent that the red hunting coat be worn only by gentlemen 'of independent means'. [71]

In the old days there had been little difficulty in recognizing a gentleman, but it was becoming harder. Many of the newcomers looked like gentlemen and sounded like gentlemen. In fact, looking and sounding like a gentleman was becoming the chief criterion in determining a gentleman for most practical purposes, but this was not good enough for the hunting field, where a very delicate relationship had always existed between the gentle and the non-gentle.

In an apparent paradox, therefore, as the hunting field became more popular, old-line hunting men, not willing to abandon their favourite diversion in the face of the growing number of newcomers, began to retreat to greater and greater social exclusiveness. Even as 'Harry Hieover' wrote in the late 1840s, the situation was changing, and by 1854, the same author was complaining of the swarms of 'jackeens who only began hunting yesterday, and keep as many hunting coats (or perhaps more) than horses'. [72] During the sixties and seventies whatever had remained of the openness disappeared in many hunting countries. By the late seventies it was gone forever. In 1880, *Bell's Life* advised would-be hunting men to be sure to obtain introductions to local people before venturing into a country, for 'to the stranger unknown to anyone, and especially if the individual by his own choice or misfortune carries with him anything of the snob or the *parvenu*, there will be very little bending from the most rigid rules of etiquette'.[73]

Many of those who turned to hunting in those years had been taken in by the myth of hunting egalitarianism that hunting men had so carefully cultivated. They had heard and read of the easy camaraderie of gentlemen and farmers, and were, therefore, surprised to find that when they turned to hunting they were not met with the same welcome. 'A', who called himself a gentleman, 'though in business', complained to *The Field*, in 1878, that though he had been a member of two hunts for the previous twenty years, he was only really accepted by the members of the one that, being near town, had many businessmen as members.[74] A 'German gentleman' from Hamburg, signing himself 'G.F.M.W.P.', complained in a similar vein some years later, prompting the editors of *The Field* to confront the issue head on. 'G.F.M.W.P's' letter, they wrote,

> raises the whole question as to how far participation in what may be termed a public amusement, like hunting, is in itself, a passport to society. Owing to the altered condition of things, the answer will certainly be in the negative. Adventurers, and persons who are singularly destitute of honour in their own country, are sufficiently numerous to make men shy of taking up with strangers.[75]

Meeting a man with hounds, they declared, meant no more than passing him in the street.

People like 'A' and 'G.F.M.W.P.' had failed to see that, though the hunting field provided the opportunity for the free mixing of classes, hunting alone could not ensure that the mingling would take place in the absence of a shared sense of community. The local hunting tradesman or farmer stood higher in the eyes of the hunting gentleman than his non-hunting compatriot. He was a 'good fellow'. But the real basis for the intercourse of classes was the absolute knowledge, on both sides, of the respective position of each. The newcomer to the field dressed and talked like a gentleman, but, without an introduction, who was to know who he was? He could be an 'adventurer ... destitute of honour in his own country'. He could even be a cutlery manufacturer from Sheffield.

Meanwhile, hunting men could go on talking of the sport as the unifier of classes because, at least, it unified the classes that really mattered. None of the foregoing should make us lose sight of the fact that, in many countries, the old 'natural hunting men' – country gentlemen and farmers – still made up the backbone of the hunt and would continue to do so until economic conditions made it impossible for many of them to go on.[76]

The agricultural prosperity that benefited landlord and farmer alike enabled members of both classes to keep their hunters and turn out regularly with hounds. Though the general trend toward the consolidation of farms meant that there were fewer farmers, it also meant that those who were left were wealthier and better able to afford the sport. If anything, the participation of farmers in the field increased during the third quarter of the nineteenth century. A leading article in *Bell's Life in London* in 1874 went so far as to call hunting the '*special* sport of the farmer class'. [77] Though this cannot be taken to mean that most farmers hunted, for they almost certainly did not, hunting was, nevertheless, still the only field sport that openly welcomed farmers, and in which they participated in any numbers. Game laws still restricted their shooting and fishing, while coursing was popular only in certain districts.

The wealthier farmers, and especially the younger men among them, were even taking to the sport in a far grander style than had their predecessors, and began appearing in scarlet coats by the 1860s. [78] Some farmers even started subscribing to hounds, though this was still very rare and was to remain so. When a number of hunting farmers collected nearly twenty-eight pounds to aid the South Durham in 1881, it was described as 'a novelty... in hunting subscriptions, and greatly appreciated at the time'. [79]

The grandest hunting farmers remained those who lived in the Brocklesby country on the Lincolnshire wolds. They were among the wealthiest farmers in the country, and many of them lived in a style associated far more with the gentry than the farmer. They almost all rode in scarlet, and there were often as many as sixty to eighty out in the course of a day. [80] The Brocklesby farmers were famous throughout England, but there were many more modestly situated hunting farmers in every part of the country. There were countries in which they predominated, and some in which they were almost alone in the field. In the 1850s, the South Essex was largely a farmers' hunt, though the depression drove most of them from the field. In the seventies, the Craven field was made up largely of farmers, as was that of the East Essex. [81]

In 1898, the Bilsdale Hunt, a pack in the North Riding of Yorkshire, was engaged in a boundary dispute with a neighbouring pack, and when the dispute was submitted to the Master of Foxhounds Association for arbitration, the hunt compiled statements from old followers of the hounds in order to establish its precedence to the coverts in question. Only three of the statements were from men styling themselves 'esquire' or 'gentleman'. All the rest were farmers, retired farmers, carriers, blacksmiths, and other 'humble' country people, and almost all of these claimed to have hunted or followed 'regularly' or 'often'. [82]Some of these may well have followed on foot, since the statements are often unclear on this point, but the statements, and the choice of people to make statements, indicate clearly that in the North Riding, at least, hunting remained an essentially popular amusement throughout the century.

Farmers and other 'humble' hunting men continued, of course, in a subordinate social position. Hunt breakfasts still often served them only after the gentlemen had eaten. [83]Local professional men and tradesmen also continued to turn out as they had before. [84]Even the clergy were still to be found in the field, though it became increasingly awkward for them. The old sort of hunting parson had, of course, largely disappeared along with his counterpart, the old sort of hunting squire, but his replacement, often a younger son of the gentry, and a former public school and university man, could still regard sport as a perfectly normal part of his life. As we have seen, the Rev. Charles Kingsley, one of the foremost apostles of 'muscular Christianity', was an ardent foxhunter who saw the sport as a great builder of moral character. 'I know that He has made me a parish priest', he wrote, 'and that is the duty which is nearest, but did He too let me become a strong, daring, sporting wild man of the woods for nothing?' [85]

The debate over the propriety of clergymen hunting flared briefly in 1859, with the *Saturday Review* taking the middle position that there was nothing wrong with clergymen hunting *per se*, provided, of course, that it did not interfere with their parochial duties, but the possibility that some parishioners might be scandalized if their parson hunted, they added, made it wiser for clergymen to work off their surplus energies in foreign travel, which would give them 'a field where they can go through any amount of hard work, kill any amount of game to the glory of heaven, and attain any human measure of moral activity', — an ironic reference to Kingsley and his school. [86]But as late as 1913, when a memorial window was erected in honour of a clergyman killed in a hunting accident, Cosmo Gordon Lang, Archbishop of York, could state: 'Some people might find it difficult to understand how there could be a close connection between hunting and the life of a Christian clergyman, [but hunting] was a form of sport which developed some of the finest qualities of human nature — courage, endurance, readiness to face risk, comradeship, and honourable courtesies', and which drew together, 'the various classes of the countryside'. [87]

Archbishop Lang's strained encomiums aside, however, there is no question but that hunting clergymen definitely felt on the defensive by the seventies, and whatever they might have said about the virtues that hunting fostered, or the community of interest it provided with their parishioners, there were many people who, though not opposed to hunting, were opposed to it for their parson. [88]

The continuing presence in the field of the old hunting classes meant that in many countries a dual structure of hunting men existed, side by side, but rarely mingling. Insulated within the old familiar hunting society, the hunting establishment could afford to live as though things had not really changed. Though they could not help but be aware of the crowds of newcomers, they could largely ignore their significance. Secure in their positions, they did not realize that the entire basis of the sport had radically changed.

CHAPTER 5

HUNT COUNTRIES

The enormous growth of interest in hunting just described was accompanied by a parallel growth in the organization of the sport. In its earliest days, foxhunting had existed with little formal organization, but by the first third of the nineteenth century hunting people had evolved an often complex system of organization governing almost all aspects of the sport. Packs of hounds and the countries over which they hunted took on an existence of their own, totally distinct from the personalities of the men who hunted with them. Once the private property of a country gentleman, subject to his will alone, the hunt became a semi-public corporation able to perpetuate itself no matter what became of the man at its head, subject to the wishes of many, and governed by a comprehensive code. During the years in which hunting was becoming a national sport it was also becoming a great national institution. This institutionalization extended both to the pattern of hunting over England as a whole, and to the organization within each hunting district, or country, as it was called. Though it will be convenient to examine each of these two separately, it must be kept in mind that certain questions – the rights of land and covert owners, for example – fall partly within each category.

The need to arrange for the organization of the sport over the country as a whole was prompted by the fact, already alluded to, that, unlike shooting and fishing, foxhunting could not be restricted by property boundaries. Even if the owner of a pack was able to find foxes on his own land, which was not always the case, it could not be expected that the foxes in their flight would remain there. Since the sport could not hope to survive if every chase had to be stopped as soon as the fox crossed the line into another man's property, some arrangement had to be worked out to allow the sportsman to ignore ordinary property considerations. In the eighteenth century, it had generally been believed that a hunt had the legal right to pass over anyone's land in pursuit of a fox. In 1786, this belief was strengthened by the case of *Gundry v. Feltham*. Feltham, a huntsman in Dorset, followed a fox onto Gundry's land and damaged his property. He justified his right to be there on the grounds that the fox was a noxious animal, which had to be destroyed for the good of the community, and that hunting him with hounds was the only way of doing so.

Justice Buller, before whom the case was heard, found in favour of Feltham. 'The question on this record', he wrote,

> is, whether the defendant is justified in following the fox all over another man's grounds. The demurrer admits that which is averred in the plea, namely, that this was the only means of killing the fox. This case does not determine that a person may unnecessarily trample down another man's hedges, or maliciously ride over his grounds: if he does more than is absolutely necessary, he cannot justify it; and such circumstances are a proper subject for a new assignment. [1]

Despite the clear limitation of the principle in this case, *Gundry v. Feltham* was in fact taken to mean that property rights did not exist so far as hunting was concerned. Nevertheless, for the purposes of local peace, masters of hounds tried not to appear too careless of the rights of at least the major landowners in their neighbourhoods. Thus we find Lord Euston, later the third Duke of Grafton, writing to the Marchioness de Grey in 1791:

> As I am persuaded of your Ladyship's desire of conducing to the innocent amusement of your neighbours, I scarce feel an apology necessary for the liberty I have three times in the course of the last month taken of hunting upon your manors near Silsoe, at the same Time I feel it necessary to inform your Ladyship that I have done so, lest it should be represented to you that I have taken Liberties inconsistent with the attention due to your Ladyship. [2]

In 1809, however, any doubts that might have been left by *Gundry v. Feltham* were finally settled by the important case of *Essex v. Capel*.[3] In this rather curious case, the Earl of Essex sued the master of the Old

Berkeley Hunt, the Hon. and Rev. William Capel, who also happened to be his brother, when the hounds, after being warned off, entered his property, leading to the breaking of several fences. Citing *Gundry v. Feltham*, Capel's counsel claimed that the trespass was justified. Not surprisingly, the counsel for Lord Essex argued that, far from hunting to keep down the population of foxes, the Old Berkeley took the field solely for amusement, and that, in fact, foxes were preserved for that very purpose. [4] Lord Ellenborough on the bench, agreed with the plaintiff. In his decision he stated:

> The defendant stated in his plea, that the trespass was not committed for the purpose of diversion and amusement of the chase merely, but as the only way and means of killing and destroying the fox. Now if you was [sic] to put it upon this question, which was the principal motive? Can any man of common sense hesitate in saying that the principal motive and inducement was, not the killing of vermin, but the enjoyment and diversions of the chase? And we cannot make a new law to suit the pleasures and amusements of those gentlemen who choose to hunt for their diversion. These pleasures are to be taken only when there is the consent of those who are likely to be injured by them, but they must be necessarily subservient to the consent of others. [5]

Essex v. Capel settled the law that followers of foxhounds were subject to the normal rules of trespass, and several subsequent decisions established that the master of hounds was responsible not only for damage caused by himself, his hounds, and his servants, but also by the people who accompanied them, or by those going out with his hounds even if he were not himself present. [6]

The reaction of hunting men to this new limitation on what they had thought to be their rights took several forms. On the one hand, it made them all the more careful not to offend influential landlords. Masters of hounds regularly began asking landlords for permission to hunt over their land. [7] They were also careful to avoid giving offence to any landowners when it came to damaging their property, though they were often less careful when it came to the property of farmers. [8]

On the other hand, *Essex v. Capel* was not allowed to seriously interfere with hunting. Although after 1809 the law was firmly on the side of anyone who sought to bar hounds from his land, rural custom was firmly against him. Anyone who sought to close his land to hounds found himself subjected to the strongest pressures, which few but the most secure in their social and economic position could long endure.[9]

If anything, hunting men began to take a sort of perverse pride in the fact that their custom was in opposition to the law. It demonstrated, they felt, the unique position that foxhunting held in the community, that it was able to exist even though the law was not on its side. They rarely lost the opportunity to point out that though the law of property gave landowners the right, 'by the *law of honour* no gentleman would prevent his neighbours from taking their accustomed diversion, when the inconvenience would be so trifling to himself'.[10]

Entirely distinct from the whole question of the right of hunting men to pass over the land of others, however, was the question of the right of a pack of hounds to look for a fox. This second question was far more troublesome for many hunting people than the first, and it was to solve this that the elaborate system of hunting 'law' and hunt territories evolved.[11] A glance at a hunting map of England today will reveal that the country is divided into the territories or 'countries' of the various established packs of hounds. Within the territory of a pack, only that pack and no other is permitted to draw for a fox, though if a hunted fox should run from one country to another, he may be followed until he goes to ground, escapes, or is killed.

The reason for this limitation arose out of simple convenience. As hunting grew in popularity, it became necessary to restrict the number of packs of hounds hunting in any given area. In the early eighteenth century this was not a problem. There were relatively few packs of hounds, some of them hunting large expanses of country on an irregular basis. As late as 1810, for example, the fifth Earl of Berkeley hunted a country stretching from Scratch Wood, near Wormwood Scrubs, five miles from London, nearly to Bristol.[12] Still other large areas were not hunted at all, or were hunted by informal packs that appeared for a short time, hunted hare or fox or both, and disappeared. Under these conditions there was little cause for concern, for the prospects of competition among packs was slight. As hunting increased in popularity toward the end of the eighteenth century, however, the prospect of clashes increased, and the present system of hunting countries began to take shape. Precisely when or how this began is impossible to determine. The prime consideration in most places was simply precedent. If a pack was known to have 'always' drawn particular coverts, these coverts belonged to it.[13] Thus Lady Ossory recorded in her journal:

7 Oct 1772 – Ld. R. Spencer & Mr. Crewe went out a Fox Hunting on the other side the Wear, to assert ye rights of the farming woods hunt & killed their fox...

8 Oct 1772 – Ld R.S. & Mr. Crewe went a second time to assert the rights of the farming woods hunt & were met by Earl Fitzwilliams did not kill their fox which was supposed to give said Earl great pleasure. [14]

By about 1800, the principles of hunting law had begun to be formulated, and recognizable hunt countries had taken shape. The basic organization of hunt countries as we know them today dates from about this time, though the fine details of the system were still being worked out many years later. In 1806, Peter Beckford, still the only man to have written extensively on hunting, and hence the recognized authority on the subject, was appealed to by the Old Berkshire Hunt and produced a memorandum on hunt law. There were, he claimed, three distinct rights to a hunting country, 'Original, Acquired, and by Sufferance'. [15]

The original right belonged to the covert owners, but, he stressed, once a pack of foxhounds was established in a country with the consent of those owners 'an acquired right is then obtained, of which the said pack cannot afterwards be deprived, unless by an uncommon misconduct on the part of those concerned in the management of the hounds, the Proprietors themselves should think fit to deprive them of it'. [16] The third right, 'right by sufferance' referred to the temporary right that a pack might from time to time acquire to the coverts of a neighbouring hunt. It drew those coverts with the knowledge that if the original pack wished, it would have to relinquish them.

These principles, Beckford claimed, were based upon 'common sense' and were, in fact, to form the basis of hunt law as it evolved in the nineteenth century, but at the time Beckford wrote, and for many years thereafter, they were imperfectly understood by many. The rights of covert owners, for example, remained unclear for at least forty years. Beckford correctly noted that original right over coverts belonged to the men who owned them. The etiquette of hunting required the master of hounds to request the permission of the covert owners to draw, and this was generally done at the beginning of each season. [17] What was not clear was how far the owners' rights extended once they had granted them to a master. Did they have the right to withdraw them and offer them to another? Clearly, so far as property law was concerned, they had, but equally clearly, that law as unsatisfactory so far as hunting was concerned.

If any landowner could dictate what pack of hounds could draw the coverts on his land, the end result would be chaos. Not only could this result in a crazy-quilt pattern of hunting, with small holdings hunted by one pack in the centre of a country hunted by another, it could also lead to rapid changes of rights, with the master of hounds dependent upon the shifting preferences of the covert owners. Under these circumstances there would be few men willing to undertake the mastership of a pack of hounds. Hunting law, therefore, established the principle that though a covert owner could deny a master permission to draw his coverts, he could not then offer them to the master of another pack. If the owner was dissatisfied with the management of the hunt within whose boundary his coverts lay, his only alternative was to have no one draw them. [18]

The need to place hunting law on an established footing gained new urgency with the increase in the number of packs in the first thirty or forty years of the nineteenth century. As more country gentlemen began to feel the need to have their neighbourhoods regularly hunted, the old extensive hunting countries were carved into newer, smaller ones that could be hunted more intensively. In 1832, for example, the Hon. Henry Moreton, later Lord Ducie, master of the Old Berkshire, found his country too big to hunt regularly by himself, and so arranged to give up a part, which was formed into a new country known as the Vale of White Horse. [19] Sometimes these splits were arranged amicably, but they could also lead to controversy and dispute. [20] In the 1830s and 1840s disputes such as these increased greatly in number and excited the interest of the hunting world. [21] There was no established method for settling them, and some threatened the peace of the countryside. A dispute between Lord Gifford of the V.W.H. Hunt and T.T. Morland of the Old Berkshire in 1844-45, for example, aroused such emotions that violence between members of the two hunts was prevented only by the quick action of a few cool heads. [22] In the face of these disputes, hunting people began to urge the formation of an official body to settle conflicts. [23] There was some precedent for this. The parties to some of the disputes had called upon 'neutral' masters of foxhounds to arbitrate, and where this was done, the disputes were settled amicably. [24] Since the 1820s, masters of hounds had been holding a dinner in London each spring, and in 1841, plans were made to form a regular association of masters. Though the idea seemed to excite a great deal of enthusiasm, it somehow fell through. [25]

Not every hunting man accepted that masters of hounds should have the right to arbitrate, of course, [26] but sentiment for this sort of solution continued to grow through the thirties, forties, and fifties. [27]Finally, in 1856, the first steps were taken to formalize these arrangements. Following that year's dinner of masters of hounds, five of them [28]met at Boodle's Club, which, because it drew much of its membership from among country dwellers, was known as 'the country gentleman's club', and they petitioned the managers of the club to establish a committee of members who were, or had been, masters of foxhounds to settle any questions submitted to them. [29]By August of that year, the committee was established and published its first set of rules. Membership on the committee was open to any member of Boodle's Club who was, or had been, a master of foxhounds, and the committee members agreed to look into any disputes referred to it. They had no authority to compel anyone to submit a dispute, but they did require that all parties to a dispute agree to be bound by the committee decision if they wished to refer a dispute. They also required each member of the committee to agree to refer any dispute in which he was involved, on pain of expulsion. Finally, they agreed that if there was a dispute between hunts as to the rights to draw a covert and the hunts refused to submit the dispute to them, they would, nevertheless, inquire into the case if the owner of the covert in question requested it. [30]

Although the committee's first attempt to arbitrate a dispute was a failure, [31]it gained widespread acceptance in the hunting world. Parties to disputes took to submitting detailed statements of their side of the case, over which the stewards of the committee often deliberated at great length, before delivering their opinion. [32]

In 1881, the committee severed its association with Boodle's Club and became known as the Masters of Foxhounds Association, opening its membership to all past and present masters, whether members of Boodle's or not. Otherwise its constitution remained the same as that which had been adopted by the M.F.H. Committee in 1856. [33]

Hunt law did not apply only to disputed territory. By the middle of the nineteenth century, an elaborate code had grown up governing the relations between neighbouring countries. The origin of most of this code is obscure. It was never expressly formulated by anyone but grew out of local custom and usage. By the time such mid-century authors as Vyner and 'Cecil' put it into print, it had already been accepted by masters of hounds. Most of the rules governed what a hunt might do if it chased a fox into another country; a few examples will suffice to give an idea of what they were like. If, for example, the fox escaped in another country, hounds could not draw for a new one but had to return to their own country to draw again. If the fox was found to be making for a known earth in another country, a whipper-in could be sent forward to try to head the fox back, but he could not actually stop the earth, nor could he go to it before the fox was actually making in its direction. Should a fox go to ground in another country, the primary rule was that the earth could not be broken in any way to get to him. However, if he was in a hole so shallow that he could be bolted or drawn with a common hunting-whip, it was permissible to do so. He could also be bolted by a terrier, provided the terrier belonged to the master of the hounds and was, therefore, with them, but it was illegal to borrow a dog for this purpose. [34]

The increasing institutionalization and formalization that marked relations among hunts was also evident within hunting countries, which, as the result of parallel developments, were taking on an existence independent of the master who headed them.

In the early eighteenth century, virtually all packs of foxhounds were private packs. That is, they were the property of a single man, who kept them primarily for his own amusement and the amusement of his friends. Masters, in fact, often considered their hunting a very private thing; such company as they had, they had by choice rather than of necessity. [35] We find, for example, that Sir Edward Littleton, who hunted in Staffordshire in the 1770s, often sent cards announcing the meetings of his hounds to approximately seven houses in the neighbourhood, but did not feel the need either to tell anyone else where his hounds would meet or even to tell these favoured few all his hunting days. [36]

These private packs could vary in size and pretension from a few couple of nondescript hounds kept by a yeoman farmer to the great packs kept by the families of territorial magnates like the Dukes of Rutland and Beaufort. Though these packs were often known by a territorial name, they were more commonly known by the name of the master. A list of hunts published in 1821, for example, included 'The Duke of Rutland's hounds' and 'Lord Yarborough's hounds' rather than 'The Belvoir' or 'The Brocklesby' as they were also known. [37]

As hunting grew more popular, however, resulting in the increase in both the number of packs and the average expense of keeping a pack in the style that was becoming expected, it became far more difficult to locate enough men who were both willing and able to take on the responsibility themselves. This led, therefore, to the appearance of subscription packs, in which the costs were shared among a number of subscribers. We know that Meynell accepted subscriptions as early as 1761, though he never had more than a handful of subscribers, who did little more than help him in supporting the hounds. [38] The earliest attempt that I have found to form a pack of hounds supported entirely by subscription was made in 1788, with the foundation of the Quarley Hounds near Andover, Hampshire. [39] There may have been earlier attempts, but the practice remained uncommon for some time. Though subscription packs began to be more than an oddity between 1800 and 1810, they were generally regarded as far inferior to private ones. For one thing, they lacked some of the snob value that attached to a pack headed by a great magnate. The master of such a pack was as aware of this as his followers. When the Marquis of Tavistock became master of the Oakley Hunt in 1809, for example, he refused to accept subscriptions though, according to his father, the pack cost him half his income. The Duke of Beford wrote that year to Samuel Whitbread on his son's behalf, declining Whitbread's offer of aid, for 'in the estimation of the world I am a much richer man than Ld Spencer, yet Ld Althorpe is censured for taking a subscription for the Pychely [sic] hounds'. [40] Even more important, it was feared that a subscription pack lacked the permanence of a private one and occasional melancholy announcements of the demise of subscription packs seemed to bear this fear out.

Since, in addition, few sportsmen wanted to pay for their sport if they could get it for nothing, a private pack, preferably one kept by succeeding generations of the same family, was the most desirable. These, however, were increasingly difficult to come by, and more and more countries found themselves turning to masters who accepted at least a partial subscription. By 1845, the *Sporting Magazine* was able to list only fourteen packs out of over one hundred that were supported entirely by the master, [41] and, though this list was not complete, [42] it did indicate that, as Robert Vyner had written four years previously, 'a committee is the order of the day; the new mode of doing things by subscription is introduced'. [43]

The mere fact that a master took a subscription did not necessarily mean that the character of his country was markedly different from one headed by a man who did not. Nevertheless, the introduction of subscriptions was one of the things that contributed to the greater institutionalization of hunt countries, for it introduced a new element into the hunting picture, the subscriber and his representatives.

In the very early days of the sport, the hunting of a country rested upon the agreement of two parties, the master and the covert owners. Anyone who chose to follow the hounds might do so, but he was, in theory, totally extraneous to the arrangement. When masters began to take subscriptions, there was no immediate change in this model. The master who took a subscription was, in theory, in precisely the same position as the master who did not, the only difference between them being that the latter received help from his friends in supporting the expense of his hounds. Most of the early subscription packs were, in fact, essentially private. Like Meynell's, they began as private packs in which the master was forced to accept subscriptions somewhere along the way. Some of these packs even resembled the great hereditary packs, for they remained in the same family and were handed down from father to son for generations. [44]

There were, however, even in the very early days of subscription packs, some, like the Durham County Hunt, which were founded by the agreement of a group of subscribers to organize a pack of hounds for their neighbourhood. When this was done, the master, though he was still expected to hunt like a private gentleman, might find his freedom of choice somewhat curtailed. In return for an annual subscription of 800 guineas, for example, George Baker of Elemore Hall, first master of the Durham County Hounds, agreed in 1798 to 'keep a pack of Foxhounds to consist of Thirty five Couples which shall hunt three times a week regularly during the season to be attended by a Huntsman and Whipper In properly mounted'. [45] It was not expected that the subscriptions would completely pay all the hunting expenses, and all excess expenses – which could be considerable, as Baker's successor, Ralph John Lambton, was to discover [46] – had to be borne by the master. Not all agreements between masters and their subscribers were as explicit as the one signed by Baker, [47] and even the most restrictive of them gave the master a certain freedom of choice. Nevertheless, a new element was introduced.

The subscription system was not the only influence that contributed to this change within hunt countries. A second stimulus was the need to ensure the continuance of the hunt when the master chose to step down. This, too, was a contingency for which the original model of the private pack provided no answer in most countries. In the case of an hereditary pack, of course, there was no problem. On the death of a Duke of Beaufort, his heir succeeded to the hounds as naturally as he did to the title, thus ensuring that the Duke of Beaufort's country remained the Duke of Beaufort's country. In other early countries there was no such provision, and the decision of a master to step down could easily lead to no hunting at all. Often a pack would be assembled, hunt for a season or two, and then disappear, leaving no trace. The Quarley Hunt, for example, disappeared soon after its foundation, leaving no successor to hold its country together, and only the chance survival of its agreement has led to our knowing that it ever existed.

The increasing interest in foxhunting, which led in the opening years of the nineteenth century to the development of fixed hunting countries, also meant that sportsmen were increasingly interested in making sure that their neighbourhoods would be hunted regularly. The only way to do that was to ensure that there was always a pack of hounds in the country, for should a country fall vacant, its outlying coverts were sure to be snatched up by neighbouring masters.

The simplest way, besides inheritance, of ensuring the continuation of a hunt was for the outgoing master to name a successor and turn his hounds over to him. The new master would, of course, have to go through the formality of requesting the permission of the covert owners to draw their coverts, but this would rarely be refused. In this way, Lord Sefton succeeded Meynell at Quorn in 1800, though he brought his own pack of hounds with him. [48]The retiring master could not always be counted on to arrange for his successor, however, nor could the local sportsmen depend on a new master offering to hunt the country, and so they took the matter into their own hands. On the prospects of the country falling vacant, the interested sportsmen would meet to see what arrangements could be made for the future. This organization quickly became more formal, however, especially in countries where a committee was also needed to arrange for the collecting of subscriptions. By 1820, certainly, most countries had at least a rudimentary organization, even if it was little more than an informal committee of local sportsmen. In some countries it was more than rudimentary, and the trend was for even more organization. In 1823, for example, Sir Bellingham Graham was invited by the subscribers of the Albrighton Hunt to bring his hounds into their country and to become its master at a subscription of £1000 per year. [49]By 1830, however, the subscribers had decided that it was far too risky to depend on finding a master with his own pack, and a subscription was raised to buy a pack of hounds to be kept permanently in the country, and to be lent to whoever wished to take the mastership. [50]

The constituency of these committees varied from pack to pack. If a subscription was collected, the subscribers certainly had a say, as did the covert owners, even if they did not subscribe. In 1825, for example, the

Warwickshire Hunt called together subscribers and covert owners to choose a new master. When, at one meeting, some covert owners were told that they had no right to vote because they did not subscribe, it was generally considered a breach of propriety. [51] Tenant farmers generally were not represented on hunt committees, except in those packs run almost entirely by farmers. The need to keep farmers friendly to the sport did, however, ensure that in most packs farmers were informally consulted on some issues. [52]

The result of these developments was that by 1830, and even earlier in many cases, there existed an independent organization entirely distinct from the master of hounds and his establishment, and in part, at least, from the covert owners as well, an organization that was to exist virtually unchanged for the rest of the century. What the relationship between this organization and the master was to be, will be discussed in the next chapter.

Meanwhile, a word or two on the question of hunt finance is in order, for the maintenance of these increasingly independent hunt countries depended upon the expenditure of often considerable sums. The costs of hunting a country could vary. In 1826, Colonel John Cook, whose experience in keeping hounds had extended from 1800 to 1813, estimated that the costs of hunting a typical country ranged from £1170 per year if it were hunted twice per week, through £1625 for three days per week, to £1935 for four days per week, if no professional huntsmen were kept – £300 more if one was. [53]

By 1903, G. C. Ricardo, who had been master of the Craven, estimated that an average pack cost £2110 per year to maintain, exclusive of earthstopping and poultry damage, expenses that could add anything up to another £500-£600 per year to the cost. [54]

These estimates were valuable as guidelines for prospective masters and were generally accurate as far as they went, but they hid the great variation that could occur. During the 1839-40 season, for example, the Cleveland Hunt, a trencher-fed pack in the North Riding of Yorkshire, was able to hunt for a total expenditure of £90 18s. 8d. [55] The Cleveland, of course, was an exception to the general rule, having no kennel expenses to meet, and its records did not take into account the sums spent by individual members in keeping hounds. That same season, however, the West Somerset Hunt, a regularly kept pack, spent approximately £500, [56] while the Northumberland Hunt spent over three times as much. [57] An idea of the wide variation in the amount of money spent by different hunts may be gained from table 1.

Table 1: Representative costs of maintaining a hunt

A. At midcentury

Season	Hunt	Cost
1849-50	Atherstone	£2014 7s.
1848-49	Heythrop	£1489 7s. 3d.
1851-52	Essex Union	£476 6s. 6½d.

B. In the 1870s

Season	Hunt	Cost
1876-77	Meynell	£3889 1s. 5d.
1877-78	Oakley	£2244
1876-77	Hampshire	£1945 11s.
1876-77	Braes of Derwent	£253 1s. 8d.

Source: Wilson, *Green Peas at Christmas*, pp. 88-89; Heythrop Hunt MS Minute book; Essex Union Hunt MSS, Essex Record Office, D/DU 655; *Field*, LI (January 12, 1877), p. 38; Oakley Hunt MSS, Bedford Record Office, X213/61; Hampshire Hunt MS Minute Book; G. A. Cowen, *The Braes of Derwent Hunt* (Gateshead on Tyne, 1955), p. 172.

The variations in the cost of hunting depended upon many factors. The number of days hunted determined the number of hounds and horses needed. The style in which the establishment was kept, the quality of horses bought, the salaries paid the hunt servants, the quality of their uniforms, and the physical nature of the country, which determined the sums needed for earth-stopping or maintaining coverts, all influenced the final expenditure, as did the personal whims of the master. In the shires, where everything had to be done in first-rate style, the expenses were naturally the highest. Shire packs had to compete for the finest huntsmen, mount them in the best style, and hunt to suit the wealthy people who made up the field. In 1821, Sir Bellingham Graham was given £4000 with which to hunt the Quorn, a sum unheard of in any other country.[58] In 1890, the subscription collected was close to that sum, and the master must have spent a considerable amount of his own money in addition.[59]

These sums were merely the amounts spent for yearly operating expenses. In addition, there could be periodical large expenses to place an extra burden on the subscribers. The Worcestershire and North Cotswold Hunts, for example, built new kennels in the late 1860s, at a cost of £4745 and £2700 respectively, which had to be raised by selling shares in the ownership.[60]

Raising the large sums of money that maintaining a hunt required, usually from subscriptions of from ten to fifty pounds, was a constant struggle in many countries. Most fortunate were those that could count on one or two large subscribers for most of what was needed. In others, potential subscribers had to be sought out, and prominent members of the hunt had to be urged from time to time to increase their contributions. The minute books of subscription packs record almost annual crises, as the subscriptions fell a few hundred pounds short of the expenses or the amount due the master, and special subscriptions had to be raised or the master convinced to accept less than had originally been agreed upon. [61] The sad plight of the East Sussex Hunt, which was broken up in 1843 and the establishment seized for taxes, [62] was not shared by others, but one can hardly blame hunt treasurers for envisioning a similar fate on many occasions.

Nevertheless, despite these periodic crises, hunting continued without interruption. Most of the money needed was generally forthcoming from someone in the neighbourhood, and the style and amount of hunting could be trimmed or expanded to suit the state of the hunt treasury. That the fate of the East Sussex was not shared by other hunts, testifies to the importance of the hunt in the eyes of local sportsmen.

CHAPTER 6

MASTERS AND SERVANTS

R. S. Surtees once observed that the ideal master should have 'the boldness of a lion, the cunning of a fox, the shrewdness of an exciseman, the calculation of a general, the decision of a judge, the purse of Squire Plutus, the regularity of a railway, the punctuality of a time-piece, the liberality of a sailor', [1] and a host of other qualities. But all these, he went on, would be to no avail unless the master also had 'that indescribable quality' of being a gentleman.[2] Few masters, needless to say, measured up to this ideal, but Surtees was not far wrong in his estimate of what the office demanded. The Master of Foxhounds was the most important man in the hunt country. His duty, simply put, was to arrange for and oversee the hunting of the country, but behind that simple description lay an almost infinite variety of tasks.

First among them was the overseeing of all the day-to-day business that hunting demanded. Though he had servants to do much of the dirty work, it was his responsibility to ensure that the kennels housed a good pack of hounds in hunting trim, that they were well fed and trained, and ready to take the field. He also had to see to it that he, and more especially his servants, were well mounted, for the huntsman, if not the master, had to be able to keep up with the hounds at all times and over all terrain. This was a year-round job, for it was during the off-season that the details of breeding, whelping, and buying hounds and selecting horses had to be carried on.

Next the master had to take charge of keeping the country well stocked with foxes. This involved more than a simple knowledge of natural history or even of which dealers were most discreet and had the best foxes for times of shortage.[3] It also meant that he somehow had to manage to induce all who lived within the country to help with preservation. Farmers had to be persuaded that foxes did not kill poultry and that hunting crowds never damaged a field of wheat. Game preservers had to be convinced that foxes and pheasants could live amicably side by side.

As the personification of the sport in his neighbourhood, the master had to be cordial to all and careful to offend no one, for any personal animosity toward him could easily turn into a vendetta against the sport.[4] He had to attend numerous dinners, and he was forced to entertain numerous people with whom he might not otherwise have associated. Farmers had to be given gifts of game and their wives new dresses and local tradesmen had to be patronized liberally.[5] He had to take care not to be involved in local feuds or politics nor to wound the sensibilities of the proudest country squire. If he took a subscription, the master had to do all he could to ensure that the subscribers were kept happy, but at the same time he had to exercise control over the members of his field to keep them from interfering with the hounds, or causing unnecessary damage to the crops of a short-tempered farmer. If this were not enough, the master was held responsible for the state of the sport in his country. If the hounds had trouble in finding, or lost the scent, if the huntsman was unable to keep up with his hounds, or even if the foxes did not provide good runs, it was likely to be laid at the feet of the master.[6] Finally, he had to see to it that the bills were paid, and it was the rare master who found himself able to depend entirely upon subscriptions for this. As Lord Petre told his successor with the Hertfordshire Hounds: 'Remember ... after all this, you will never have your hand out of your pocket, and must always have a guinea in it.'[7]

Like the total cost of hunting a country, the costs to the master could vary considerably. The new master faced his greatest expense at the beginning of his career, when, depending upon whether his new country had its own pack of hounds, he might be called upon to spend up to several thousand pounds to purchase hounds, horses, and other equipment. A pack of hounds could cost anything from £800 to £3000 or more after about 1810.[8] The most ever paid for a pack was 3170 guineas for $20\frac{1}{2}$ couple in 1870.[9] These prices, of course, were for packs that had already been assembled. If the master chose to build up a pack himself from odd lots of hounds, his costs were likely to be less, but it would take years to assemble a matched pack.

Horses for the master and servants were another major expense. 'Scrutator' estimated that ten horses were sufficient for the master, huntsman, and whipper-in in a three-day-per-week provincial pack.[10] Many packs, however, had more. At one hundred guineas per horse, an average price for moderate hunters through most of the nineteenth century, even ten horses meant an expenditure of an additional one thousand guineas. Much of this, of course, could be recouped at the end of the master's term.

The yearly operating expense also varied, though it seldom fell below several hundred pounds. William Wilson, for example, who received a subscription of £1800 in 1849-50 to hunt the Atherstone country, considered that he was getting off cheaply when the expenses of the hunt only reached £2104.[11] Nicholas Snow, who hunted the Exmoor in the 1870s, received only £100 per year to pay the expenses, which reached £400.[12] Even the masters of the Braes of Derwent, whose total expenditure remained below £300 per year between 1872 and 1885, generally had to pay at least half that sum themselves.[13]

Many masters, however, found themselves paying considerably more than that. T. T. Drake, who resigned the Bicester in 1866, received a subscription of £1250, but found himself paying over £1000 per year out of his own pocket.[14] The Hon. T. W. Fitzwilliam took the Fitzwilliam Hunt in 1881 at a promised subscription of £1650 per year, the full amount of which he never received.[15] The expense of the hunt in 1881 was £3753.[16] Albert Brassey, son of the railway contractor, took £1500 per year from the Heythrop from 1873 until 1918, and paid all poultry, covert, damage, and earth-stopping fees himself. Even at a conservative estimate, the hunt must have cost him £1500-£2000 per year.[17] The great shire packs often cost their masters even more. Lord Althorp spent between £4000 and £5000 per year on the Pytchley between 1808 and 1818,[18] and Lord Annaly spent £2700 per year, exclusive of the keep of his own horses, on the same pack one hundred years later.[19]

Though few masters expected that their subscriptions would cover their expenses, they, naturally enough, tried to squeeze as much out of their subscribers as they could, and many carried on a running battle with their committees for years. The masters of the Hampshire Hunt, for example, 'resigned' annually to pressure the committee for more money, and it came to be expected that they would; hence the following entry in the hunt minutes: 'Mr. Deacon's letter of Feb. 2, 1874 . . . was read signifying his (annual) resignation.' [20]

In the face of this enormous task, it is astonishing that anyone would have wanted to take on the responsibilities that being a master of foxhounds conferred. In fact, however, few countries ever had more than temporary difficulty in finding a master, and it often seemed that as soon as one man stepped down, there were two more clamouring for the chance to take his place. A love of the sport was the reason why some men became and remained masters. For others, however, the answer lies in the fact that being a master had its rewards as well as its liabilities. Though Lord Willoughby de Broke, himself a master of hounds, might have exaggerated somewhat in ranking the M.F.H. second only to the Lord Lieutenant in the hierarchy of county society, [21] to be a master of hounds meant being a man of considerable status and importance.

So far as we are able to tell, virtually all of the earliest masters of hounds were local men who kept their hounds for their own amusement and that of their neighbours. They were generally landed proprietors, but they did not necessarily have to be. The Rounding brothers, Tom and Dick, innkeepers at Woodford, Essex, for example, kept a pack of foxhounds in the 1790s and were accepted by the local gentry, but they were curiosities. [22] As we have seen, Meynell himself was one of the first exceptions to the rule, but even he needed the benefit of his fashionable contacts to overcome the natural suspicion of the local landowners toward a stranger. By the year of Meynell's retirement, the situation had not changed. Of the sixty-seven men who held the office of master in 1800, [23] only five were not local men. One of these five was Lord Sefton of the Quorn, which always drew its master, like its followers, from outside; and a second was a Mr Snow, a London banker who headed the Old Surrey, [24] another pack that was out of the ordinary because of its close proximity to London. This left three packs, the Pytchley, Thurlow, and Warwickshire, headed by John Warde, John Cook, and John Corbet, respectively, each of whom was developing a national reputation.

One outgrowth of the increased popularity of hunting in the opening decades of the nineteenth century was that masters of hounds drawn from outside the local country became more common. There were two reasons for this. First, the increased demand for masters could not always be satisfied within the country itself, and secondly, the new craze for the sport had produced a group of men, often young and wealthy, who, having tasted the delights of hunting, began to wish for the opportunity to show what they could do with a pack of their own. They were aided in fulfilling this wish by the growing institutionalization of hunt countries. It would have been difficult for a stranger to carve out a new territory for himself with no local connections to help him along. With 'ready-made' countries already established, however, often with kennels and stables built, and coverts well stocked with foxes, most of the initial problems of beginning as a master were already solved.

The new type of master had begun to appear by 1800. The first of them was John Warde, a country gentleman of Squerries Court, Kent, who began as a master in his native county around 1776, hunted in Oxfordshire in 1778, and then kept hounds continuously from 1797 to 1825, hunting the Pytchley from 1797 to 1808, the New Forest from 1808 to 1814, and the Craven from 1814 to 1825. [25]

Warde was the prototype for many of the new masters who began making their appearance in the opening years of the nineteenth century. John Musters, of Colwick Hall, Nottinghamshire, who began his career in 1798 and hunted five countries down to 1845, was the first of the new generation to take to keeping hounds. In 1806, Thomas Assheton Smith began the fifty-two-year career that was to see him master of three countries, and in 1810, George Osbaldeston, who was to ride at the head of no less than eight hunts in the next twenty-five years, first kept foxhounds. Musters, Assheton Smith, and Osbaldeston, though personally unlike in many ways, were the three greatest examples of the new school of master, and they inspired many imitators. They were the best known foxhunters of the first third of the nineteenth century, and their place in foxhunting legend is secure today.

Assheton Smith [26] was the oldest of the three. He was born in 1776, a descendant of the Assheton family, of Ashley Hall, Bowden, Cheshire. The family was very wealthy, with estates in Hampshire and Carnarvonshire. [27] He was sent to Eton, where he distinguished himself, by taking part in the most savage fight in the school history. His opponent was John Musters, the second of our trio of masters. He then went to Christ Church, Oxford, and on coming down from the university, went to hunt in Leicestershire, where he soon acquired a reputation as one of the boldest riders to hounds even in that distinguished company. It has been said that when he visited France during the Peace of Amiens, Napoleon introduced him to his officers as 'le premier chasseur de L'Angleterre'. [28] Though he sat in Parliament in the Conservative interest for Andover and Carnarvonshire and was an active improver on his estates, most of his life was devoted to sport, and he was generally considered the finest rider to hounds of his day. He made his first appearance as master in 1806, at the head of the Quorn, which he hunted until 1816. From 1816 to 1824 he was master of the Burton Hunt in Lincolnshire, and in 1824 he founded the Tedworth Hunt near his Hampshire estates and settled down to hunt his home country as a resident country gentleman until his death in 1858. He ventured out of his home territory once, in 1840, when he was invited to bring his hounds back to the Quorn country for a day's hunting. Over two thousand horsemen turned out to see hil, making any serious hunting impossible. One of the two thousand was Prince Ernst of Saxe-Coburg, who thought the crowd had come to see him. [29]

John Musters, the only son of John Musters, of Colwick Hall, Nottinghamshire, was born in 1777. Like Assheton Smith he was sent to Eton and Christ Church, and in 1805 he married Mary Anne Chaworth, the heiress of Annesley, who was the 'Mary' of Byron's 'The Dream'. Musters served as master of the South Nottinghamshire country three times, from 1798 to 1814, 1835 to 1841, and 1844 to 1845. In between he hunted the Badsworth for the 1814–15 season, the Burton in 1815, the Pytchley from 1820 to 1827, and the Southwold from 1841 to 1844. [30]

Assheton Smith and Musters hunted several countries, but spent most of their careers in their home country. George Osbaldeston, the youngest of the three, was an itinerant, pure and simple. Osbaldeston was born in 1786, the son of a Yorkshire squire who died when he was very young. [31] After attending Eton and Brasenose College, Oxford, Osbaldeston began his hunting career with a pack of harriers in his native Yorkshire around 1807. [32] He first took foxhounds in 1810 as master of the Burton, which he hunted until 1813. He then hunted Musters' Nottinghamshire country from 1813 to 1815, Derbyshire from 1815 to 1817, the Quorn from 1817 to 1821 and again from 1823 to 1827, the Hambledon in 1821-22, the Thurlow from 1822 to 1823, and the Pytchley from 1827 to 1834.

Osbaldeston's great drive for success and notoriety made him the finest all-round sportsman of his day. He was famous as a cricketer, pigeon-shot, steeplechase rider, and foxhunter. On his death in 1866, *Bailey's Magazine* called him 'the greatest sportsman the world ever knew since the days of the Assyrian Nimrod.' [33] He was know all through England as 'Squire' Osbaldeston and when someone once asked, 'squire of what?' the answer was 'Squire of England.' [34] The great hold hunting had acquired over the imaginations of sportsmen fed Osbaldeston's great vanity. He belittled both Musters and Assheton Smith in his autobiography, accusing Musters of training his hounds to bay at a rabbit hole after losing their fox, to make the field think the fox had gone to ground, [35] and told with delight a story of how Assheton Smith failed to 'accomplish his purpose' with a Melton prostitute. [36]

Musters, Assheton Smith, Osbaldeston, and some of their imitators were responsible for a new development. Not content to give up the smallest share in the management of their hounds, they dispensed with a huntsman and hunted the hounds themselves. There were always many hunting men who felt, perhaps rightly, that the practice smacked too much of showing-off and that the hunting was generally better with a professional carrying the horn. Nimrod, whose class feeling would not let him admit that a professional huntsman was necessarily better than an amateur, [37] nevertheless wrote that too many gentlemen huntsmen would be the 'bane of hunting'. [38] Though there were always bold young men, and older ones too, eager to try their hand at hunting their own hounds, gentlemen huntsmen remained a small minority throughout most of the nineteenth century. The example set by Musters, Assheton Smith, and Osbaldeston of masters from outside the hunt country did, however, gain wider acceptance, and was one more contributing factor in giving hunt countries an existence of their own. By the end of the 1830s, hunt committees had even begun advertising for masters in the national and local press. The Heythrop Hunt placed the following advertisement in two Oxford papers, *Bell's Life*, the *Northampton Herald*, the *Globe*, and the *Morning Post* in 1838:

> At a numerous Meeting of the Members of the Heythrop Hunt held at the White Hart Inn – Chipping Norton on Wednesday the 19th of December – Mr. Langston announced his intention of giving up the Management of the Hounds at the Close of the Season. The Meeting Resolved to offer £1000 per annum exclusive of Earth-Stopping, Rent of Kennel and Stables & Coverts to any gentleman who will undertake the management of the Hounds and Hunt the country four days a week. Lords Vaux, Redesdale and Churchill were appointed a Committee to receive offers – and the meeting was adjourned to Saturday the 19th of January when the manner in which the Country is to be Hunted next Season will be finally determined upon. [39]

The tone of the notice, making it sound more like a news story than an advertisement, was necessary to protect the dignity of the office. Many of the early advertisements either took this form or were published as letters from readers. [40]

The practice of advertising for a master grew more common through the forties and fifties. By the 1860s, any pretence that the notices in the press were not advertisements began to disappear. The New Forest Hunt sent an advertisement to *Bell's Life* in 1851, which began: 'We understand, to the great regret of the gentlemen of the country that the Mastership of the New Forest Hounds has become vacant....' [41] In 1869, however, their advertisement concluded: 'All applications to be addressed to Captain Martin Powell.' [42]

There was rarely any difficulty in filling the vacancies. The opportunity to hunt a pack of foxhounds appealed to many young men, and Osbaldeston and Assheton Smith were followed by a host of imitators. Some were successful. Most, like Lord Suffield, who had one disastrous season with the Quorn in the 1830s, [43] were not, and after a short career, retired to take their hunting as a humble member of the field.

Nevertheless, most countries continued to look at the outside master as a last resort, much preferring to fill the mastership with a local man. [44] In the great majority of cases, hunts were successful in persuading a local man to take the job. A rough count of ninety-three men who held the office during the 1850-51 season, for example, reveals only fifteen who were not local men, and one of these, Colonel C. T. Tower, of Weald Hall, Essex, master of the Durham County, was the grandson of George Baker, a Durham man who had been the first master of the pack. [45] As late as 1885, when the pressure of the agricultural depression might have been thought to drive packs to strangers in order to survive, a similar rough count reveals only 29 out of 146 masters with no local connections. [46]

Not only did local men predominate, but many hunts tended to draw their masters from members of the same families. The Essex, for example, was hunted by the Rev. Joseph Arkwright and his son, Loftus, the South Notts by John Musters and his grandson, John Chaworth Musters, and the Hambledon by three generations of the Longs of Preshaw. [47]

Even a master drawn from the body of the country, however, was likely to find himself in a somewhat ambiguous position as a result of the growing institutionalization. With a committee and subscribers to please, and with increasing numbers of sportsmen to criticize his every step, he could no longer be considered the independent gentleman he had been during the eighteenth century. On the other hand, it could hardly be imagined that anyone would take on the mastership of a pack of hounds with all its concomitant expense and toil without being assured of at least some independence.

Generally speaking, the model of an independent gentleman hunting his own hounds was the most congenial to foxhunters. Not only was it most convenient, relieving them from much of the responsibility; it also seemed most fitting. It suited their conception of a society based upon mutual dependence and deference, in which sport was provided by the largesse of one gentleman towards his friends and dependants. Every effort was made, therefore, to ensure that the master, by virtue of his office, retained the authority that had originally been his by virtue of his ownership of the hounds. Thus, in 1821, Henry John Conyers of the Essex Hunt offered to return the subscriptions when he took his hounds home after becoming angry at the behaviour of one member of the field, but the subscribers refused to accept, and expressed the hope that he would 'consider himself as much at liberty in respect to the direction of the Hounds as if he received no subscriptions'. [48] Similarly, the forms that were followed were often designed to give the appearance, at least, that the master was an independent agent. In the New Forest Hunt, for example, though the hunt owned both the kennels and the hounds — an arrangement that was becoming far more prevalent during the nineteenth century to prevent the pack from being split up each time the mastership changed hands — the master, nevertheless, had to pay rent for the use of the kennels, or failing that, had to pay to keep them in repair. [49]

Nevertheless, in many countries, the master's independence was being eroded. It was becoming increasingly accepted in hunting circles that the master, even if he did not accept a subscription, had an obligation to his followers. [50] If he did receive a subscription, and moreover, if he entered into an agreement as to the way he would hunt the country, his obligation was all the greater. In 1856, for example, a great scandal in Cheshire demonstrated the new position that many masters found themselves in. Captain Arthur Mainwaring, master of the Cheshire Hounds, had written an indiscreet letter to a married lady. The lady herself had been indiscreet enough to allow her husband to discover it, and he, in turn, had been so indiscreet as to let the story of the letter become public. [51] Mainwaring was asked to resign as master, and when he refused, a number of the Cheshire covert owners closed their coverts to him. [52] Since much of the country was closed to Mainwaring, the hunting naturally suffered, and the subscribers attempted to withhold the subscription from him. Mainwaring, who had taken the hounds under a three-year agreement, claimed that they had no right to do so. The subscribers, on the other hand, claimed that the agreement implied, though it did not state, that he was to hunt the country efficiently, and since this was no longer possible, the agreement was void. [53]

The dispute was the first to be submitted to the recently formed M.F.H. Committee of Boodle's Club, which in 1857, decided in favour of the subscribers.

All hunting is carried on by sufferance from the owners of land over which the sport is pursued. The good feeling which prevails towards fox-hunting has allowed a right to accrue to the members of a Hunt to make arrangements for hunting a district, in which the owners of land who are not hunting-men seldom interfere; but still all is sufferance. The Subscribers may therefore be held to have given him the good will of the country which the Hunt possessed when he entered into the management, and which he must, on his part be held to have been bound to do nothing to impair. [54]

The 'Cheshire Difficulty,' as it was known, demonstrates two things. First it shows that a master of hounds could no longer be considered as merely a private person. He had become a public figure whose private morality was the concern of the entire hunting country. Secondly, and more important, it showed that the master of a subscription pack acted as the agent of the subscribers, whose store of good-will he acquired. In return for subscriptions, the subscribers had the right to demand that the master perform in a satisfactory manner, and, failing that, they had the right to withdraw their subscriptions.

In some packs, steps were taken to make the master more responsive to his followers. The New Forest Hunt, for example, adopted a resolution in 1866, allowing the club to call the master to account if members complained. [55] By the 1880s, the Oakley Hunt had removed from the master any role in the breeding of the hunt-owned pack, placing it in the hands of a committee of members. [56] Many hunting people welcomed the new arrangements. Anthony Trollope, for one, applauded the fact that by 1865 most masters accepted subscriptions. 'The ordinary master of subscription hounds is no doubt autocratic,' he wrote, 'but he is not autocratic with all the power of tyranny which belongs to the despot who rules without taxation.' [57]

The power that the master was to wield was never definitely settled and varied from hunt to hunt and master to master. The master with old ties to the hunt and country was likely to have more authority than the newcomer; the man who took little or no subscription was a freer agent than the man who depended on a generous subscription. The two extremes were stated by Sir Richard Sutton, master of the Quorn from 1847 to 1856, and H. W. Selby Lowndes, master of the Bilsdale from 1897 to 1900. Sutton, who took no subscription, was once asked by a member of his field to draw certain coverts. He replied: 'Gentlemen, I have but one hobby; it costs me £10,000 a year – and I go where I like.' [58] Selby Lowndes, writing to a brother master in 1897, complained: 'I am placed the same as all Masters of subscription packs, I am more or less a servant.' [59] Most nineteenth-century masters fell between these two extremes.

If the role of master changed somewhat over the course of the nineteenth century, the group from which he was drawn both changed and did not. With some notable exceptions, masters of hounds at the end of our period continued to be drawn from the same class that provided them at the beginning: the landed gentry and aristocracy, and those who sought to enter their ranks. In 1881, the editor of *The Field* devoted a leading article to what he saw as the changing social status of masters of hounds. At one time, the status of the class from which the M.F.H. came, he claimed, determined the status of the office. Now, he noted, the opposite was the case, and the obligation of the sporting world toward men who assumed the mastership made the office an 'invaluable introduction' for the newly-rich man desirous of entering county society. [60] To a certain extent he was correct. Subscribing handsomely to the local hounds and taking the responsibility of the mastership was undoubtedly a quick way for the newly-rich to gain acceptance. What he failed to realize was that that had always been the case. Among the 'squires' who kept hounds in 1800, for example, we find Sampson Hanbury, of Poles, master of the Puckeridge, whose grandfather was 'the greatest tobacco merchant of his day' and who was himself active in the brewery firm of Truman and Hanbury. [61] In nearby Essex, a pack of subscription hounds was under the mastership of Sampson's brother Charles, a London banker. [62] At the head of the Old Surrey that same year, as we have seen, was a Mr Snow, another London banker. [63] The head of the Thurlow was Colonel John Cook, who was to become famous as the author of *Observations on Fox-Hunting*, and whose father was a well-to-do Hampshire merchant. [64] Throughout the course of the century as new blood flowed into the gentry, so it also flowed into the world of foxhunting, and often the origins of it were unknown to much of the sporting public. Sir Tatton Sykes, fourth Baronet of Sledmere, who hunted the family hounds in Yorkshire from 1824 to 1853, was generally considered the prototype squire by most of his contemporaries. He affected out-of-date clothing and language and devoted himself to sport, [65] but he was only one generation removed from the family banking and trading concerns in Hull and had himself been articled to a firm of attorneys in Lincoln's Inn Fields. [66] J. J. Farquharson, who hunted Dorset at his own expense for fifty-two years from 1806 and was generally regarded as the paragon of country squires, was the son of a Scot who had made his money as an East India merchant before buying land in the county. [67] Harvey Combe, who hunted the Old Berkeley and Old Berkshire countries in the 1820s and 30s, was the son of Alderman Combe, who had abandoned £500 per year in Hampshire land to become head of the brewery firm of Combe, Delafield and Co. in London. [68]

In 1850, 'Cecil', a leading sporting writer, claimed that fewer than six of the nearly one hundred masters in England did not derive the principal amount of their incomes from land. [69] That year the roll of masters included James Morrell of Headington Hill, master of the Old Berks and son of the founder of the Oxford brewery. [70] It also included two members of the Villebois family of the brewery firm of Truman, Hanbury and Buxton. A third member of the family had been master of the Hampshire and Hambledon Hunts, and all three were considered typical country gentlemen. [71] Three packs that year were headed by bankers, [72] and one by a manufacturer of china and glass. [73]

During the course of the century the process accelerated, as more fortunes were made, and this was duly noticed by the editor of *The Field*. By 1885, when the depression had driven many agricultural landlords to withdraw as masters, no fewer than 21 of 146 masters in England had recent or current connections with business of one sort or another. There were seven bankers, [74] two shipowners, [75] two manufacturers, [76] three colliery owners, [77] one stockbroker, [78] one writer and journalist, [79] two members of a family of Cornish landowners, bankers, and shipowners, [80] one brewer, [81] and the sons of a railway contractor [82] and a bookmaker. [83]

Most of these men, however, even if they maintained connections with the businesses that had brought them money, lived as much as possible the life of country gentlemen. Though they may have been late in coming to the land, buy land they did, and some of them became considerable land owners. [84] They were new members of the landed classes, but members nevertheless. They interested themselves in the usual local affairs like the yeomanry cavalry and the bench of magistrates, to which thirteen of them belonged. If there was any difference between these men and the men who had preceded them into the ranks of the gentry earlier in the century, it is not so much that there were more of them, but that they represented the new ways in which Englishmen were making money. Their predecessors had been bankers and brewers, two occupations traditionally found in the countryside. The new men, however, included shipowners and iron founders.

Occasionally a well-to-do farmer might head a pack, but they were generally men just one step removed from the gentry themselves. John Parker, who headed the Worcestershire in the 1820s and 1830s, for example, was a tenant farmer on the Spetchley Estate, but held a commission in the Worcestershire Militia, and with John Somerset Russell – later to be Sir John Pakington, and still later, Lord Hampton – fought the last recorded duel in England. [85] Most farmer-masters, moreover, confined their activities to packs in which farmers made up most, if not all, of the followers. [86]

The real home of the farmer-master was the North, where large areas of Yorkshire continued to be hunted by farmers' packs, some of them trencher-fed, to the very end of our period. These Yorkshire masters could range in type from the grandest to the most humble. Thomas Parrington, for example, was a well-known North Country agricultural and sporting figure through much of the nineteenth century, and must almost be considered a member of the gentry. His father farmed the entire parish of Middlesbrough, Yorkshire. Thomas was for many years, from 1835, honorary secretary of the Cleveland Hunt, managed and hunted the Hurworth Hounds in the 1860s, and was master of the Sinnington Hunt in the 1880s. [87] At the other end of the scale were men like John Andrew, master of the Cleveland from 1817 to 1835, who was a smuggler as well as a farmer, [88] or the George Bells, father and son, of Chop Gate, Bilsdale, blacksmiths and farmers, who were masters of the Bilsdale from 1830 to 1853. [89] As late as 1885, nine regular packs of hounds were hunted by farmers, all of them in the north except for the Lamerton in Cornwall and the Newmarket and Thurlow in Suffolk. [90]

During the 1860s and 70s, hunting writers began to complain of impecunious army officers or charlatans with no money taking packs, hoping to live on the subscriptions, padded out with clever horse trading. [91] These mysterious figures made fine material for stories, and one of Surtees' most memorable characters, Facey Romford, was modelled on them, as was Captain Glomax in Trollope's *The American Senator*. No doubt occasional examples of this type turned up. Lists of masters occasionally contain an unidentifiable Captain This or Major That, and there was the case of the ex-groom named Walker, who, under the name of Marsh, was master of the Vine in 1858. [92] Nevertheless, these men never lasted long and made little impression. The depression effectively eliminated most of them, as masters with money became all the more important. [93]

These, however, were exceptions. The prototype master of hounds remained the country gentleman, and it was from that group that most masters of hounds were drawn. Though many of them may have had several sources of income, the land remained important. [94] Only twenty-six of the ninety-three men who headed packs in 1850 do not have their families represented in the New Domesday Survey of twenty-four years later, while sixty of them owned or were members of families owning over one thousand acres. In 1885, only twenty-six men were not represented, and eighty-eight men or their families owned over one thousand acres, seventy of these owning over three thousand acres. [95]

Important as the master was, the day-to-day work of the establishment was done by the hunt servants in his employ. The most important member of the hunt staff was the huntsman. His duty was to take charge of the hounds in kennel and in the field. He bred them, selected them, often fed them, nursed them, trained them, and hunted them. He was expected to know each of the up to 150 hounds in his care by name, to know their idiosyncrasies, and the extent to which they could be depended upon in the field. He often was able to tell one hound from another merely by their voices when they were hidden from his view in drawing a covert, and the good huntsman could, on the basis of this knowledge, decide whether or not the hounds had actually found a fox. In addition to his skill with hounds, the huntsman had to be wise in the ways of foxes, and above all, to be an able and fearless horseman, for he had to be up with his hounds at all times during a run to make sure that they caught their fox. It was a hard, arduous, and often dangerous job, but it could also be a glamorous and exciting one, and for the son of a local labourer, or even the son of a farmer, it offered opportunities not to be had in any other way. Hunt service became a tradition in some families. The Smith family, for example, hunted the Earl of Yarborough's hounds for generations. The Goodalls, three Stephens, two Franks, and two Wills, served eleven hunts. The Hills served seven. [96]

The huntsman occupied an ambiguous social position. He was, technically and in reality, a servant. His demeanour was expected to be that of a servant, and he could be dismissed if it were not. In 1849, for example, the Vine whipper-in was advanced to huntsman following an injury to the regular huntsman. He lasted only a short time, however, being dismissed for 'forgetting himself on being remonstrated with by one of the members of the hunt'. [97] He often had to suffer interference from ignorant members of the field in silence though he knew it might lose the fox, [98] for it was the job of the master, not the huntsman, to control the crowd, [99] and on days when the master was not out, the huntsman missed his presence. In 1864, the Court of Common Pleas ruled, in the case of *Nicol v. Greaves,* that a huntsman was a menial servant, requiring only one month's notice for dismissal, rather than the one year that many sportsmen had supposed. [100]

Nevertheless, he was a servant of an especially favoured sort. He was generally a local, and in some cases, a national celebrity, who associated on terms of familiarity, though not equality, with some of the highest in the land. When, for example, Tom Firr, long-time Quorn huntsman, retired in 1898, he was presented with a cheque for £3200, which had been collected from 380 subscribers led by the Prince of Wales, the Dukes of Beaufort, Rutland, Portland, and Somerset, the Bishop of Peterborough, and many others of equal prominence. [101] In the absence of the Duke of Rutland, Frank Gillard, Firr's contemporary with the Belvoir, entertained the Empress of Austria in his parlour after a day's hunting. [102] This celebrity, especially if the huntsman also had a reputation for being a 'character', could often lead to his being forgiven for occasionally losing his temper with a social superior. [103]

Assisting the huntsman was the whipper-in, whose main job was to keep the hounds together in the field, discipline them, and also occasionally assist in the stables. [104] Most whippers-in aspired to carry the huntsman's horn themselves one day.

A huntsman generally received a cottage near the kennels, coals, hunting clothes, and a salary, which varied from pack to pack. Around 1800, he received around £40 to £50 per annum. [105] This rose by mid-century to around £80 to £100 per year [106] and could reach as high as £200 by the end of the century, though it rarely did. The salary of a first whipper-in was generally about 65 to 75 per cent of that of a huntsman, that of a second whipper-in about 50 per cent. [107] In addition, a huntsman could count on receiving tips from members of the field. It was customary to tip the huntsman anything from half-a-crown to a pound from time to time, especially if hunting with a strange pack. [108] A special favour, like receipt of the brush, mask, or pads, called for a special tip. [109] Tips could amount to a considerable sum, especially in a non-subscription pack, where the members of the field were spared the expense of subscribing. Bob Price, huntsman to the Croome in the 1870s, once collected over seventy-five pounds one Saturday before Christmas. [110]

Upon retirement, the huntsman could generally count upon a presentation of some sort, generally a piece of plate and some money, which could range from the £70 collected in 1889 for the first whip of the South Durham [111] to the over £3000 received by Firr. Some hunts purchased annuities for servants, as the Heythrop did in 1865. [112] If he had been in the service of one man for a long time, the huntsman might also receive a pension or a cottage, as Will Long did from the Duke of Beaufort in 1855. [113]

A huntsman's job, however, was a dangerous one, and not all huntsmen were as fortunate as some of those who have been mentioned. One frequently comes across appeals for aid for the families of injured huntsmen, or for retired huntsmen themselves in need of money. [114] As early as 1848, suggestions had been made for establishing a benevolent society for hunt servants, [115] and these suggestions recurred from time to time, though there were those who opposed the idea. Delabere Blaine, for example, felt that it was a slur on country gentlemen to suggest that they did not look after their old servants, and that a society would injure the sport by removing the desire to excel. [116]

In 1871, however, a society was established. The Hunt Servants Benefit Society was governed by a board consisting of masters of foxhounds and a few hunt servants, and provided illness, retirement, and death benefits for its 'benefit members' — hunt servants who paid premiums ranging, for a thirty-year-old man, from 14s. 1d. to £5. 4s. 9d. per year for the various kinds of benefits. [117] Membership in the society became a 'badge of respectability', for in order to join, every hunt servant had to produce a certificate of good conduct from his master. [118] The society also enrolled honorary members, hunting people who contributed five pounds to aid the society's funds. Contributions for the society were solicited constantly by the sporting press, and in many hunts, committees, often of women, were set up to collect money. [119] Money was also raised through amateur theatricals, and, starting in 1880, an annual cricket match was played at Lords between a team of huntsmen and a team of jockeys for their respective benefit societies. [120] By 1877, the society had invested around £10,500 and enrolled 276 benefit members and 1750 honorary members. [121]

Huntsmen and whippers-in, with their scarlet coats and spirited horses, were the aristocrats of hunt service. There were also humbler men, like grooms and stable attendants, who contributed to the sport. The most invisible of these was the earthstopper, who had to rise between midnight and two in the morning to stop the earths in the area to be hunted the next day. Though originally the earthstopper, who generally did other jobs like ratcatching or gravedigging as well, [122] was employed directly by the hunt at a set fee for each earth stopped, by the end of the nineteenth century most hunts entrusted the job to farmers and gamekeepers, each of whom stopped the earths on his land for a flat fee, which he lost if the fox went to earth. [123]

Finally there were those who were not strictly hunt servants but who made their living performing services for hunts and hunting men. Most notable of these were the 'roughriders' who schooled young horses with hounds or broke wild ones. The most famous roughrider was Dick Christian, who rode in the shires in the early nineteenth century and who was featured prominently in the books of 'The Druid'. Christian received twenty guineas per season and fifteen shillings per ride to be retained on a regular basis, or one pound per ride for occasional services. He rode as many as twenty fresh horses in a week and generally had three out in a day. [124] On slow hunting days, the Meltonians often would send Christian ahead as a 'fox' in order to give them a hard run. [125] In his old age, Christian was supported by a fund set up by hunting men. [126]

The work of masters, committeemen, and hunt servants was a year-round task. Much of it went unnoticed by the great majority of those who turned out to hunt; to them the hounds were a convenience that they took for granted. Without this work, however, hunting could not have exerted the great influence over rural life which we must now consider.

PART III

THE VIEW FROM WITHOUT

CHAPTER 7

HUNTING AND RURAL LIFE

Had foxhunting merely been the concern of those who hunted, it would hardly have been significant enough to warrant much attention, no matter how wealthy or prominent its followers, or how deeply they felt about their sport. But hunting was not solely the concern of the approximately fifty-thousand men and women who rode to hounds in any given year. [1] From its earliest days, foxhunting was woven inseparably into the pattern of English rural life. Men who had never ridden to hounds, and who never would, took an interest in 'their' local pack and its doings, often with pride, sometimes with dismay, but rarely with indifference. If only because anyone's field could quite literally become the hunting field, no one with an interest in agriculture could safely ignore hunting, but the interest often ran far more deeply than that. The hunt was not merely incidental to rural society, it was a legitimate and integral part of it, and there were few who could imagine rural England without foxhunting. The class of people most directly affected by hunting, whether the individual members of that class hunted or not, were the farmers; their relations with the hunt will be discussed in greater detail in the next chapter. But everyone else in the neighbourhood was likely to have his life touched, to some degree, by the hunt, and it is to these other people that we shall first turn.

Though people could be affected by the sport in many ways, and though hunting people often spoke of hunting in other than sporting terms, we must not lose sight of the fact that the primary purpose of the sport was entertainment. Those who rode to hounds, however, were not the only ones who were entertained. Hunting, with its scarlet coats, baying hounds, and spirited horses, was above all a spectacle; unless there happened to be a military unit quartered nearby, it was often the only spectacle that country dwellers were likely to see. No one could ignore a foxhunt if it passed by, and many went out of their way to be sure to see it. In the early days, when packs of hounds were fewer and travelled about hunting vast territories, the arrival of the hounds in the neighbourhood was often a looked-for event of the first magnitude. William Cobbett described the excitement in a village in Surrey at the prospect of a visit by the hounds in 1825:

> Wyndham's FOXHOUNDS are coming to Thursley on Saturday. More than three-fourths of all the interesting talk in that neighbourhood, for some days past, has been about the anxiously looked-for event. I have seen no man, or boy, who did not talk about it. There had been a false report about it; the hounds did *not come;* and the anger of the disappointed people was very great. At last, however, the *authentic* intelligence came, and I left them all as happy as if all were young and all just going to be married. [2]

Almost a century later, the hounds still had the same attraction. 'An interesting event', wrote the farm labourer, Fred Kitchen, about his schooldays in the West Riding of Yorkshire,

> was when the hounds met at the Hall. Then the children would be taken to see the meet. Whether it went down as a lesson in natural history, or what it was, I don't know, but it was an interesting lesson, watching the pink coats arrive on their prancing horses, and the dappled hounds trotting round the whipper-in. [3]

The meet of hounds often attracted hundreds of onlookers, from the very aristocratic, who attended on horseback or in carriages, to the very humble, who came on foot. If it were a 'lawn meet' — a meeting on the grounds of a great country house — the attraction could be even greater, for, in addition to the spectacle of the hounds and horsemen, there was the prospect of free food and drink provided by the owner of the house. A lawn meet at a great country seat, like the opening meet of the Duke of Beaufort's hounds at Badminton, was a major social event for the entire neighbourhood. The annual 'Badminton Lawn Day' attracted huge crowds of onlookers of all classes including foreign princes. [4] Owners of great houses would often ask the master to meet at their house and draw nearby coverts to mark some celebration of their own, or in honour of guests that might be staying in the house.⁵

Sometimes a special meet might be arranged at a town or village just for the purpose of putting on a show for the local people. In 1861, for example, the North Warwickshire hounds met at Coventry Railway Station 'for the especial gratification of the distressed weavers'. Thirty to forty thousand people are said to have turned out that day. ⁶The Boxing Day meet used to attract the largest crowds, partly because it was a holiday, partly because an old tradition named St Stephen's Day (December 26) as the day on which all were free to kill any game they wished. ⁷ The Pytchely Boxing Day meet of 1841, for example, attracted 1500 foot followers. ⁸

When the hounds moved away from the place of meeting and trotted off to the first covert, some of those who had come to view the spectacle would return home or to their work, but not all. The drawing of the first covert was yet another recognized spectacle, and, again, there were many who crowded round the covert, often to the great annoyance of the master and huntsman, to see the hounds find their fox and to watch the field of horseman gallop away. Even after the fox was found and the chase began, the horsemen were not the only ones to follow hounds. An active man who knew the country and was wise to the way in which foxes ran could often manage to see a fair amount afoot by judiciously cutting corners and taking advantage of the high ground, which offered good vantage points. Many who followed on foot were farm labourers who did not turn out to hunt but who joined in the chase for a short time when the hounds ran past where they were working. 'There is a little hop-garden,' wrote Cobbett, 'in which I used to work when from eight to ten years old from which I have scores of times run to follow the hounds, leaving the hoe to do the best that it could to destroy the weeds. ⁹ Many an older labourer did likewise, and though few could afford to lose their wages by following for more than a very short time, even that provided a rare and pleasant break from the day's work. ¹⁰ If the labourer risked losing wages, there was always the chance that he might make a shilling or two catching a loose horse or opening a gate; more, if he happened to be nearby when some special labour was required, like digging out a fox that had gone to ground. ¹¹

Farm labourers were not the only ones to follow, however. We must not forget that there were craftsmen, like weavers, who did not work in factories and who, if they were fond of seeing a little hunting, could still arrange their own work so as to allow them an occasional day's outing. [12] There were even those few who were more than occasional foot followers, but who could be expected to turn out day after day, and often walked many miles just to be able to follow hounds for even more miles. Like the hunting sweep, these men often became established as local characters and were frequently dependent upon whatever money they could earn in the field, supplemented by charity from the members of the hunts to which they were hangers-on. Sam Curnock, or Cornock, for example, the son of a Gloucestershire weaver, turned out regularly with the Duke of Beaufort and Earl Fitzhardinge in the 1840s, wearing a cast-off coat of whichever hunt he was out with. In addition to the tips that he was able to collect, he eked out a living performing odd jobs for Lord Fitzhardinge, including carrying around notice of the unadvertised meets to the gentlemen of the neighbourhood. [13]

The presence of large numbers of foot hunters was not necessarily welcome to the master of hounds. No matter how well-behaved they were, they were far more likely to interfere with sport than to contribute to it. Even one man on foot in front of the fox could head him, causing the hounds to lose the scent. Several hundred could prevent them from ever finding it again. [14] The foot people were not always 'well-behaved', at least by the standards of the master. There were many — out for a good time in the fresh air, to enjoy the spectacle of the chase, and to let off steam — who were not above crowding the hounds in covert or at a check, heading foxes, or halloaing without having seen the fox, sometimes as a result of error, sometimes to annoy the 'swells', sometimes to lure the huntsman and pack closer so they could get a better look, and sometimes just for the fun of shouting. [15] Will Goodall, the Belvoir huntsman from 1842 to 1859, used to give ale and sometimes a half-crown to country people if he had not caught them heading foxes or giving false halloas during the course of a season. [16]

The way a master dealt with these crowds of onlookers went a long way toward determining his popularity with the ordinary people of the neighbourhood; and on that popularity could depend his success as master, for few people went out of their way to preserve foxes for a master they did not like. George Osbaldeston and Sir Harry Goodricke both had to contend with the crowds of Leicestershire stockingers and weavers who would turn out *en masse* when the Quorn met in their neighbourhoods. Osbaldeston generally tried to bully them into order and was not averse to resorting to force. He and his men fought with bystanders with alarming regularity, both in the Quorn country and in the Pytchley, where he was involved in a row with the Northampton shoemakers at the Pytchley Hunt races. It is no wonder that he rarely had the cooperation of the foot people or that he found it difficult to keep his countries stocked with foxes. [17] Sir Harry Goodricke, on the other hand, was one of the most popular of Quorn masters, both with the members of the field and with the bystanders, and one of the sources of his popularity was his tact with the stockingers. [18]

For the purist, 'hunting' meant the sport seen in the field, but there were many, like the women in Surtees' 'Doubleimupshire', for whom the hunt was a 'grand nucleus of society — the promoter of balls, breakfasts, dinners, races, and conviviality of all sorts.' [19] For them, the exploits of the master on the dancing floor or at the dinner table were far more important than his exploits in the field. The role of hunting as a social centre of this type need not detail us long, but we must not lose sight of the fact that hunting served this function. Hunts sponsored balls, dinners, breakfasts, hound shows, and races, all of which contributed to the style of life of a neighbourhood, and all of which were eagerly awaited by local residents.

Much of the social life associated with hunting centred around the hunt club. Clubs had originated in the days when packs hunted a large territory and moved from one part of their country to another. For the convenience of those sportsmen who followed the hounds, clubs were established in different parts of the country to provide stabling and lodging. [20] When countries became smaller, clubs lost this function, but they remained as a social adjunct to the hunt. Not everyone who followed the hounds belonged, nor, in many cases, did all the subscribers. Membership in the club, which could generally be gained only through balloting, was limited to the gentry. [21] In addition to its social function, the hunt club often raised a subscription to pay earth-stopping, damage, or covert expenses. [22]

The hunt ball was often one of the major social events for the gentry of a neighbourhood. The practice of giving a ball, often at the end of the season and in conjunction with the hunt races, dates from the eighteenth century [23] and became even more common in the nineteenth. The ball was usually sponsored by the hunt club, and invitations were generally limited to those with some claims of gentility. Wives and daughters of 'yeoman and tradesmen' had been invited to the Pytchley Hunt Ball in 1826, [24] and some other hunts did the same, [25] but so egalitarian a step never caught on. When the daughters of J. R. Coupland, the Quorn master, gave a ball for the townspeople of Melton Mowbray in 1872, it was considered a 'novel', but on the other hand, 'appropriate' idea. [26]

Hunt dinners attracted a wider social range than did the balls, often because they were generally limited to men only, and so the danger of introducing ladies to unsuitable company did not arise. But there were various kinds of dinners. There were those limited to members of the club and their guests, dinners given by the hunt for farmers, or great public dinners to commemorate an event like the retirement of a master, which all classes of people attended. [27] Dinners, like breakfasts, often attracted people who had no other connection with the sport. The opportunity for a celebration, an assembly, or a dinner was not to be scoffed at in small town or village society, and so, the hunt's celebration could become everyone's celebration. The fiftieth anniversary of J. J. Farquharson as master of the Dorset Hounds in 1856, for example, was celebrated as a public holiday in the town of Blandford. [28] Hunt activities could even serve the cause of charity. Mr Jorrocks' sporting 'lectors' for the benefit of the Handley Cross Infirmary [29] had their counterpart in the booklet of maps and fixtures published by the Suffolk Hunt in 1851 for the benefit of the Suffolk Hospital. [30]

In addition to social events, hunting gave birth to a number of ancillary sporting events, such as horse and hound shows and races, which acquired a life of their own, independent of their source. Horse racing on an informal basis had been a part of the hunting scene from its very beginning. By the end of the eighteenth century, a number of hunts had taken to organizing an annual race meeting for their followers, [31] and the practice became almost universal in the nineteenth. These races were an immensely popular local event, drawing great crowds.

What is the most striking, however, about the place of hunting in rural life in the nineteenth century was the extent to which its influence was felt in matters having only remote connections with the hunting field *per se*. In some cases, the influence was exerted through the normal functioning of the sport. As a consumer of local products, an employer of local labour, and a lure for outside money, the hunt played an important role in the economy of several parts of the country. Tradesmen, especially in those parts of the country that drew hunting people from outside the immediate vicinity, were strong supporters of hunting because of the business it brought them. Of the £2400 subscription collected by Sir Reginald Graham as master of the Cotswold Hunt, for example, £500 came from the tradespeople of Cheltenham.³² Hotels in the town, especially if they used the hunt's name in their advertisements, each contributed about £25.³³

In many cases, however, the influence of hunting only existed because the hunt was a convenient peg upon which to hang other matters. When, in 1859-60, for example, apprehensions about the foreign policy of Napoleon III led to the formation of volunteer militia corps throughout the country, nothing was more natural than for hunting men to form irregular cavalry units organized around their hunts. The followers of the Oakley and Fitzwilliam Hunts set the fashion by forming a corps under the Duke of Manchester, and other hunts followed suit. The London Light Horse Volunteer Corps was organized around hunting men who lived in London. 'Hunting', commented the editor of *Bell's Life*, 'leads almost insensibly into mounted volunteering.'³⁴

Hunting was one of the few institutions in pre-Victorian and Victorian England whose organization was essentially geographical, taking in all who lived in an area, irrespective of class or occupation. For that reason it was often the point at which local interests or grievances came to the surface. Because it was a highly visible institution, and because it was identifiable with local personalities, it could become a symbol of local pride. Because of its close connection with the land and its identification as the sport of those connected to the land, it could become a symbol of the rural way of life.

Consider, for example, the great emotion aroused by the events leading up to the resignation of J. J. Farquharson as master of the Dorset hounds after over fifty years of service. Farquharson succeeded to the country in 1806, when large countries were the rule, and over the years had steadfastly refused to part with any of it, even though much of the country could not have been hunted fairly according to the more modern notions.³⁵ His latter years as master were, therefore, marked by a succession of acrimonious disputes with neighbouring masters and with residents within his borders who wished to see the country divided. The last of these disputes took place in 1857, one year after Farquharson celebrated his fiftieth anniversary as master. When he refused to relinquish certain coverts, after having received a petition asking him to do so, he found himself warned off by two large landowners who had sponsored the petition. Faced with this, Farquharson chose to resign, and his resignation became a *cause célèbre* in Dorset. With regard to the petition that had sparked the dispute, the *Dorset County Chronicle* editorialized:

We are glad to say that looking through the names attached to the document in question we find that it is not a Dorsetshire petition at all; but that headed by the Lord Lieutenant of Somersetshire, it is a *Somersetshire requisition* in every sense of the word, every one of the signatures, save *three,* being Somersetshire signatures. The aim of the Lieutenancy we can easily appreciate, as well as the political and personal ambition which may also be amongst the motives for this Somersetshire attempt to ride roughshod over the Yeomanry of Dorset. But surely that gallant band of fox-hunters will rally round their ancient Squire and never suffer him to be overborne. [36]

The Farquharson affair was trivial in the scheme of great events. It indicates, however, that strongly held feelings often materialized around local objects of pride like the hunt.

When local politics were involved, the feelings could become even stronger. The wise master of foxhounds, particularly if he was not a local man, was careful not to get involved in politics, for in the end the result could only be harmful to hunting. But try as he might, he could not always be successful, for politics, like hunting, was a grand entertainment, even for those who did not take a direct part. The interaction between politics and hunting might begin on either side. As a vital part of local society, the hunt was as natural a place as any for local political feeling, often having nothing to do with hunting, to manifest itself. As an important local interest, on the other hand, hunting could significantly affect local politics.

In 1811, for example, Sir William Manners barred the Belvoir from his lands because the Duke of Rutland, its master, had put up a candidate for Grantham in opposition to him. The prohibition was not lifted until the duke withdrew his candidate, prompting the *Sporting Magazine* to comment that this was the first candidate to be returned to the House of Commons by foxhunting. [37] He was not the last.

In 1851, political feelings again surfaced in the hunting field, this time with overtones of greater national significance, when Sir Robert Peel, the son of the recently-deceased statesman, was barred by farmers from following hounds over their land, because of their indignation over a letter that the baronet had sent to *The Times*. At a protectionist meeting at Tamworth soon after his death, the elder Sir Robert Peel had been assailed in very strong language. On their way home from the meeting, some of the protectionists were set upon and beaten by Peel's supporters, an action the younger Peel had seen fit to praise in a letter to *The Times* as a 'spontaneous burst of indignation which greeted those musty pilgrims of protection'.[38] The farmer who was the first to bar Peel was finally prevailed upon to withdraw the prohibition in the interest of the hunt, and Peel returned to the field, no doubt disabused of any notion that he might have had about the hunting field being a place where the cares of the everyday world could be forgotten.[39]

The influence of the hunting field upon politics could be even more striking. We must never forget that local interests, grievances, and personalities were often likelier to sway voters than were the grand national issues. Few politicians, unless they represented thoroughly urban constituencies, could afford to alienate foxhunters if they wished to keep office. Even in the days before the League against Cruel Sports, hunting could be an issue in politics. Two elections of the 1860s − the North Essex election of 1865 and the North Leicestershire election of 1868 − illustrate the way that this could come about.[40] In neither was foxhunting a decisive issue. In both, however, hunting attracted major attention and provided much of the excitement, if not the substance, of the campaigns.

Charles DuCane, of Braxted Park, Witham, Essex, M.P. for North Essex, was an ambitious young Conservative. He came of a family that had represented the county off and on since the eighteenth century, and had been member for North Essex since 1857.[41] Since his first important speech in June, 1858,[42] he had taken an increasingly active role in Parliamentary debate, and his political future seemed bright. He was also, as befitted his position in the countryside, one of the largest subscribers to, and a guarantor of, the East Essex Hunt.[43]

On February 14, 1865, as the preparations for a general election were beginning, a letter appeared in the Liberal *Essex Telegraph*. Over the signature 'A Tenant Farmer', the writer accused DuCane of a belated attempt to curry favour with the tenant farmers, who he had alienated by increasing rents and overpreserving game. He pointed to DuCane's having just dismissed Robert Partridge, who, as DuCane's agent, had implemented these unpopular measures, as proof. As if DuCane's behaviour as a landlord were not bad enough, the letter went on, 'let us see too what he has done for our prince of field sports − hunting'.

Is it not a fact that there is, or was, in Braxted Park, a cave in which foxes were shut up in order that the same might not interfere with his excessive game preserving?

Is this the way to encourage our national sport of foxhunting?

Surely the members of the Hunt can appreciate such an example of sympathetic feeling with them in their love of the chase. [44]

Though the election was still months away, DuCane lost no time in answering the charges. He dashed off a letter to the *Telegraph* denying all the accusations. [45] He also arranged to have copies of several letters he had received and written on the subject inserted in the local papers, and included statements in his defence by his gamekeepers, as well as a letter from Richard Marriott, the master of the East Essex, written at the time of the alleged 'cave' incident, in which the master acknowledged that he knew and approved of it. [46] Of the two accusations made by 'A Tenant Farmer', and later repeated by Partridge in a letter to the local papers, [47] the one that tenants were leaving DuCane's estates because they could not recover damages caused by overpreservation of game was perhaps the more alarming to him. The votes of the tenant farmers were important to secure his re-election, and they were likely to be swayed more easily by the relationship between DuCane and his own tenants than by the less vital topic of DuCane's practice with regard to foxes. But DuCane was also well aware of the damage that could be done him with all segments of the community by the accusations regarding foxes, and the refutation of the charges occupied much of his attention for the ensuing three weeks. He wrote an article in his own defence which was published as if written by the editors of the *Essex Gazette*. [48] Following the publication of this, he had one of his tenants send a letter, which, in fact, had also been written by DuCane, to the local papers, praising him as a landlord and fox preserver. [49]

It would be difficult to assess the extent to which the controversy affected the outcome of the election, which was eventually won by DuCane. What is unquestionable is the importance both sides attached to it. Though the Conservative *Essex Standard* declared the whole issue 'a simple and unmitigated absurdity', and referred to the 'folly of hanging the result of a county election on a question of the greater or less ease used in the preservation of foxes,' [50] it was alone in dismissing it all as 'folly'. All the other participants, aware of the great emotion that hunting could arouse, treated the controversy accordingly. The passionate language used by one side was matched or even surpassed by that of the other. 'The honourable member stands charged with having systematically bid defiance to the recognized duties and amenities of his order', thundered the *Essex Telegraph*. [51] 'A Lie which is half a truth is ever the blackest of lies', countered the *Essex Gazette*. [52]

DuCane, probably more confident on the issue of fox preservation than on that of game damage, [53] nevertheless could not have looked forward without some nervousness to the meeting of the East Essex Hunt that he called for the purpose of explaining his position. [54] The great issue of the campaign of 1865 was the tax on malt. But for a month, all else took second place to questions of game preserving and foxhunting, and the controversy even found its way into the national press; [55] eleven years later, the question was not forgotten. [56] It is also significant to notice that party affiliation in no way affected the issue. The Liberal paper first took on the role of the spokesman for the foxhunting interest, though the Conservatives were not slow to profess equal zeal for the sport.

The North Leicestershire election of 1868 is yet another example of the fact that where foxhunting was concerned, party lines meant little, though in this case we can see the beginnings of a Radical dislike of hunting, based not on any aversion to the sport itself, but on an identification of hunting people, whether Liberals or Conservatives, as the representatives of an essentially conservative political and social order.

As befitted a county so closely associated with foxhunting, the two official Conservative candidates in the dual-member constituency were two men whose own association with the sport was well known. Lord John Manners was the brother of the sixth Duke of Rutland, hereditary master of the Belvoir Hunt. S. W. Clowes, though not a Leicestershire man, had been master of the Quorn from 1863 to 1866. The constituency was so solidly under the influence of the Duke of Rutland that the Liberals did not bother to contest the seat, but the excitement of a contest was not to be denied the local inhabitants. C. H. Frewen, a member of a prominent and wealthy local gentry family, declared himself an independent Conservative candidate, and proceeded to campaign hard. Fighting lost causes and generally making a nuisance of himself were nothing new for Frewen. He had unsuccessfully contested the seat since 1857. [57] Two years previously he had attempted to bar a congregation from part of its parish church in order to assert his rights as lord of the manor. [58]

The election of Lord John Manners was a foregone conclusion. The contest very quickly became one between Clowes and Frewen for the second seat. The great national issue of the campaign was the disestablishment of the Irish Church. The great local one was the political influence of the House of Rutland. On the first, there was no difference of opinion between Frewen and Clowes.[59] It was on the second that Frewen chose to make his stand. Accusing Clowes of being the nominee of the Rutlands, he put forward his candidacy as a means of breaking the stranglehold of the duke's family on local politics. Most local opinion, whether it favoured Frewen or not, saw his candidacy in the same light.

Polling was due to begin on Friday, 20 November. On the preceding Saturday, 14 November, the leader column of the *Leicester Advertiser* referred the attention of its readers to another page for what it called, 'the greatest curiosity in electioneering correspondence that we have ever met with'. There, under the heading 'Leicestershire Men, *Read, Mark and Understand*', was the following letter, dated 9 November, from C. H. Frewen to the Duke of Rutland:

> I think it is always best under *all* circumstances to act in a fair and straight-forward manner, and this is the reason I am going to trouble your Grace with this letter, particularly as you are master of a pack of Foxhounds.
>
> I do not think that Mr. Clowes's prospects of success in North Leicestershire are very encouraging, but there is a decided feeling with many that if he should be draged [sic] in to represent the foxhunting interest, why then, the sooner foxhunting is put an end to the better, – and if it should happen that he get in some of us intend to do our best to clear the country of foxes, *which can very easily be done*. When poor men have been turned out of their land because they dared to vote for me in 1865, we shall be quite justified in taking this course.
>
> A gentleman of large landed property in the county said to me only on Saturday, 'that it was monstrous bringing forward a man who had no property in the county, and who had only been here a few years as a foxhunter, and who was shortly going to leave the country'.
>
> I have written in the same tone to Mr. Tailby and Colonel Lowther in order that they may know what our intentions are, and if such a state of things should be brought about, the foxhunters will then have nothing to complain of, as they will have been informed beforehand what our intentions were.

The letter concluded with the postscript:

> If there was any *great* difference in our political opinions, or if Mr. Clowes was an owner of property in the county things would be very different. The Conservatives in this county have lost two seats through

their own foolish conduct – the Borough of Leicester and South Leicestershire – both of which they had previous to the election in 1865, and if they loose [sic] any more seats they will only have to thank themselves for it. [60]

Up to this point hunting had not entered the campaign. The Radical *Leicester Mail* had referred to Clowes as 'the foxhunter' on more than one occasion and had criticized foxhunting magistrates for neglecting their judicial duties during the hunting season, [61] but even the *Mail* saw fit to publish the weekly list of hound meetings.

The reaction to Frewen's indiscretion was prompt. In a masterpiece of unfortunate timing, Frewen arrived in Melton Mowbray to address a meeting on the Monday following the publication of the letter, only to be greeted by a mob with a fox's brush and mask on a pole. He was forced to duck into the railway station for shelter. [62] Similar scenes occurred in other places. At the hustings at Loughborough, one of only two polling districts in which he did not come third, [63] he was greeted by a noisy crowd waving foxes' heads and traps. The newspapers that supported Clowes, of course, had a field day with Frewen's letter, offering it as proof of his lack of fitness for office. [64] The Liberal *Chronicle* maintained a discreet silence, and the Radical *Mail* clearly wished that the letter had never appeared. The *Mail*, which might have been expected to exploit Frewen's letter to the fullest, did no such thing. Perhaps its editors knew only too well that the tenant farmers could not be expected to go along with it. When the excitement of the election had passed, they looked back over what Frewen had done. 'Men write things in haste and under natural irritation which they would recall', [65] was their only verdict.

Frewen himself was made of sterner stuff. Though he denied being a vulpicide, and, in fact, claimed to be a supporter of the sport, he remained on the attack, accusing local hunting men of riding rough-shod over the farmers, and asking whether foxhunting was a qualification for election to Parliament. [66] His boldness did him no good. When the votes were counted, Lord John Manners, to no one's surprise, topped the poll with 3296 votes. Clowes had 2092, Frewen, 1750. [67] It was the worst defeat of Frewen's political career. As in the case of DuCane three years earlier, it is difficult to assess the effect that the foxhunting letter had on the result. The election was an unruly one, and Frewen charged that tenants were threatened with eviction for voting for him. [68] That some Leicestershire farmers were dissatisfied with the way hunting was carried out in the county is quite clear. [69] Whether they voted for Clowes out of fear of their landlords or out of dislike for Frewen's extreme position is hard to determine, but vote for him they did. Certainly, the Rutland influence cannot be discounted, though the great difference in the number of votes gathered by Manners and Clowes indicates that it helped Clowes far less than it did Manners. Clowes himself was not helped, especially among those Leicestershire men who resented the influx of outsiders into the hunting field, by being from outside the county.

Two things are quite clear, however. The first is that the foxhunting issue provided most of the excitement of an otherwise uneventful contest. The second is that everyone involved was convinced that the publication of Frewen's letter did him great harm. He himself claimed that it was solely responsible for his defeat. [70] The *Mail*, which, speaking more out of hope than knowledge, had predicted a victory, acknowledged that the letter had hurt him. [71] 'A Liberal Elector' wrote to the *Mail* claiming that many Liberals who voted for Frewen did so on Liberal principles, but that on personal grounds they would have preferred Clowes, who conducted himself as a gentleman throughout. [72] Characteristically, Frewen had the last word. Hounds were barred from the Frewen estates at Cold Overton, [73] and in Oakham County Court, William Tailby, M.F.H., was forced to apologize for crossing Frewen land without permission. [74] It must have been some consolation for his defeat.

No one would claim that the Essex election or that of Leicestershire was a significant event in the political history of the nineteenth century. They do, however, remind us that great national events often took second place to the more personal issues of local interest, and among these, foxhunting cannot be discounted.

CHAPTER 8

FOXHUNTERS AND FARMERS

The relationship between foxhunting and farmers epitomized more than anything else the peculiar nature of hunting as a social institution, for it was here that hunting people and non-hunting people came into closest contact, and it was here that the idealized picture of hunting society was brought into its sharpest and most clear-cut contrast with everyday reality.

The farmer had a definite image in the iconography of foxhunting, and that image changed very little in the more than one hundred years between Hugo Meynell and the great agricultural depression. Farmers, so far as hunters were concerned, fell into several categories. First, and most admired, was the farmer of the 'old sort', the crusty, hard-working, well-to-do but deferential old man who always wore top boots, and who rose early to put in a hard day's work before taking his one or two days a week hunting. He loved sport, preserved foxes, and always had a mug of ale or piece of cheese ready to offer any passing sportsman. Second, there was the younger farmer, often the son of the first, who was wild, had ideas above his station, and often aped the manners of his betters, but was a good sportsman for all that, and who would, as likely as not, settle down to become one of the good old sort himself. Finally, there was the grumbler, the man who hated foxes and hunting. More than likely he was a transplanted city man.[1] To each of these there was a definite way to act. The first had to be respected and shown consideration, though he might also provide a chuckle or two behind his back. The second needed to be put in his place from time to time, but generally was to be treated well. The third was beneath contempt.

In no other field sport was the farmer as directly involved as he was in hunting. Despite the great outcry over the game laws through most of the nineteenth century, he was relatively unconcerned with shooting unless he had the misfortune to rent land in an over-preserved part of the country, in which case his crops might suffer from the depredations of game. Otherwise, his only contact with the sport, unless he did a bit of shooting himself, might be the occasional gifts of game that he received from his landlord or other local gentry. But even the great majority of farmers who did not hunt had a vital interest in the doings of the local pack of hounds.

The foxes themselves could be a matter for concern. There was little doubt that foxes would long since have been destroyed as harmful predators were it not for their preservation for hunting. No farmer liked to have foxes around, for they killed his poultry and even his lambs. Secondly, where the fox led, the hounds followed, and this, more often than not, was over the farmer's fields and pastures. In the wake of the hounds came the sportsmen – as many as five hundred or more in the fashionable countries – and in the heat of a good run, few stopped to consider the damage they did.

On the face of it, therefore, hunting would appear to have been an unmitigated social and economic evil as far as farmers were concerned. That they did not generally consider it so through most of the nineteenth century was a result of three factors: the general prosperity of farming throughout the period of hunting's greatest popularity, the care taken by foxhunters to gain the good will of farmers, and the general belief that hunting was an integral part of rural life that benefited all country dwellers 'from the peer to the peasant'.

From the very beginning, foxhunters recognized that the existence of hunting depended, to a large degree, on the good will of the farmers. Moreover, most of those who hunted depended to a greater or lesser degree on the prosperity of agriculture for their own livelihood. Respect and consideration for farmers, therefore, was a major tenet of foxhunting creed. 'You should also endeavour to gain the good will of *the farmers*', wrote Colonel John Cook, for 'if any respectable body of persons suffer from hunting, it is them; and I think it not only ungentlemanly, but impolitic, to treat them in the field, or elsewhere, otherwise than with kindness and civility.' [2] Nimrod, characteristically less disposed to consider the question of kindness to social inferiors in the abstract, considered the more practical aspects of the problem. 'To every man who is a foxhunter', he wrote in 1822,

> it is well known how much it is requisite for a master of hounds to stand well with the yeomen and farmers of his country. They have much in their power, and to them Mr. Meynell was uniformly civil, *and even polite.* [3] [Italics mine.]

The debt that hunters owed to the farmers, however, was balanced in the minds of most sportsmen by the debts that the farmers owed to hunting. The two were often considered together as an example of the community of interest shared by all rural people. In addition to the more general argument that field sports, by keeping gentlemen resident in the country, benefited the whole country, the specific benefits to the farmer were frequently pointed out. The number of extra horses kept for hunting, it was argued, created an increased market for the farmers' hay, oats, and beans, spreading money through the agricultural community. [4]

Another supposed advantage of hunting was that by creating a demand for horses, it gave the farmers yet another source of income, the breeding of hunters. Since the best way to show off hunters was by riding them to hounds, it provided the farmers with a perfect opportunity to combine business and pleasure. [5] There were some few, notably the tough-minded Surtees, who admitted readily that most of the money spent on hunting found its way into the pockets of the horse and forage dealers, rather than those of the farmers, [6] and the farmers themselves were able to see that they were not getting rich from hunting, but it was not until the agricultural depression acted as a catalyst to unleash long submerged feelings that these opinions were given general currency.

In addition to enumerating the benefits the farmers gained from hunting, the hunting apologists were also careful to stress that hunting caused very little serious damage or inconvenience to farmers, and that whatever damage was done was quickly paid for if the farmer wished it, but that most farmers, being great lovers of hunting, would not dream of claiming compensation. That this ideal did not exactly describe the reality of the situation is hardly surprising. We cannot, however, help but be struck by the fact that despite the strains that existed between farmers and foxhunters, hunting, which, in fact, depended on the good will of the farmers for its very existence, never came under any serious threat from them until late in the nineteenth century. The farmers were not fools, nor were they meek and docile. They were aware of the realities of the situation and knew, in addition, their powers to change that situation. That they used those powers rarely and always with moderation until they saw a major threat to their own existence is eloquent testimony that, on the whole, hunting enjoyed the good will of most farmers.

The farmer's involvement with the hunt was not limited to its occasional incursions onto his land. The organization of hunting in any hunt country was far more all-pervading than that. Though the visiting sportsman might only be aware of the hunt's existence during the course of a day's sport, the residents in the country were far more aware of the behind-the-scenes organization and planning. Before turning to the far more dramatic picture conjured up by the image of hordes of horseman flattening all in their path, let us turn first to the calmer but no less important ways in which a hunt might affect the lives of those who lived within its boundaries.

The most basic of these was in the matter of preserving foxes. To the non-hunting farmer, as we have seen, foxes were a nuisance, and he would gladly have killed them all. In order, therefore, to induce farmers to preserve foxes, which, in its simplest form, simply meant to refrain from killing them on sight, various means were adopted. The simplest of these, especially in the late eighteenth and early nineteenth centuries, but persisting in many instances well into the Victorian age, was undisguised social and economic pressure, generally exerted through the farmer's landlord. A copy of a letter from a 'nobleman of considerable property, to his Agent in Leicestershire' was printed in the *Sporting Magazine* in 1793 and was widely reprinted thereafter. 'I must desire', it stated,

> that all those tenants who have shewn themselves friends to the several fox-hunts in your neighbouring counties; viz. Lord Spencer's, the Duke of Rutland's, Mr. Meynell's, Lord Stamford's, &c. may have the offer and refusal of their farms upon easy and moderate terms; and, on the other hand, that you will take care and make very particular inquiry into the conduct of those tenants who shall have shewn a contrary disposition, by destroying foxes, or encouraging others to do so, or otherwise interrupting gentlemen's diversion, and will transmit me their names and places of abode, as it is my absolute determination, that such persons shall not be treated with in future by me, upon any terms or consideration whatever.... I shall ... use my utmost endeavour to induce all persons of my acquaintance to adopt similar measures: and I am already happy to find, that three gentlemen of very considerable

landed property ... have positively sent within these few days, similar directions to their stewards.[7]

There is no evidence as to who the author of the letter is, or whether, in fact, it was ever really sent. It is clear, however, that instructions of this type were generally considered a legitimate influence that a landlord could exert over his tenant. The letter was reprinted in a number of places, and no foxhunter ever saw the need to defend the man who wrote it.

Pressures of this type continued to be exerted throughout the nineteenth century. Masters of hounds regularly wrote to landlords, asking them to use their influence on their tenants to see to it that foxes were preserved, and, with some exceptions, the landlords were glad to oblige.[8] As late as 1884, when a farmer in Northumberland killed some foxes that had taken some of his lambs, the first reaction of the hunt secretary was to refer the matter to the man's landlord.[9]

This sort of pressure could only be effective when farmers killed foxes openly, and had the added disadvantage of causing ill-will towards hunting, precisely the opposite of what the sportsmen wanted. Most country gentlemen – and they were the dominant class in hunting throughout the nineteenth century – wanted nothing more than peace and harmony in the countryside. It was far more to their advantage to conciliate farmers than to attempt to intimidate them; if farmers suffered by having foxes in the neighbourhood, common sense dictated that foxhunters do their best to minimize the farmers' losses, if they could not eliminate them altogether.

Foxhunters began by attempting, as much as possible, to live up to one of the basic rationales of hunting, that it existed to keep foxes in check. No one, of course, really believed this, but the hunts did try, as much as was possible, to find and kill foxes that were particularly troublesome. There are, for example, numerous entries in the diaries kept by members of the Smith family, huntsmen to the Earls of Yarborough, beginning: 'We went to a complaint.'[10] It was customary for farmers to appeal to the hunt in this way,[11] and one of the arguments in favour of digging out hunted foxes that had gone to ground was that farmers would only preserve foxes if they felt confident that the hunted ones would be killed.[12] But by the very nature of fox preservation, these methods could not be successful. Instead, the custom developed, in the early nineteenth century, of paying compensation to farmers for poultry and lambs killed by foxes. In many hunts, though, the claims were not paid out of the regular hunt funds, but out of a special fund, often collected by a committee or club expressly organized for that purpose. [13] The poultry fund, though it generally was administered in as businesslike a manner as any other aspect of hunt finance, was always viewed as something extra. Unlike damages directly caused by the hunt, for which the hunt could be held legally responsible, the poultry fund was a moral, rather than a legal, obligation. It was 'what one did' to keep the people happy, much as one sent one's tenants gifts of game. In the only instance on record that a farmer actually sued for compensation for fox damage, the Oswestry County Court ruled, in 1890, that poultry funds were entirely voluntary, and that hunts were not legally liable to pay anything. [14]

Not unnaturally, this view of the obligation to pay for poultry damage manifested itself on the part of many foxhunters as an unwillingness to pay any damages at all, and a tendency to view any who claimed damages as tricksters and liars. [15]

Many who did not accuse poultry claimants of downright fabrication tended to look at claims as exaggerated, or blamed the farmers for carelessness in allowing their poultry to be eaten by foxes. 'Poultry thus allowed to run wild in woods must get destroyed', [16] wrote one Oakley committeeman to another in 1836. Some foxhunters refused to admit that foxes ever killed lambs or poultry at all, [17] but these were in a minority.

The major problem in dealing with poultry claims was that, while the hunts admitted no real liability, the farmers could not substantiate their claims. Fowls eaten by foxes could not be produced as evidence and the informality of the procedure, in any event, left the farmer no real means of redress other than vulpicide, though the power of this must not be underestimated. The usual procedure was for the farmer to come to whoever handled poultry claims in his district and claim a loss. The hunting man, in turn, would try to talk him down, and finally a price would be agreed upon. A. G. Bagot, for example, in his series of hunting sketches, included one of 'Mr. Boulter', the hunt secretary, who had the great accomplishment of being able to charm farmers' wives out of submitting poultry claims, though at Christmas, of course, he saw to it that the farmers got a hamper of game and a bottle of sherry. [18]

The Burton Hunt, as late as 1875, tried to do away with paying compensation altogether, 'but as far as possible to compensate for the damage by presents of game to be sent out by the Master', [19] but this system, though it might have been satisfactory in better times, was not calculated to please farmers with the onslaught of the agricultural depression. The Taunton Vale Foxhounds, who had, in 1888, admitted tenant farmers to the hunt committee, hit upon a far more pleasing method of avoiding squabbles, by printing and distributing a 'tariff of payment', setting forth a standardized set of payments that would be paid for lost poultry. But this was done at a time when the old informal values of country society, of largesse and deference, were increasingly being rejected under the impact of hard times for landlord and tenant alike. [20]

Beyond simply refraining from vulpicide, farmers could assist in fox preservation in more positive ways. The farmer who was friendly to hunting was probably the most effective fox preserver in the countryside. His daily tasks took him around and through his fields, he was in a position to know where foxes had their earths and where litters were bred, and he could see to it that they were not disturbed until the hunt met in the vicinity.

Preservation went even further, of course, especially in those parts of the country where artificial means had to be resorted to to ensure a plentiful supply of foxes. In those areas – primarily, though by no means exclusively, the open grass areas of the Midlands and other grazing districts – it was necessary to plant new gorse coverts or enclose existing ones to provide places for foxes to live. Farmers were often called upon to plant or keep one of these coverts on their holdings. Customarily, they were paid rent by the hunt in order to compensate them for what they lost by not farming the land. Covert rents were a major item in the yearly expenses of the Quorn, for example, where the open pastures, ideal though they were for hunting, were less than ideal for the breeding of foxes. [21] These coverts were often a source of friction between the hunt and the farmer on whose land they were planted. Often the arrangements for their planting or preservation were made between the hunt and the landlord, without deciding who was to pay the covert rent or fixing the amount to be paid. [22] Even if the rent were paid, many farmers objected to having a covert on their land because it meant more foxes and the likelihood that the hunt would cross their fields more times than might ordinarily be the case. Unless he owned his own land, though, a farmer needed the support of his landlord in resisting the attempt to plant a covert. [23]

Fox preservation was not the only way in which farmers could be called upon to aid the hunt. One of the most widespread customs was that of walking puppies, which, like preservation, involved many people who lived within the hunt's boundaries, not merely farmers. Not all hunts bred their own hounds, but it was generally agreed that in order to build up a first-rate pack and keep it that way, it was necessary to engage in extensive breeding over many generations. This was one of the advantages seen in a long association between a hunt and a master, or preferably, a great family like those of the Duke of Rutland and Beaufort, where continuity would secure the quality of the pack.

In packs where breeding took place, it was generally arranged for the puppies to be born in February, and they were kept with their mothers until May.[24] The problem of what to do with them then arose for they were too young to begin their training until the following year, and no hunt had the facilities to care for them. It became customary, therefore, to send the puppies out to be kept by people in the country until the following spring, when those who survived were brought back to the kennels where the decision could be made as to which would be kept and which disposed of.[25] This custom was known as sending the puppies out to walk, and those who received them were said to walk a pup. During the time a man walked a pup, the expense of keeping it fell on him; the hunts were thus spared the expense of having to rear as many as 160 puppies

The availability of good walks was a prerequisite for successful hound breeding, and a master or committeeman who had the ability to prevail upon people to walk puppies was much sought after. Puppies were walked by people of all classes, but by far the great majority of them were walked by farmers. For a farmer, walking a puppy was not generally an arduous task, and could often be done at no great expense or trouble. Even before masters began giving prizes for the best puppies walked each year,[26] farmers often took pride in 'their' pups and followed their exploits in the hunting field avidly.[27] At its best, the custom could be one of the strongest ways in which hunting bound classes together in the countryside. It gave the farmer, even if he did not hunt, a stake in the fortunes of the local pack, and, by enabling him to contribute actively to the welfare of the pack, it raised his social status at a time when to give was a mark of position.

This is not to say that all farmers were willing to walk pups. Various means were resorted to to induce them to do so. The task was easiest for the master who was a large landowner in the hunt territory, who could usually count on using his influence with his own tenants, either informally or as part of the rental agreement. At Berkeley Castle, Gloucestershire, the seat of the Earls Fitzhardinge, the tenants were obliged to walk one or two puppies yearly according to the extent of their farms, and the

John E. Ferneley: Thomas Goosey and the Belvoir Hounds

John E. Ferneley: Full-Cry

Henry Alken: Earth Stopper

James Seymour: Full-Cry

Henry Alken: The Death

Henry Alken: The Kill

Phiz: Amongst the Leicestershire Bullfinches

Henry Alken: Fox Hunting, Breaking Cover

Henry Alken: Fox Hunting, Full Cry

James Seymour: The Duke of Richmond and Gordon's Hunting Party at Goodwood

Lynwood Palmer: Hugh Cecil, 5th Earl of Lonsdale, and Grace his wife

VIVE LE SPORT!

English Friend (to Foreigner of distinction). "THE FOX HAS BROKE, AND GONE AWAY!"
Foreigner of distinction (who has been galloping about the rides, to his immense satisfaction). "AHA! HE IS BROKEN, AND GONE AVAY! HAT A PITY! ZEN I SUPPOSE IT IS ALL OVARE, AND WE MUST GO HOME!"

"THE CHESNUT HAS SURELY BOLTED? JOE!"
"AY! AY! SIR, HE B'LONGDD TO A COSSACK IN THE CRIMEA, AND THERE AIN'T NO HOLDING OF HIM WITH BRITISH CAVALRY IN HIS REAR."

Reproduced by kind permission of 'Punch'

Henry Alken: Breaking Cover...10 o'clock...Rather difficult

Thomas Rowlandson: Hunting Scene. An aquatint

gamekeepers visited each of them in turn to inspect and report on the condition of the walks. In the early nineteenth century, Lord Monson's tenants were expected to walk puppies from the Burton Kennels, and when he was master of the North Devon in the 1870s, the Hon. Mark Rolle used to walk forty-eight couple of puppies per year among his tenantry.[28] Perhaps the most extensive puppy walks were those of the Duke of Rutland. During the 1880s, he could send out up to one hundred couple of puppies every year, and no tenant was asked to take more than one every other year.[29]

In the matter of pups, as with everything else, conciliation was greatly to be preferred to compulsion, and throughout most of the nineteenth century, many farmers were only too glad to walk a pup, especially since associated with the practice were such things as prizes for the best pup, usually awarded at an annual dinner for farmers and puppy walkers, which was generally one of the most anticipated events in the local social calendar. The ability to find walks for his puppies was generally considered a mark of the popularity of the master.[30]

The one issue that, more than any other, had the potential for creating hostility between farmers and foxhunters, and hence that had within it the greatest potential for the ultimate end of hunting, was the behaviour of the hunts in actual pursuit of the fox. Nothing amazed foreign visitors to England more than the apparent willingness of farmers to allow their land to be ridden over by huge fields of horsemen. Hunting writers themselves often expressed surprise at this. 'We must say, and greatly to their credit we say it', wrote Surtees,

> that it really is astonishing the damage and inconvenience farmers put up with every year, and the extraordinary good grace with which they do it. It is not the grumpy, passive acquiescence, that looks – 'I'd break your head if I durst' – but the sheer downright permission to do what the exigencies of the sport require.[31]

Surtees was right to be astonished. Whatever we may think of the rhetoric of hunting, the fact remains that foxhunters did cross farmers' fields in pursuit of the fox and that few tried to stop them.

The farmer, of course, had a measure of protection from *Essex v. Capel*, but his rights under that decision could be circumscribed by the particular provisions of his lease and the wishes of his landlord. Sporting rights were generally reserved by the landlord, and these could include the right of the owner, or anyone named by him, to cross the land with hounds. [32] Hunting, as most hunting men liked to boast, however, depended for its existence, not upon law, but upon custom; while custom recognized that the hunting man was obligated to show consideration for the property rights of the man over whose land he rode, it also dictated that this obligation could be subordinated to what Surtees called 'the exigencies of the sport'. [33] The ambivalent nature of this custom is perhaps the facet of hunting most illustrative of its peculiar ethic.

It is important to realize from the outset that hunting was organized so as to do the least damage to farming. The duration of the hunting season was dictated entirely by the seasons of agriculture. Though the opening day of the season was traditionally the first Monday in November, the regular season was preceded by a training period known as 'cubhunting'. The first day of cubhunting was determined by the harvest. The hounds could not generally come out until the crops had been gathered; if they did, they could not be allowed to interfere with farming. 'During Cub Hunting', wrote Will Smith, the huntsman, in his diary for 1816, 'I have kept no account of Sport in consequence of being so much confined to the Covers and not being able to run over the Country, from the great quantity of corn being so very late cut.' [34]

Hunt etiquette was strict in its prohibition of riding over sown wheat. The expression 'ware wheat' was taken into upper-class slang as meaning 'be careful, you are about to do something wrong'. But, significantly, the term used by hunting writers in treating the question was that hunting men must avoid 'unnecessary' damage, thus opening up the question as to what damage was necessary. The general construction put on 'necessary' damage was that anything that was necessary in order to maintain one's place in a run with hounds was acceptable, anything else was not. In 1869, *Baily's Magazine* cautioned its readers that when hounds were running fast, no one objected to a rider getting to them by the quickest route, but that at other times one ought to have a thought for the farmers. [35]

It is not that hunting men were malicious, but in general they were callous toward the property of farmers. It was not that the rights of farmers were, in themselves, unimportant, but that they were of secondary importance to the real business of life, hunting. The man who would cold-bloodedly tear down another man's fence on a non-hunting day would have been criticized by foxhunters as much as by anyone. If he did it in the middle of a fast run with the Quorn, however, their only reaction would have been to follow him through the gap. [36]

Damage to fences was the single most common sort of damage that hunting men were guilty of, and they never acknowledged any responsibility for it. For all the many sporting prints showing great fields of foxhunters sailing over fences, the number who had the skill and courage to do so was very small. Lady Augusta Fane tells of the Meltonians of the 1830s, who, when the formidable 'double-oxer' fences were coming into general use in Leicestershire, used to send their grooms out the night before hounds met to saw almost through the rails so that they would break easily when jumped upon. [37] *Baily's Magazine*, advising its readers on hunt etiquette in 1867, told them that if a man dismounted to lift a locked gate off its hinges, the rest of the field must wait for him to remount and go through first. [38]

The general feeling about fence breaking may best be epitomized by an anecdote from Nimrod. Out one day in 1825 with the Hampshire Hunt, Nimrod fell into conversation with a farmer who told him:

'There is one fault about the gentlemen who follows these hounds – *they breaks the fences, but they never mends them.*'

'My good fellow! You cannot expect gentlemen to mend every fence they break down when they are hunting.'

'Oh, *there is one way of mending them.* What do you think of a leg of mutton and good bowl of punch?' [39]

Here, in a nutshell, was the attitude of many hunting men. The land was there to be hunted over. It was given to them for that purpose, and it was their natural, if not their legal, right to do so. If fences were broken, they had to be fixed, but it was hardly their place to do it. Behind the rhetoric, behind the assertion that hunting men owed much to farmers for allowing their gates to be smashed, was the attitude that farmers, after all, owed much to hunting, and a gate or two was not too much to expect in return for the privilege of having hunting men in the country.

The attitude emerged clearly during the great wire controversy of the early 1860s. The use of wire in fences was probably introduced sometime in the 1850s; by 1860 enough of it was in use to worry hunting men. [40] What especially worried them was not wire fences, but rather the practice of threading a strand or two of wire through an existing hedge in order to strengthen it. This was a cheap and easy way of mending fences, and as such recommended itself to farmers. Wire used in this way was almost invisible and created a great hazard for anyone trying to jump the hedge or even more to someone trying to crash through it. By 1862, the use of wire had become widespread enough to cause a near panic among foxhunters; one prominent sportsman called the use of concealed wire 'as inhuman and illegal' as spring guns. [41] Reports of accidents caused by wire began appearing in the sporting press in great numbers, and suggestions were made as to what to do about the growing menace, which had become especially widespread in the grazing areas of the shires.

The first reaction was one of anger and resentment towards the farmers who had dared to interfere with hunting. Let the landlords tell their tenants that, after a certain day, any wire found in fencing will ensure a notice to quit the farm, and all the wire would speedily disappear, wrote one correspondent to *The Field*. [42] Others took the same tack. In December, 1862, a 'Lincolnshire man' suggested that perhaps the best solution would be for masters of hounds to defray the cost of taking the wire down for the course of the season, [43] but so radical a statement was met with silence. Even those who urged sportsmen to consider the farmers' side of the question only suggested that bluster was not the answer, and that the farmers would take the wire down themselves if asked politely by local men of influence. [44]

The following season (1863–4), the controversy heated up in earnest. Two hundred 'landowners and sportsmen' of the Midlands, led by the Duke of Rutland, issued a circular at the beginning of the season, calling on farmers to stop using wire. [45] The circular aroused emotion on both sides. *The Field*, calling it 'temperate, earnest and comprehensive,' [46] urged the landlords to go even further, and evict farmers who used wire. [47] Farmers were incensed. E. A. Paget, a farmer at Thorpe Satchville, near Melton Mowbray in the Quorn's most popular and crowded 'Friday country', sent off an angry letter to *The Field* explaining that fencing was one of the largest expenses on farms in grazing countries and went on to condemn attempts by sportsmen to coerce farmers into taking down their wire. 'This is not the way to keep up the popularity of fox-hunting amongst the yeomanry of England, upon which, I may say, its very existence depends', he wrote.

> The nobility and gentry who hunt in the shires have, it appears to me, a simple remedy for the evil in their own hands. Let them not be afraid of putting those hands in their pockets. . . . If foxhunters are too selfish, too near to pay for their own amusement, they deserve to lose it. [48]

The Field disagreed, claiming that such payments would only be an inducement for farmers to put up wire. [49]

The Field was the most violent in its opposition to the proposal that sportsmen pay for taking down wire, but it was joined by *Baily's Magazine*. [50] The proposal met with approval from the *Mark Lane Express*, a farmers' periodical, [51] and even *Bell's Life in London* had suggested a similar solution. [52] The *Sporting Magazine* took a middle position, calling upon hunting landlords to bar wire from farms on their estates but to assume the expense themselves. This, they said, referring to the circular issued by the Duke of Rutland, would do more good than 'signing round robins, which are guiltless of one word about compensation'. [53] Meanwhile, as the paper war continued, and hunting men in the shires were aiming themselves with files and hatchets to cut through the hated wire, [54] conciliators were working behind the scenes, and by the end of the season most farmers had been convinced to take down the wire at their own expense, in return for which, sportsmen contributed money for increased prize money given by the Leicester and Waltham agricultural society. [55] Following this brief flurry of excitement, the subject of wire died down. Many landlords began to bar its use, and, except for occasional flashes of interest when wire appeared in one place or another, little was heard of the controversy until it reappeared under the pressure of the agricultural depression. [56]

What is most striking about the anti-wire arguments was the strong element of righteous indignation and moral rectitude they contain. Hunting men were so absolutely convinced of the benefits they conferred on the countryside, they could brand any attack as selfish. Paget could therefore be accused of trying to put an end to an amusement that benefited the whole country, 'for a paltry consideration'. [57] So convinced were hunting men of their superior moral position that they could find it perfectly natural to expect that if wire disrupted hunting it should not only come down, but someone else owed it to them to assume the expense of taking it down. If the farmers could not do it, the landlords ought to.

It is also noteworthy that this dispute centred in the shires, for it was there that the artificial character of hunting was most apparent. Paget and others like him were quick to point out that most of those who hunted in the shires were not resident gentry but strangers who came only for the hunting, had no interest in the land, and, in fact, spent most of their money with large dealers, rather than local men. [58] Even the *Sporting Magazine* recognized the truth of this and placed the blame on the faceless nobody who hunted because it was fashionable, contrasting him to the real hunting man, the backbone of country society. [59]

In fact, hunting had already reached a stage in many parts of the country where the old assumptions were no longer valid. Hunting had ceased to be a local, informal amusement, and while farmers and other local people still benefited somewhat by hunting, the growth of a class of merchants serving hunting people meant that local suppliers benefited far less. Though many farmers still hunted, the increasing number of strangers in the hunting field meant that it was no longer as pleasant as it once was. Non-hunting farmers, especially, resented great hordes of strangers galloping over their land – strangers who had little time to spare to talk to them and who could never be seen at the farmers' dinner afterwards.

Although these conditions already existed, they did not yet cause the problems and bitterness they were to cause two decades later. Times were still prosperous, and the problem was still apparent only in a few places. The old assumptions about the benefits of hunting, therefore, were not yet seriously challenged by most people. Most farmers still accepted that hunting was a good thing, and still welcomed the hunt over their land. The *Mark Lane Express*, for example, while supporting the right of farmers to use wire in their fences, nevertheless stressed the fact that farmers had always been friends to hunting, 'as we hope they always will be'. [60]

Why it is that hunting men generally accepted the responsibility to pay for damage to crops and livestock, but not for fence damage, is one of those mysteries which may never be explained. It may be that fence damage was such a common occurrence that no hunt could survive financially if called upon to pay for every fence knocked down, while crop damage was much less common. Certainly the mores of hunting condemned riding across crops, while the jumping of fences was one of the chief attractions of the sport. For whatever reason, the distinction existed. As we shall see, however, many of the same assumptions that characterized hunting men's attitude on the question of fences were equally common with regard to crops.

There is no question but that hunting men in general were kinder towards the farmers' crops than they were towards his fences. But, of course, it was far easier for them to be. Since, as we have seen, the hunting season was the winter, there were few crops to ride over, with the exception of new sown wheat. Since riding over wheat was far less pleasurable than riding over grassland there was little temptation to do so. Furthermore, it was ingrained in the minds of most hunting men that to ride over standing crops was as awful a crime as could be committed in the hunting field. It is true, nevertheless, that in their attitude towards crops many hunting men displayed the same callousness and lack of thought that they did towards fences. Larking over fields was condemned in any case, but when it came to a conflict between the 'exigencies' of the sport and the crops, the crops often suffered, and so did the poor farmer who might try to stand between the charging horsemen and his fields. 'For some years', wrote a landlord to the Oakley Hunt committee in 1834,

> the Hunting has been conducted in the north of Bedfordshire in so unsportsmanlike a manner, and some of my tenants (and other farmers also) have not only suffered damage, and remuneration has been promised to them which was never paid, but they have also been [illegible] with such gross language that I feel it necessary, in defence of my tenants, to request from you some information upon this point. [61]

The attitude of many hunting men emerges clearly in an account of a run by 'H.H.', a regular correspondent of *The Field*. The hounds crossed a field, and someone yelled 'ware wheat!',

> a custom which seems to be exceedingly prevalent in this country. It is the duty of everyone who hunts to avoid unnecessary damage, and all real sportsmen do so; but the cry of 'Ware wheat', 'Ware swedes', and so forth, becomes somewhat tantalizing when heard at intervals of every half-mile or so during a run. But perhaps the Surrey farmers are more thin-skinned in this respect than in most countries. I know no one rode the wheat on Monday wilfully, *if firmer going was to be found*, for in places it went somewhat heavy withal. [62] [Italics mine.]

Clearly, the determining factor in 'H.H.'s' mind was not the condition of the wheat, but the state of the going, the 'exigencies' of the sport.

Hunting men even attempted to convince the world that it somehow benefited crops to be ridden over. There was a favourite story among them that was told and retold with minor variations of time and place. A particular field, went the story, was so trampled and cut up by foxhunters that it appeared likely that no crop would grow. When the farmer sent in no claim, the master sent him a cheque for the amount that he estimated the field would have produced. The farmer, however, returned the money, for, far from being a total loss, the field produced the best crop on the farm. [63] Perhaps the last word on this subject, as on so many, may be left with Mr Jorrocks:

Some labour 'ard to make themselves believe that it increases the crop to ride over it, and many a hargument I've held with farmers in favour of that position myself, but no man, who treats himself to a little undisguised truth, can make himself believe so, unless, indeed, he is satisfied that a drove of hoxen would improve the prospects of a flower-garden by passin' a night in frolicsome diwersion. [64]

The self-righteous attitude of foxhunters also emerged clearly during the great rinderpest epidemic of 1865-66. At a time when stringent measures were adopted all over the country to limit the movement of cattle and other animals, hunting men, far from limiting their activity, went so far as to claim that the stopping of hunting would impose further hardships on the already hard-hit farmers. [65] A bill to limit the movement of animals, which had, in its first version, a clause to control dogs 'at large,' was amended to exclude 'dogs under the control of [their] owner, or his or her servant or servants', so as not to apply to hounds, even though the control over a pack of hounds in full cry might be considered negligible. [66] Even *The Times* reprinted a *Field* editorial that attempted to show that hunting did not spread the disease. [67]

I would not wish to give the impression that hunting men were, in this case, especially callous to the wishes of farmers. Most agreed with *Baily's Magazine* [68] that sportsmen should be guided by the wishes of the farmers in the matter. A number of packs stopped hunting early when requested by local farmers, but even many of the farmers supported the continuation of hunting. [69] But other farmers, as the season progressed, came to have second thoughts, and several masters of hounds indicated that they would stop early. [70] Meanwhile, the sporting press continued to offer 'proof' that hunting did not spread the disease, [71] and the sportsmen on the Flintshire–Shropshire border were incensed by a landowner who ordered foxes killed on his estate when it was found that they liked to burrow down to where the slaughtered cattle were buried. [72] Few farmers seemed disposed to follow the example of Lord Denman and warn hounds off their lands, though in Yorkshire many banded together to urge an early end to hunting. [73]

Though the 1865-66 hunting season may have ended slightly earlier than usual for some packs, hunting was generally unaffected by the rinderpest. [74] The significance of this is not that hunting men continued hunting in the face of evidence that they spread the disease, or against the wishes of the farmers. It is rather that hunting men, and many farmers as well, needed overwhelming evidence that hunting did in fact spread cattle plague before they were willing to stop. In the face of what was generally conceded to be a national disaster, justifying the most stringent measures; in the face of the real possibility that hunting might spread the disease; so convinced were they of the beneficial results of hunting that they were not willing to give the opposition the benefit of the doubt. They continued, except in those places where they were expressly requested not to.

This reaction by many of the farmers themselves leads to the question of just what the reaction of farmers was to hunting in the days before the agricultural depression. It is difficult to offer generalizations about such a large group of people, but several points may be made.

First, as may be expected, the reaction of farmers differed from time to time and place to place. Some farmers strongly supported hunting and were vocal about their support. There are numerous instances on record, for example, of farmers subscribing to present a testimonial to a master of hounds or to a huntsman. [75] Less immediately obvious, but still significant, was the fact that vulpicide, though by no means as rare as some hunting apologists liked to pretend, was the exception rather than the rule. As we shall see, farmers were never slow to manifest their dissatisfaction in this way, and foxhunters, when they wanted to be honest with themselves, were well aware of this. Plentiful foxes were always taken as a sign that farmers were satisfied.

There is ample evidence to show that, on the whole, most farmers accepted hunting and even welcomed it as a natural part of country existence. Even the majority who did not hunt generally viewed the hunt as a pleasant diversion if they came across it. The spectacle of the meet, the farmers' dinner, and the occasional presents of game were all looked forward to. The major farmers' periodicals supported hunting, even, as we have seen, in times of stress like the wire controversy of 1863. [76]

On the other hand, as we have already seen, relations between hunting men and farmers were not always as pleasant as the hunters would have us believe. On the whole, though, it may be said that opposition to hunting by farmers was generally founded on specific grievances and personal dislike, rather than on any determined antipathy to hunting. More often than not, any widespread opposition to hunting may be blamed on specific actions by hunting people. George Osbaldeston's arrogance so angered the Quorn farmers and landowners, for example, that they cleared the country of foxes, causing him to depend on a weekly supply of bagmen from London. [77]

Farmers might even react against hunting because of actions by their landlords or others, having little to do with hunting. Lord Stamford, master of the Quorn, was once threatened with vulpicide when local farmers felt he had unfairly evicted a tenant over a non-hunting matter. [78] In 1891, a number of Scottish farmers who had settled in Hertfordshire barred the hounds from their land following a dispute between them and some local hunting farmers over the question of whether a frozen pond was to be used for skating or curling. [79] Vulpicide could also result from a feeling that poultry or damage claims were not being properly paid, as was the case in Devon in 1827 and Surrey in 1836. [80] Even farmers who favoured hunting could become vulpicides if they were dissatisfied with the way in which the hunt was carried on. There were the Warwickshire farmers in the early nineteenth century, for example, who were angered by the fact that the fixtures were so arranged that farmers who had to attend Coventry Market on Fridays were deprived of their day with the hounds, and so drove the foxes out of that part of the country. [81]

The great difficulty about assessing vulpicide by farmers is that by far the greatest amount of it was done secretly. Although there was certainly far more of it than most foxhunters chose to admit, the social pressure not to destroy foxes was great enough that most vulpicides did not openly admit it. Those who did were generally careful to point out that they were not systematic vulpicides, but only trying to kill a specific fox or foxes that were making free with their poultry or lambs. What is certain is that in bad times for farmers vulpicide increased, [82] and as we shall see, anti-hunting sentiments reached their peak in the agricultural depression. Finally, many farmers who were not openly against hunting may have quietly 'regulated' the number of foxes on their land, making sure that there were enough to provide sport, but no more. [83]

More open than vulpicide were attempts, of one sort or another, to keep hounds from crossing one's land, but, here again, most examples that have come to light are specific responses to particular local grievances. Large-scale, organized attempts were extremely rare, largely because of the necessity for cooperation by landlords in any movement of this type. It was an organized movement of farmers and landowners, for example, that led to *Essex v. Capel*. It is significant, however, that even here the farmers and landowners complained of specific grievances and were careful to avoid any direct attack upon hunting on general. [84]

The circumstances leading to *Essex v. Capel* were, however, uncommon. Though important for establishing the legal right of a landholder to bar hunting men from his lands, *Essex v. Capel* did not set a precedent that was widely followed. There were, of course, farmers who closed their land to the hunt, and these sometimes ran the risk of physical assault by enraged sportsmen. Some farmers, rather than resorting to law, tried to bar them physically and found themselves up before the bench for assault. [85] Magistrates, though bound to support the law against trespassing, could sometimes see a far worse crime in opposing hunting. Thus at Leamington Petty Sessions, in 1862, a farmer, who sought to prevent a foxhunter from coming over his field, by threatening him with a gun, received a strict lecture from the bench:

> You, as a farmer, residing in a fox-hunting country, must know there is a certain courtesy shown in the hunting field. Even though in strict law this may be a trespass, yet it would be overlooked in a spirit of courtesy, which I may say extends throughout the length and breadth of the country. [86]

Some farmers, who, for one reason or another, could not bar the hunt, tried the next best expedient of trying to bar the foxes. One Quorn farmer, during the mastership of Sir Harry Goodricke (1831-35), used to turn out his labourers to stand on one side of the covert to scare the fox from breaking in their direction. [87] Sir Bellingham Graham's diary recorded the incident of the 'confounded farmer' in the Atherstone country who gave him misleading information about which way a fox had gone in order to prevent the field from riding over his farm. [88] In 1829, a farmer in the Hambledon country stood in the covert to be drawn holding a gun, and threatened to shoot the fox if anyone rode over his wheat. [89] Several days later, another farmer in the same area put his harriers into the coverts to keep foxes from staying there. [90]

Despite many examples of this type, the number of farmers who openly attempted to bar hounds from their lands was small. They would, of course, have preferred not to have their land ridden over; they were not fools after all. But generally, they were reasonably happy to see hunting men continue in their neighbourhoods. High farming and the growing number of sportsmen combined to make hunting more troublesome than it had been earlier in the century, and this called for greater patience on the part of farmers and greater tact on the part of hunting men, but there was no open break. One of the reasons for this was that many farmers were willing to accept the ideal that hunting was beneficial, even though many of the supposed benefits were more apparent then real.

The greatest benefit the farmer received from hunting was undoubtedly social. It would be a mistake to underestimate the value of farmers' dinners, races, prizes, and the like to the life of the countryside. The farmers' dinner was the principal way in which the hunt expressed its gratitude to the farmers over whose land it rode. As an institution it dated from the earliest days of organized foxhunting and it grew in popularity as time passed.[91] Some hunts made the dinner a regular part of their activities; in others, the dinners were more informal, and might be given by the master or simply by an ordinary member of the hunt as his contribution to furthering good relations.[92] These dinners, which often included awarding prizes for puppy walkers, were another means of furthering the idea that hunting promoted a meeting of classes on fairly informal terms and that even non-hunting farmers were a part of the local hunting community, though, like Nimrod, many hunting men who attended probably did so more out of a sense of duty than from any great desire to mix socially with farmers.[93] The sponsorship of a farmers' race at the annual hunt race meeting was another fairly common method of cementing relations between hunting men and farmers. The Atherstone Hunt Club gave a special horse show for farmers in the hunt country.[94] Lord Penrhyn, of the Grafton Hunt, used to sell his prize shorthorn cattle to local farmers at reduced prices.[95] Henry John Conyers, master of the Essex, once presented new dresses to the wives of all the farmers in the country in order to keep them well disposed toward hunting, especially since it was they who had charge of the poultry.[96]

Hunting also gave to the farmer a certain social importance that he might not have otherwise had. The wise master, especially if he was not a local man, made it his business to find out as much as he could about all the farmers in the district. A memorandum, dated 1869, from Wharton Wilson, master of the V.W.H., to his successor, Sir William Throckmorton, included a list of all the farmers who held land in the country, together with suggestions for keeping each happy, ranging from gifts of game or gin to going to breakfast at the farmer's house.[97] Attention of this sort paid to farmers could not help but dispose them to look kindly on the hunt.

The direct economic benefits that hunting was supposed to provide for farmers were less important in cementing relations between farmers and foxhunters, because, though they were an important argument in the arsenal of hunting apologists, most farmers did not receive them. To be sure, some farmers did benefit, especially in the early days of the sport and in those parts of the country where hunting remained relatively informal. The account book of a farmer on the estate of H. J. Conyers, master of the Essex Hunt, for example, included among the receipts for 1814: '5 Loads Hay for hunters £22–10–0', '2 Hacks for Hunt £15–12–0', and '3 Hunters at Grass £21–12–0'. [98] In most countries, however, farmers benefited less.

If we turn first to the question of horsebreeding, the facts are clear. Despite the high prices that hunters could fetch, these prices almost never went to farmers. Unlike race horses, which might fetch high prices as colts because of their breeding, hunters, which were usually only part thoroughbred, could only bring high prices after they had proven themselves in the hunting field. Since horses were rarely hunted before they were five years old, this meant that the horse had to be reared for five years, broken and trained for hunting, and then ridden to hounds to be shown off, before the owner could expect to get more for him than he could for an ordinary saddle or cart horse. Few farmers could afford to do this. There were some exceptions, as we have seen, but even these generally well-to-do men raised only a few horses at a time, and kept them for their own hunting, hoping that the horse might catch the eye of a wealthy sportsman. [99]

In 1825, Nimrod tried to convince farmers that raising hunters could be made to pay, but was answered by a farmer who produced figures to show that when he tried to do just that, he lost an average of £35. 9s. on each horse. [100] Though Nimrod attempted to rebut these figures, even on the basis of his own the profit would have been very small – less than ten pounds per horse after five years. [101] Even 'Harry Hieover', who had written that farmers benefited from hunting, advised hunting men against buying horses from them, saying that though they could be had more cheaply from the farmers than from the dealers, they were generally not worth the money. [102] Only resident sportsmen, it must be added, were in a position to buy horses from farmers. The growing number of outsiders, of course, had little recourse except to the dealers, since they were hardly in a position to know of good horses in the possession of farmers.

Throughout the course of the nineteenth century, hunting men and others urged farmers to breed hunters [103] but these urgings generally fell on deaf ears. In fact, the breeding of any type of horse was never popular among English farmers, and many horses had to be imported. [104] There was always a shortage of good hunters, and this shortage kept the prices high.

Farmers probably made more money selling forage than they made by breeding horses, but here, too, the benefit to farmers was much less than hunting apologists would have us believe, and for similar reasons. Hunting was undoubtedly responsible for the consumption of large amounts of hay, beans, and oats, but few hunting people obtained these things directly from the farmers.[105] Farmers were simply not in a position to serve the needs of hunting men directly. Non-resident sportsmen were almost forced, and resident sportsmen found it far more convenient, to go to dealers who were able to deliver, offer credit, and age the oats and beans.[106] As we shall see, some laudable attempts were made under the pressure of the depression to find ways of bringing farmers and prospective purchasers together, but these only point up the lack of any such arrangement previously.

Though farmers must have known that they were making no money from hunting, they rarely questioned the sport because they had no real reason to do so. If they gained little from hunting, most of them lost little, and those who lost more knew what to do about it without making a fuss. A trap set here or there, a strand of wire in the proper place, solved the problem quietly. Meanwhile, his son enjoyed an occasional day out with the hounds, the master was generally civil to him, and besides, hounds had always been in the neighbourhood.

This was to change in the 1870s.

CHAPTER 9

THE OPPOSITION

The acceptance, not to say devotion, that hunting received should not blind us to the fact that there were those who looked upon it in a less favourable light. Though the anti-cruel-sports movement, so much a part of any consideration of hunting today, did not seriously attack hunting until the very end of the period under discussion, there were always active opponents of the sport.

Through much of the eighteenth century – when foxhunting had not yet attracted the great attention it was to receive in later years – the opposition, as befitted the relative obscurity of the sport itself, tended to be relatively mild and was based largely upon the image of hunting as the pastime of the country-bumpkin squire. As has already been noted, men of fashion, polish, and intellect looked down on hunting men and considered them hardly more intelligent than their horses, and perhaps less so than their hounds. While the poet Cowper's hatred for 'the reeking, roaring hero of the chase' [1] was in part the result of his perception of the hunting man's cruelty, there were those who disliked him merely for reeking and roaring. Lord Chesterfield spoke for them all when he described English hunting as fit 'only for bumpkins and boobies'. [2] William Shenstone's mid-eighteenth century assessment that 'the world my be divided into people that read, people that write, people that think, and foxhunters',. [3] was to survive long after the vagaries of fashion had separated those who wished merely to be fashionable from those whose dislike for hunting was deeply felt.

Men like Chesterfield, of course, were not really opponents of hunting, they simply disliked it. They held those who enjoyed the sport in contempt, but probably would not have devoted any great energy to bringing about its extinction. There were, however, those who disliked the sport not because contemptible people took it up, but because they felt that hunting made men contemptible, or, at the very least, kept them from being admirable. According to some of these men, hunting led naturally and inevitably to drunkenness, gambling, profanity, idleness, and profligacy. [4] Leaving aside those few who saw all amusement tending to those ends, it is not difficult to see whence they derived their ideas. To some extent at least, drinking, gambling, and general boisterousness were associated with hunting, not because hunting brought them about, but because they were the pastimes most naturally turned to by the all-male, hearty types that peopled the early hunting field. Hunting men, eager to promote the image of 'good fellowship' they associated with their sport, were, in a way, their own worst enemies in this regard. The numerous pictures of 'jolly sportsmen' sitting round the table over port, which appeared regularly in the *Sporting Magazine* and elsewhere at the end of the eighteenth and beginning of the nineteenth centuries, all reinforced the image of hunting men as riotous and drunken. The reports that reached the country of the doings at Melton, with its cock-fighting, gambling, prize-fighting, and prostitutes, completed the picture. That is why there were those who saw the hunting field as less than a fitting place for clergymen. William Gilpin, it will be recalled, ruled out hunting not only because it was cruel, but because it was 'riotous', and because the hunting clergymen would be likely to find himself in unseemly company. [5] Even after hunting became divorced in the popular imagination from drunken orgies, pious people of the more serious persuasions tended to disapprove of hunting, if not for its outright profanity, then at least for a frivolousness akin to profanity. [6]

We have already seen how, from Beckford's day onward, hunting people attempted to contradict that image. Any slur on the manners and intellect of hunting men was sure to be met by a reply from one of them, pointing out the 'refinement' that foxhunters had achieved. 'I have attempted to shew that fox-hunting and ignorance are not synonymous', wrote Nimrod in 1825, [7] and other hunting men followed suit. [8] As hunting increasingly became the sport of the fashionable, much of this criticism died out. It became especially difficult to continue damning the sport as fit only for boors when women began to appear in the field, for their presence indicated to all that the manners of hunting people had undergone a great change. It was possible, of course, to continue to attack hunting people as unintellectual, but by the middle of the nineteenth century, they no longer bothered to take notice of these attacks. They knew themselves to be as cultured as any in the country, and whatever their personal inclinations, they knew that hunting had its own men of letters, like Charles Kingsley and Anthony Trollope. They knew, too, that the editors of the weighty reviews, from the days of Lockhart and Nimrod on, were favourable to the sport. At the other end of the scale, *Punch*, generally so willing to deflate pretentiousness, had nothing but kind words for hunting. [9]

Far more serious were the attacks that claimed hunting wasted time that could be put to better use. Because hunting had long been justified on the grounds that it kept country gentlemen resident on their estates, where they were needed to perform their duties, hunting people were particularly sensitive to any allegations that hunting left them little time for these duties. [10]

It was not just the country gentleman who could be considered to be wasting his time if he went hunting. For him, at least, there was the excuse that he was not expected to work for his living. The farmer or tradesman who hunted, or even the labourer who was distracted by hounds as he worked in the fields, had himself and his family to support. There had always been those, including a few within the hunting community itself, who looked upon hunting farmers as the symbols and products of unrestrained vanity, decadence, and unbridled extravagance. [11] When city people took to hunting in greater numbers, they, too, were condemned by some who felt that their time could be far better put to making money. [12] As for labourers, hunting might make them 'restless and unhappy, and ... unfit to pursue their quiet and industrial occupations'. [13]

The most notable attack on hunting as the cause of neglect of duty, because it attracted the most attention, was a letter which appeared in *The Times* in 1858 on the death of Thomas Assheton Smith. [14] The writer, who signed himself 'X', professed no dislike for hunting *per se*, and admitted to a respect for Assheton Smith's talents. It was the waste of these talents, in fact, that was the cause of 'X's' complaint. A man has a right to hunt, he wrote, but 'has he a right to consider that this may fairly absorb the whole of his energies, and that as a moral agent the purpose of his existence is completely satisfied by success in the field?' It was bad enough, he went on, that Assheton Smith squandered his own time and talents, but he was also the cause of others doing the same thing. Perhaps even worst of all to 'X', however, was that Assheton Smith was a relic from the past, who had no place in the modern age with its new emphasis on progress and hard work. 'Such a man', he wrote,

> is, at the present day, like an insulated fragment of some former period of society inserted in the scene, pleasing perhaps from its picturesque associations, but wholly uncongenial with the objects round it, and looking strange and uncouth simply because it has unfortunately slipped out of its proper place.

'X' was right. Assheton Smith was a survival, a relic of a wilder age. The man who had ridden to glory in the Billesdon Coplow run of 1800 was, in some ways, out of touch with the increasingly urban, disciplined spirit of 1860. What 'X' failed to realize, however, was that Assheton Smith, who in many other respects was completely up-to-date, was not alone in his harking back to an earlier time. Hunting itself was, by 1858, out of its time, and was to continue to be so for another fifteen years at least.

'X's' letter had touched a sore point and drew responses not only from those who had known Assheton Smith,[15] but from sporting writers as well, all of whom tried to prove that Smith did not live for hunting alone.[16] The controversy provoked a *Times* leader, which, while affirming the paper's belief that, in its time and place, hunting was a valuable 'part of the English social system', nevertheless expressed 'a strong feeling against any exclusive and tyrannical excess'.[17]

Though attacks on hunting men for neglecting their duties seemed tailor-made for political or social radicals less interested in the sport itself than in its place as a symbol of the old social order,[18] hunting, largely because of its egalitarian tradition, never attracted the fury of radicals in the same way that shooting, with its structure of repressive game laws, did. As we have seen, many early radicals, like William Cobbett, were staunch supporters of the sport.[19] Later radicals may well have disliked hunting as a symbol of the upper classes, but saw little to be gained in attacking a sport that was generally well regarded by the tenant farmers, the only class whose members had a legitimate grievance against it. Only in Ireland, where the sport was seized upon as a symbol of the English oppressors, did opposition to hunting become a popular rallying point for radical politics.[20]

To the modern mind, of course, most of these arguments are

insignificant compared with the issue of cruelty to animals, but though the opposition to hunting on the grounds of cruelty was never absent during the period under consideration, its real impact upon hunting throughout most of the nineteenth century was virtually nonexistent. Although concerted attacks were raised from time to time on other field sports, hunting always remained comparatively untouched. Not only was hunting the most entrenched of all the British field sports, it was also, in the eyes of even its severest critics, one of the least cruel.

Different ages, of course, have had their own conceptions of cruelty. It is hardly surprising to find that a society that tolerated cock-fighting, bear- and bull-baiting, dog-fighting, and monkey-fighting was unsqueamish when it came to so relatively bloodless a sport as foxhunting. But we must not be too quick to jump to conclusions, for ideas of what constituted cruelty could change. There were those, for example, who considered foxhunting, where the contest between fox and hounds was neither as even or 'voluntary' as that between two game-cocks, to be far more cruel than cockfighting. [21] Even in the eighteenth century, however, there were those who opposed hunting on the grounds that it was cruel to animals. A religious tract, published in 1776, for example, argued against hunting, though it was by no means clear whether the author opposed all hunting or just the hunting of gentler animals like hares. [22] Less ambiguous was the poet Cowper, whose hatred of hunting and hunting people emerges clearly in several of his poems, most notably in 'The Task':

> ... – Detested sport,
> That owes its pleasure to another's pain;
> That feeds upon the sobs and dying shrieks
>   of harmless nature ... [23]

But though Cowper and others like him [24] wrote against hunting, their work attracted little sympathetic notice.

It was not only that eighteenth-century people were prepared to accept far more cruelty than we are, but that for the great majority there was simply nothing cruel about a foxhunt. The idea that cruelty to animals was somehow undesirable was not unknown. Indeed, to judge by their statements, eighteenth-century sportsmen liked to consider themselves among the leaders in any movement to eradicate cruelty altogether, and consistently attacked cruelty to domestic animals. [25]

Horses and hounds were, in fact, the major concern of the anti-cruelty forces in the early days of foxhunting. When Peter Beckford published *Thoughts on Hunting* in 1781, he was denounced in the *Monthly Review* for recommending that foxhounds be flogged and hanged. The criticism so affected him, that he felt obliged to add defensive footnotes to subsequent editions of the book. [26] Beckford's reception was not ignored by later writers, and up to the middle of the nineteenth century, when the practice of flogging hounds died out, writers who recommended it were careful to claim that, in the long run, it was kinder to flog young hounds to save them from the noose in later life. [27]

So far as cruelty to foxes was concerned, however, aside from the few objections already mentioned, there was an almost complete silence. The fact that the fox was a predator himself may have had something to do with this. There were more people willing to see cruelty in the hunting of the 'timid hare' than in the 'wily fox'. John Lawrence, a leading writer on animal subjects for example, opposed hare hunting, but justified hunting the fox, 'which is a beast of prey, greedy of blood, a robber prowling about'. [28] Certainly the hare, unable to fight back, was a far more likely object of pity than the fox; it is no accident that it was chosen as the quarry in such sentimental anti-hunting children's stories as *The Hare, or Hunting Incompatible with Humanity* [29] and *Sandford and Merton*. [30]

Ironically, the public recognition that hunting involved cruelty to the fox that had the most significant results came not from the opponents of cruel sports, but from those who successfully defended such popular sports as bull- and bear-baiting on the grounds that they were no crueller than hunting. [31] The fact that those who sought to outlaw bull-and bear-baiting were required to counter these arguments by maintaining publicly that foxhunting and other 'legitimate' field sports were not cruel, made it all the more difficult for them to attack hunting. Forced to choose between outlawing the far more cruel baitings and attacking hunting, they allowed hunting to survive unscathed.

There was, however, during the first thirty years of the nineteenth century, a growing feeling against wanton cruelty, and the change in opinion did not leave foxhunters unaffected. To men like Peter Beckford, the death of the fox was of paramount importance. Because the notion that foxes were vermin to be held in check had not yet died, and because it was generally believed that hounds had to taste blood frequently in order to keep them keen for the chase, a hunt with no kill at the end was considered a wasted day. [32]

But, partly because to the new sportsmen who were turning to hunting in the days after Meynell, the chase rather than the kill was most important, partly because the notion that hounds needed blood was being exploded, and partly, too, because of new attitudes toward sportsmanship in general, Beckford's opinions were falling into disrepute.

By the 1830s, the new attitude was becoming firmly entrenched. A *Sporting Magazine* author wrote, in 1832, of a vixen with a litter being accidentally killed:

> The mind of that man is not to be envied who returns from such a scene with a heart unclouded by the reflection of what those wretched cubs must undergo ere death shall terminate the horrors, the lingering horrors of sure and certain starvation! [33]

Any suspicion of cruelty to foxes was, in fact, enough to excite the ire of the entire hunting community even beyond the anger normally displayed when foxes were killed in any way other than with hounds. [34] Foxhunters were sometimes faced with the dilemma of deciding whether it was better to condemn cruelty within their ranks or to attempt to hide it in the best interests of the sport. In 1859, Thomas Marsh, master of the Vine Hunt, presented them with such a problem when he allegedly turned down a fox before his hounds on a Sunday, after having first cut off one of its legs. It is difficult to tell whether mutilating the fox or profaning the Sabbath was the more heinous crime, but the good name and self-respect of the hunting community were salvaged by the time discovery that Marsh was, in reality, a former groom named Walker. With great relief, *Bell's Life* was able to inform its readers that

> every earnest promoter of the chase will welcome the announcement that the delinquent is neither by birth nor education a gentleman; his present position is more attributable to one of those successful turns of fortune than any particular merit of his own, and thus far the stigma which would otherwise attach to the aristocratic supporters of fox-hunting is entirely removed. [35]

This new attitude toward foxes kept foxhunting relatively free from attack because foxhunters were, generally speaking, at least as advanced as most people when it came to their attitude toward animals in general, and perhaps even somewhat in advance of them in their attitude toward domestic animals. Partly because the health of their horses and hounds was of paramount importance, and partly because their romanticized picture of hunting led to a sentimentalized view of their horses and hounds, foxhunters tended to be especially solicitous of the health of their domestic animals. Grantley Berkeley, for example, a hunting man who never scrupled to abuse any human with whom he disagreed, dedicated his memoirs, in 1854, to 'convey[ing] to the booted and spurred of the rising generation a higher appreciation of the animals of their use and abuse'. [36] Similarly, the S.P.C.A. – later R.S.P.C.A. – which was founded in 1824, never took a stand against hunting, provided horses and hounds were well treated, and enjoyed good relations with the hunting community, many of whom were active supporters of the society's work. [37]

There were, to be sure, some attacks on foxhunters. There was a small flurry of interest in 1838-39, for example, when a prize was offered for the best essay on the subject of cruelty to animals. The winner of the prize, the Rev. John Styles, attacked hunting and hunting men in no uncertain terms, charging them with 'making life the sacrifice of mere amusement, and destroying unoffending and happy creatures, without any higher motive'. [38]

What is interesting about the 1839 dispute, however, is that of four contest essays that were printed, only two [39] condemned hunting. One [40] was ambiguous. The fourth found nothing wrong with the sport provided the horses were well treated and foxes were not preserved especially for the hunt. 'For what object was given the scent of the hound, and the exultation with which he abandons himself to the chase?' asked the author. [41] Clearly, even among those for whom the humane treatment of animals was of more than passing concern, there were many who saw no reason for alarm at the growth of hunting's popularity.

The debate stirred by the 1839 pamphlets did not go entirely unnoticed by the sporting community. Hunting men were careful, thereafter, to insist that cruelty had no part in foxhunting, and were just as careful to call the attention of the country to the cruel acts of non-sportsmen. [42] But beyond that, the issue lay dormant for almost thirty years, despite the passage, in the interim, of several laws on the general subject of cruelty to animals. There was a lengthy exchange of correspondence in *The Field* in 1862 on the whole question of cruelty in sport, but, characteristically, the correspondence was allowed to die out with the approach of the hunting season. [43]

The 1850s and the 1860s were, as we have seen, the years in which foxhunting made its greatest gains in popularity, the years in which it became firmly entrenched as the 'national sport'. It is not surprising that it was in those years that hunting should become increasingly visible to the eyes of reformers; nor is it surprising that, at a time when modern 'progressive' and humanitarian concerns were becoming increasingly felt, that these reformers would see hunting as a fit subject for their attentions. In 1865, Lord William Lennox had sensed that there was a growing opposition to hunting because of its supposed cruelty, [44] and four years later the storm broke in earnest.

In October, 1869, the historian, E. A. Freeman [45] contributed an article on 'The Morality of Field Sports' to the *Fortnightly Review*. This may be considered the opening round of the modern debate – a debate whose closing rounds we have yet to witness. Freeman's article was unemotional and well reasoned. The major argument came early. 'Either man or beast may be rightly put to death when need so calls for it', he wrote,

> but neither in the infliction of death nor at any other time should any pain be inflicted which real need does not call for. The infliction of death should be in the speediest way without any prolonged torture or mockery. Neither pain nor death should be turned into matter of amusement. [46]

Freeman also took note of the social justifications of hunting, that it bound classes together, kept gentlemen in the country, and provided a pastime for those who might do worse if they did not hunt. The first might be true, he claimed, but it ignored the question of cruelty. The same might be said of the second, in addition to its being a libel on country gentlemen. The third was true, he admitted, but not to the point. [47]

Freeman's article was the most substantial attack on hunting ever made to that date and fell upon receptive ears. Not only was it logical and well written, it was also the first such attack made at a time when public opinion could be receptive to it. The immediate reaction was a controversy carried on in the columns of several of the more 'serious' literary journals. The more lasting result was that the controversy Freeman touched off never disappeared, as had its predecessor of 1839. From 1870 on, critics of hunting were more vocal. Though these critics never posed a serious threat to foxhunting, hunting men, soon to face the far greater danger of the agricultural depression, were never again able to ignore the question, and several attempted to refute Freeman's arguments.

The most prominent of Freeman's opponents was Anthony Trollope – himself an ardent foxhunter – who answered Freeman in the pages of the same journal in which he had launched his attack. Beginning with a defence of foxhunters – 'no man goes out fox-hunting in order that he may receive pleasure from pain inflicted' [48] – Trollope proceeded to the main point at issue. Freeman had said killing was justified if it served a purpose. Did he, for example, justify the killing of animals to make a luxury like a lady's fur tippet? Foxhunting, claimed Trollope, was also a luxury, but far more justifiable than a tippet. [49]

Mr Freeman, in driving his theory home, seems to ignore the fact that the recreation of a people is a matter of great moment. If all England could be indulged in an amusement that would be charming, intellectual, in every way satisfactory, – some all but divine spectacle, – at, we will say, the cost of one human life, would not that human life have been well spent? But the human life would have been excellently well spared if a tortured fox could have been made to stand in its stead. With such a result, who would regret the tortured fox? [50]

Though Trollope was the most prominent of Freeman's opponents, the passage shows that he was not the most lucid of them. There were others, however, just as thoughtful as Freeman himself, and the debate raged in both the sporting and general press. [51]

The arguments of the pro-hunting writers boiled down to three basic points: first that hunting was a natural part of animal life; [52] second, that hunting men were not cruel, because they did not derive pleasure from the death of the fox, and because the fox, if he did not positively enjoy being hunted, at least felt no terror, was hunted fairly, had every chance of escape, and died a quick death, in return for which he lived a pleasant, protected life; [53] third, that though the infliction of pain was a part of hunting, the benefits gained by society from hunting were such that they excused whatever pain was necessary. This last argument, of course, was based upon their idealized picture of hunting, which we have already come across in other circumstances. In this, as in other areas, we must not underestimate the role, whether conscious or unconscious, that this idealized view played in influencing people's judgments. Time and again we find people, who otherwise might have agreed with Freeman and his supporters, unable to take the final step and declare their opposition to hunting.

The editor of the *Spectator,* for example, dismissed Trollope's 'tippet argument' for assuming that animals had no rights that people had to respect, 'which is, we take it, the precise question at issue', and asked, more specifically:

Have we the right, because we have the power, to torture an animal, because we think we can gain some good by torturing him?

But just at this point, when the reader is sure that hunting will be condemned, there is an abrupt shift:

> A fox *may* feel tortured for aught anybody can tell, but he never gives the least indication that he is so. He goes away quite confident in himself, looks back in the cheeriest manner, never loses his head, and when overtaken fights as if he rather approved of fighting, and on the whole, dies like a gladiator to whom strife is pleasure and who has no complaint to urge.[54]

Like the *Spectator*, the *Saturday Review* had no trouble in proclaiming Freeman the winner in his debate with Trollope, but it, too, stopped short of condemning foxhunting.[55] For most of the participants in the debate, hunting was too much a part of the English way of life to imagine that there was reason for it to die out. Nevertheless, from the time of Freeman's first article, the opponents of cruel sports remained far more vocal. There was a new spurt of anti-cruelty books and pamphlets which matched that of 1839.[56] In turn, hunting men had to devote far more of their time and energy to defending themselves from the charge of cruelty.[57]

Still, the new feeling against cruel sport affected foxhunting less than it did many other field sports. Hunting was simply too well entrenched in the customs of what was still the most influential group in the country to be in any great danger of being ended by any forcible or legislative means. As opponents of field sports were well aware, it was also less cruel than many. While legislation was introduced at various times against other sports, hunting generally remained safe from any direct attack. The Humanitarian League − an organization founded in 1891 that had among its objectives the abolition of cruel sports and that was constantly more radical than the R.S.P.C.A. − for example, did not attack foxhunting directly at any time before the First World War, partly because it saw no chance of success, partly because it recognized that there were many sports that were more cruel.[58] Nevertheless, both sides of the debate recognized that the future of hunting was inseparably connected to that of the others.[59]

In 1884, concerned sportsmen founded The National Sports Protection and Defence Association, whose object, according to its prospectus, was

> to so link together sporting interests that, on any sport being attacked, full inquiry may be made by a committee of leading sportsmen, and,

should such sport be found to have been properly conducted, to render assistance in opposing such attack, and that the sporting public may not be left unprepared to resist these aggressive measures. [60]

Hunting men, like Lord Lonsdale, were active in the formation of the association, which, in 1885, changed its name to the Field Sports Protection and Encouragement Association and declared its championing of five sports – hunting, shooting, horse racing, fishing, and coursing. [61]

A second result of the anti-cruel-sports movement was that the issue of cruelty was being taken seriously even by foxhunters. The changed attitude of hunting people toward foxes, which had become apparent by the 1830s, grew even stronger. Some hunting men now began not only to deny that the kill was uppermost in their minds, but to positively assert that they delighted in seeing the fox escape. William Bromley Davenport, in what was admittedly an apology for hunting in the *Nineteenth Century*, wrote:

> I confess, when I alone have come cross the hiding-place of a 'beaten fox', and he has, so to speak, confided his secret to me with his upturned and indescribably appealing eye, it has been sacred with me; I have retired softly, and rejoiced with huge joy when the huntsman at last calls away his baffled pack. [62]

All the opponents of hunting considered thus far disliked it on the grounds that, in some way, it violated their image of the good world. Their objections, though strongly felt, were rooted in morality. There were others, however, who had no objection to hunting, provided only that hunting left them alone. In many cases, however, hunting did not leave them alone, so they, too, must be classified as opponents to the sport. It was their opposition that was most felt by foxhunters, because it often manifested itself in terms as practical as its causes.

As we have already seen, the most visible group that fell into this classification consisted of farmers and other landholders who objected to their property being damaged by hunting men, but one of the great ironies of sporting life is that the one set of people who might have been thought to have the most in common with foxhunters constituted, in the main, their most consistent and most effective enemies. Though the founders of the Field Sports Protection and Encouragement Association realized that the future of hunting and shooting were to be inseparably joined, that is not the way it appeared to the large body of hunting and shooting men who so often found themselves in bitter conflict. The cause of the friction was, of course, clear. Shooting men disliked hunting because hunting interfered with shooting. The most popular and fashionable form of shooting, in which large quantities of game were driven by beaters toward the shooters who remained in one place, bagging hundreds of birds in a day, required, above all else, a vast supply of game birds and led to the establishment of game preservation on a large scale. Thousands of pheasants were reared in preserves in conditions approximating domestication, were cared for by armies of gamekeepers, and were protected by strictly enforced game laws. The possibility of foxes and pheasants living side by side was one of the most hotly contested controversies of the sporting world. Foxhunters, by and large, took the position that foxes rarely killed pheasants, and that they were only objected to by gamekeepers because they killed rabbits, which were traditionally the keeper's prerequisite. [63] Shooters, not surprisingly, took the other side. [64] As the cost of game preservation rose steadily, preservers became increasingly unwilling to jeopardize their investment or their amusement, and were unlikely to welcome to their preserves either foxes, which could kill their game, or foxhunters, who would disturb it.

The conflict of interest between hunting and shooting men resolved itself in different ways, depending upon the people involved. When the representatives of both sides were reasonable men, the two could coexist quite peacefully — each side making slight sacrifices for the sake of peace. The shooters would agree not to molest foxes, and, in return, the master of hounds would arrange his fixtures so as not to interfere with any plans for shooting. [65]

At the opposite end of the scale, there was open hostility between the two. It was not unknown for game preservers to bar all hounds from their land, as the Earl of Harborough did in the 1850s, [66] or to make it dangerous to hunt certain coverts by setting dog spears, ostensibly to protect against poachers, but effectively putting an end to hunting as well. [67] This was an extreme step but even lesser steps could make it impossible for a master to continue. Sir Jacob Astley was forced to sell his hounds in Norfolk in 1825 because of the hostility of shooters in that premier game preserving county. [68] John Musters was forced to do the same in Nottinghamshire in 1841, [69] and Captain Percy Williams resigned the Rufford in 1869, after nineteen years as master, for the same reason. [70]

Between these two extremes, there was a wide range of possibilities.

The most common practice, however, was for gamekeepers, whether acting on their employers' orders or not, to kill foxes. This was sometimes done quite openly, [71] though of course, the open vulpicide generally had to be a man secure enough in his position to be able to withstand whatever pressures were certain to be brought to bear upon him. Most preservers, however, were far less open about their attitudes to foxes and would have denied vehemently that a fox was ever killed on their land except by the hounds. A common trick was for a gamekeeper to kill the foxes, keeping a captive fox to turn out before the hounds when they drew his coverts. This served a double purpose, for besides concealing the vulpicide, the captive foxes, stiff from their captivity, were generally killed quickly, preventing damage by the horsemen. [72]

Hostility by game preservers was a constant feature of nineteenth-century hunting. There was probably an increase in hostility as the century progressed because game preserving became increasingly expensive and preservers, therefore, became increasingly unwilling to have their investments jeopardized. In the 1860s and 1870s, the number of accounts of packs facing a shortage of foxes definitely increased. [73] Some observers blamed the problem on the increasing number of city men who rented shootings and who were determined to get their money's worth, undeterred by local ties or feelings, [74] though it might have also been due to increasing hostility on the part of farmers.

Even barring deliberate vulpicide, foxhunters were likely to find that game preserving could interfere with their sport. Traps and poison laid for other vermin or predators were likely to kill foxes or hounds. It was possible to set rabbit and vermin traps so as to make it unlikely for foxes or hounds to be caught, but few keepers or poachers took the trouble, with the result that reports of trapped foxes or three-legged ones that had managed to escape from the traps by gnawing off their own leg were common, and hounds were also occasionally caught. [75]

Deliberate or accidental poisoning of foxes or hounds was not unknown in the early nineteenth century, [76] but it became far more common with the adoption, in the 1850s, of strychnine as a widely used vermin-poison. After hounds were poisoned in 1855, a gamekeeper wrote to *The Field* with instructions for laying strychnine to make it safe for foxes and hounds, [77] but, from the mid-1850s, reports of poisoned hounds increased dramatically. In 1863, an act was passed prohibiting the laying of poisoned grain, [78] and, in the following year, a companion act prohibited the laying of poisoned meat. [79] Foxhunters enthusiastically supported both measures,[80] and the second act was actually debated in terms of foxhunting, with its opponents, like Sir Edward Grogan, M.P. for Dublin, denouncing what they considered an attempt to end the farmers' protection from vermin for the sake of preserving foxes.[81] Despite the bill's passage, however, poison did not disappear from the scene, and accounts of hound poisoning continued into the seventies and eighties.[82] Some of these may well have been deliberate attempts to kill hounds, though in two cases that were brought to trial, they were not.[83]

The extent of vulpicide and related activities like hound poisoning is difficult to determine. Despite what some foxhunters liked to think, it unquestionably existed, to some extent, in most places. Preservers and farmers had too much at stake to allow foxes to multiply with no check save the inefficient one of hounds. Judging from the reports of it in the hunting press, vulpicide seems to have increased fairly steadily through the 1850s and 60s, and to have become even more common during the agricultural depression. This is as we might expect. With the spread of hunting in those years, there was a need for an ever increasing number of foxes, which, in turn, were a far greater nuisance both to the farmers, who were attempting to squeeze more and more out of each acre, and to game preservers, who were preserving far more intensively. The amount of vulpicide may seem to have increased faster than it actually did, however, for two reasons. First, as hunt countries became smaller, hunting men became far more sensitive to the amount of vulpicide within their boundaries. Secondly, since vulpicide itself was no crime, and hence appeared in no official returns, and since vulpicides rarely were open about their activities, our only sources of information about vulpicide are the accounts that found their way into the sporting press. But it was only in the years during which vulpicide appears to have increased that the press expanded to give greater coverage to day-to-day happenings. The increase in the reporting of vulpicide, therefore, may in part be a result of the increase of hunt reporting in general.

Contemporaries, however, had no doubt that there was a real increase of vulpicide, and they blamed most of it on shooters.[84] In part this is owing to the fact that shooters could generally be far more open than farmers, for they were either considerable gentlemen themselves, or else strangers to the country. It is also partly owing to the fact that the mythology of hunting demanded that farmers be portrayed as friends to the sport, who would drum one of their own number out of the local agricultural club for killing a fox even by mistake,[85] while shooting men were the selfish enemy. It is, undoubtedly, also owing to the fact that there was some truth to the belief.

The number of people who killed foxes or hounds because of a hatred for hunting and hunting men was small. There is no evidence to show that there was ever an organized campaign against the sport in England as there was in Ireland. There may well have been isolated instances of it, but they came to nothing. [86] The increase of vulpicide during the depression, as we shall see, was a sign of the dissatisfaction of farmers, and of a desire by game preservers to protect their investments at a time when game seemed one of the few crops not to decline in value.

For the vulpicide, whoever he may have been, the foxhunter had nothing but contempt. Raised to believe wholeheartedly in the beneficial effects of hunting, he could not help but take a high moral tone when confronted by anyone who deliberately spoiled the sport. Nimrod began the tradition of publishing the names of known vulpicides, [87] and his example was followed. Whenever the name of a prominent vulpicide became known, it was sure to be published in one or another of the sporting journals, and, if he were prominent in some other way – a Member of Parliament or even, to his shame, a former master of hounds – his exposure was sure to bring even greater delight. [88] Aside from public exposure, which could often lead to local feuds and the barring of hounds from the accused vulpicide's land, however, there was little else that foxhunters could do. In the long run, the greatest protection that hunting could have was that, by and large, public opinion supported hunting and condemned vulpicide. The fact that, despite more cases of fox-killing than hunting men cared to admit, hunting managed to survive with little difficulty, is proof in itself that the sport remained popular.

PART IV

AN END

CHAPTER 10

THE DEPRESSION

Even before the agricultural crisis of the seventies, there were indications that at least some farmers were less than enchanted with hunting and hunting men. As early as the 1860s, there was evidence of increasing strains in the rural community and growing tension between landlords and tenants over such matters as game preservation and land reform. [1] These tensions alone could have affected hunting, which was so bound up in the functioning of the traditional rural community, but changes in both hunting and farming had even more direct effects on the sport.

The new advances on scientific farming and the efforts by farmers to wring the utmost yield out of every acre had produced a new breed of farmers who were less than eager to have their land ridden over by a crowd of sportsmen. The great popularity of hunting, moreover, made it all the more likely that it would be ridden over often. Hunting, no less than farming, was becoming more intensive. More hunting men meant more packs of hounds hunting increasingly smaller countries, and hence, hunting the same area all the more often. They also meant a demand for more foxes, not only to satisfy the need for more days of sport, but also because the modern style of hunting, with its emphasis on short, quick bursts, was notoriously spendthrift when it came to foxes. More hunting meant more damage, more foxes meant more danger for poultry and lambs; farmers were unlikely to care for either. [2]

Commenting on this fact in 1875, the *Pall Mall Gazette* speculated about what it called the new type of 'commercial' farmer:

Men of this stamp are not very numerous as yet among the farming class, but they may one day probably become so; and should they ever do so, hunting will have to undergo some change. Hounds will have to hunt less often in the corn growing districts, covers will be wider apart, so that the same ground may not be ridden over repeatedly, and other concessions must be made to the spirit of commercial agriculture. [3]

In the normal run of things, the situation described by the *Gazette's* leader-writer, would have come to pass eventually. It probably would have happened relatively slowly, and, as it did, farmers and foxhunters might have come to an understanding with no intense feeling on either side. But the normal run of things did not, in fact, occur. Almost coincidentally with the *Gazette's* comments, English agriculture was entering a period of great trial. By the mid-1870s, the influx of foreign grain — made possible by the repeal of the corn laws thirty years earlier, but delayed by problems of transport and unsettled world conditions — was forcing domestic grain prices down, and the downward trend was accelerated in the eighties following the disastrous weather of the 1878-79 season. In the grain-growing districts the effect was dramatic. As wheat prices fell by as much as fifty per cent and other grains were affected only slightly less severely, many farmers went under. Others managed to survive only because their landlords remitted much of their rent or allowed them to renegotiate leases at lower rents. Landowners who depended on agricultural rents for most or all of their incomes were similarly hard-hit. The fall in grain prices was followed by a fall in wool prices, severely affecting a second major component of English agriculture. Contemporaries branded the fall in grain and wool prices a great agricultural depression, and saw no reason to doubt its significance for the life of the nation. Though we now know that other segments of English agriculture were affected less severely and some even prospered, contemporary opinion was not wrong in its view of the depression as a decisive event. The most striking effect of the depression, however, was not the immediate economic effect, but the far-reaching change it brought about in the structure of English society. The landed interest, which had monopolized political power and social prestige for centuries, was faced with a severe blow to the source of its wealth at precisely the time when the commercial and industrial interests were increasing both their wealth and their prestige. Even more significantly, the different fates of landed and commercial wealth did not go unnoticed by either landlord or farmer.

The economic crisis was accompanied by a crisis of confidence. In the face of the realization that the old sources of wealth were being struck down while the new ones were prospering, the foundations of the comfortable old rural community came under increasing pressure. As we have seen, hunting was inseparably bound up in that community; as we shall see, it could not remain unaffected by anything that threatened it. [4]

This is not to say that the depression was solely responsible for the events of the eighties and nineties, but there can be no question about two facts: first, the depression greatly accelerated developments whose roots were already present; second, that in the minds of farmers and landlords alike, the depression was the great villain that radically changed their lives. Certainly, as agricultural profits turned into losses, farmers, who had in the past turned a blind eye to a few chickens taken by foxes or a fence rail knocked down, began to realize that these might well represent the margin between profit and loss. Many who had been friendly to the hunt in good times began to question whether the continuance of hunting was worth the price they had to pay.

Dissatisfaction expressed itself in many ways. As we have already seen, vulpicide, on a small scale, was a means of regulating the size of hunting losses; on a large scale, it was a traditional way of expressing dissatisfaction. From the late 1870s, vulpicide increased markedly. Instead of isolated instances coming to light, reports of wholesale vulpicide in several countries began circulating. In the North Cotswold country, for example, a special meeting had to be held to consider the problem. [5] The cause of this vulpicide could not be determined, but in other countries it was far more obvious. As it became apparent that good times were not immediately in sight, farmers became far more open about their anti-fox activities. Where vulpicides in the past had gone to great lengths to conceal their crime, some of them were now all too willing to admit it openly. Samuel Whitfield, a farmer near Rotherham, in Earl Fitzwilliam's country, for example, wrote to *The Field* admitting that he had killed foxes and had encouraged others to do the same. [6] Other farmers were equally open. In 1888, a Worcestershire farmer warned off a hunting man who had trampled his corn. The offender not only refused to leave but used his whip on the farmer. The farmer took him to court, but the magistrates dismissed the case. The farmer therefore put out advertisements:

Wanted, dead foxes, must be out of the Worcestershire Hunt, shot, poisoned, or trapped, price given, £1 dog foxes, 30/- vixens – Apply

Welch, Hunt End, Redditch. [7]

It took all the tact of the master of hounds to get him to withdraw his offer.

Wire, which had generally been absent from most hunting countries since the great controversy of the 1860s, began to appear once again, and farmers who had not used it before began to warn hunting men that they would begin. [8] Some of them began using it with the express purpose of keeping hunting men off their land; [9] for many others, however, wire was just the cheapest and most convenient form of fencing, especially where landlords did not provide timber. [10] If ordinary wire were not bad enough, barbed wire began to appear in the mid-1880s, especially in stock-raising areas. [11] Paradoxically, the hard times that had forced the farmers to these measures strengthened their hand when it came to putting them into action. With more and more farms standing vacant, landlords could not afford to antagonize those tenants who remained, for they knew that if a tenant gave up his farm it would be difficult to replace him. Landlords who might formerly have exerted great pressures on tenants who interfered with hunting were now forced to remain silent.

There was, however, yet another factor that encouraged openness on the part of farmers. As we have already seen, hard times had always tended to produce dissatisfaction among farmers, and even in the best of times there were those who disliked the sport. But these had always been kept in check, not only by the external pressure of landlords, but by the general belief in the beneficence of hunting. What was new from the late 1870s, and more especially as the bad years rolled on through the 1880s, was that for the first time, farmers were beginning to go beyond a mere reflexive reaction to specific instances of grievance. For the first time, they were beginning to question the basic rationale of hunting itself. Farmers began writing, in increasing numbers, to the national and local press to express their dissatisfaction and served notice upon the hunting world that they had to be taken seriously. The letters began appearing in the late seventies, increased through the eighties, and by 1890 had turned into a flood. [12] The extent to which these newly articulate opponents were willing to go varied from man to man. Many, if not most, were careful to stress their belief in the basic soundness of hunting if carried out properly, but, even to these men, proper hunting was something very different from what had been the norm for the previous hundred years. Hard times had made it impossible for farmers to hunt, they said, the hunts were not compensating them for damages, hunting men did not buy from the farmers, and the fields were increasingly becoming the province of rich outsiders who knew nothing of agricultural custom or local men. Since, therefore, farmers gained nothing from hunting, it could not be expected that they would continue to support it. Those who wished to hunt must pay for the privilege. They must pay for the damages, and, if they wanted farmers not to use wire fencing, they must pay for that too. [13]

Complaints were aired and debated at farmers' clubs and societies. Though the Warwickshire Chamber of Agriculture narrowly passed a resolution in favour of hunting in 1889, its members felt strongly that adequate compensation should be paid and were bitter about the number of townsmen who swelled the hunting fields. [14] Their local M.P. even raised the issue in the House of Commons, asking Henry Chaplin, President of the Board of Agriculture, what the government intended to do about the relations of farmers and foxhunters, but Chaplin refused to involve the government. [15]

For the farmers, the real question was one of money. So long as they were paid for their losses, they had no real objection to hunting. Poultry and damage claims soared in many hunts. From 1873 to 1883 the Meynell Hunt in Derbyshire, for example, had been paying between £150 and £200 per year in damage claims. In 1883 the cost jumped to £354, and from 1885 to 1900 fell below £500 only four times, below £400 only once. [16] The Duke of Beaufort claimed that his poultry claims quadrupled. [17] For the first time, farmers began to claim that they deserved compensation for damage to fences as well as to crops. One farmer suggested that compensation for fences might replace that for poultry, but others wanted payments for both fences and poultry. [18]

That the farmers' grievances were essentially economic is underscored by the fact that in those countries where they suffered least they remained on best terms with the hunt. Where a master like C.A.R. Hoare of the V.W.H. was liberal with his payments, they were willing, as we shall see, to support him even against their landlords. Where crowds were small or did little damage, or where most of the land was not agricultural, as on Dartmoor or in the New Forest, there was little friction. [19] Unfortunately the demands of the farmers for increased compensation came at precisely the time when many hunts could least afford to meet these demands, and for precisely the same reasons. The farmers were not the only ones to suffer from the depressed state of agriculture. Agricultural landlords found their rent-rolls shrinking as farmers moved off the land or negotiated leases at lower rents. Those who did not have additional sources of income found it increasingly difficult to spare money for hunting. Hunts that depended upon these men for the bulk of their income found their subscription lists dwindling dangerously.

It is difficult, owing to an extreme scarcity of available records, to assess precisely the effect of the depression on the finances of most hunts. Piecing together what few figures there are would seem to indicate that in this, as in everything else, there was a wide variation over the country, and that, generally speaking, the fate of hunting depended upon the crops grown in the district. Some hunts were very badly hit. In Berkshire, the joint-masters who had accepted the Craven country in 1877 on the promise of £1650 per year resigned, disillusioned, two years later, after finding that the committee had no way of meeting its commitment and was always in arrears, at times as much as £2000. [20] Another southern pack, the Puckeridge, in Hertfordshire, also found itself in trouble. Robert Gosling, the Puckeridge master, had been guaranteed £1750 per year in 1875-76. By 1880, only £1200 could be raised, and Gosling had to give up bye-days – extra hunting days beyond the advertised ones, always provided at the master's expense – in anticipation of an even smaller subscription the next year. After 1885, the country was split, for Gosling could only afford to hunt part of his old country. [21] These packs were located in grain-growing areas that were badly hurt by the depression. Wheat and barley had been the primary crops in both, and as a result of the depression, they fell back to grass. [22]

It was not only the southern counties that were hard hit. One of the worst affected of all the hunts was the Burton in Lincolnshire, also in a grain-producing area. [23] From 1871, when the hunt had split into two, to 1879, the annual subscription had hovered at around £1400. In 1880 it fell to £855, in 1881 to £527, and though in 1882 it bounced back to £698, that was not enough. From the £1200 that had been guaranteed to the master in the early seventies, the guarantee fell to £300 in 1884. Finally, the hunt had to be given up entirely in 1888-89, though it was revived the following year with a subscription of £409 and a master willing to take only £300. [24]

It would be foolish to generalize for the entire country on the basis of these few figures, but there are other indications that a number of packs were in trouble. Lord Middleton, who had kept his pack without a subscription, was forced to ask for one in 1877. [25] The Duke of Rutland, who hunted the Belvoir country at his own expense, had thought as early as 1876 of reducing the number of hunting days from five to four a week, but reconsidered when a substantial poultry and damage fund was raised by subscription. [26] By 1891, even this was not enough, and he was forced to cut back the number of his hunting days to four. [27] George Luttrell, who had hunted the West Somerset at his own expense, had to give it up in 1881, and his followers were not optimistic about finding a successor. 'I hardly expect that they can be kept up by subscription in these days of Agricultural Depression, when all who are chiefly dependent upon land are reducing their expenditure as much as possible', [28] lamented one of them. Lord Yarborough, whose ancestors had hunted in Lincolnshire at their own expense since the early eighteenth century, could not bring himself to end that tradition, but in 1895 he was forced to sell the famous Brocklesby dog pack, keeping only the bitches. [29] Many subscription packs found themselves looking for new masters as the old ones decided to cut their losses. [30] Other masters searched frantically for ways to cut their expenses. All too often it was the poor hunt servants who had to go to the wall, as masters or other hunt members took the horn themselves to save money. [31] Other hunts found themselves faced with unexpected expenses, as members who had assumed certain responsibilities in the past were no longer able to meet them. [32]

The situation was not one of unrelieved blackness, however. Not all farmers were turning hostile. The fact that the sport was not brought to an absolute standstill testifies to that. The number of packs of foxhounds increased during the depression years; old countries split because it was difficult to find masters for the larger packs, [33] but the new smaller packs were managing to struggle through. Some packs were relatively untouched. In Derbyshire, the Meynell managed to keep its subscriptions on a relatively even keel throughout the depression, though there was a slight decline between 1877 and 1879, and another in 1889. Subscriptions, however, could only be maintained through an influx of new people into the country as the old gentry gradually retired from the hunting field, for the Meynell, too, was located in a corn district. [34] Even here, the fairly steady subscription was eaten into by rising expenses. [35] The Heythrop Hunt in Oxfordshire was another relatively fortunate pack. Though subscriptions fell £300 between 1878-79 and 1879-80, by 1881-82 they had almost regained the pre-slump figure. [36]

Most fortunate of all were packs that could count on one or two very rich subscribers, or that drew subscriptions from men relatively untouched by the depression. The Heythrop was lucky to have in Albert Brassey, son of the railway contractor — master from 1873 to 1918 — a master who never asked for more than £1500 per year and paid all poultry, covert, damage, and earth-stopping fees himself. [37] In Bedfordshire, which had been converted to corn during the boom of the early nineteenth century and suffered as a result, [38] the Oakley Hunt managed to keep its annual subscription remarkably constant from 1874 to 1885 only because they could count on steady support from a few subscribers like S. C. Whitbread, while the Duke of Bedford increased his subscription from £400 in 1874 to £600 in 1875, and finally to £800 in 1880. Even then, the remainder had to be sought among a larger number of subscribers than before. Forty-eight subscribers contributed £1653 in 1874; sixty-two contributed £1445 in 1884. [39]

The Essex Hunt managed not only to maintain its guarantee to the master, but to increase it from £1600 in 1874 to £2000 in 1882 and even to £2600 in 1887, [40] even though it was located in an affected area. [41] There was always a sizeable London contingent in the Essex field, and it may have provided some of the money. [42] The North Staffordshire, another hunt where businessmen predominated, also seems, on the basis of very sketchy figures, to have done well, increasing its subscriptions even before instituting a minimum. [43]

Whether the depression brought about a relative decline of the gentry on the subscription lists of other packs is hard to tell, for few lists have survived. Contemporaries spoke of former hunting men giving up the sport, [44] and, as we have seen in the case of the Meynell and Oakley, there was an unusual turnover among their subscribers. Probably, however, the gentry did not retire from the hunting field *en masse*. Many must have found it difficult to continue in the style to which they had become accustomed and cut back on the number of their hunters and hunting days, but it would seem that many found it equally difficult to give up altogether. [45]

Nevertheless, despite these brighter signs, and despite the fact that the firm market for hunters and the crowded fields indicated that as many, if not more, people were hunting than ever, [46] most hunting men were convinced that hard times were indeed upon them. Caught in the squeeze between the increasing militancy of the farmers and their own increasingly vulnerable position, hunting people were torn by conflicting emotions. Self-interest demanded that the attacks on their sport be beaten off, but it also demanded that the farmers be kept friendly. Not unnaturally, some of them tried to make light of the problem. All that was really needed, they claimed, was a sign on the part of foxhunters that they still had the farmers' welfare at heart, and the farmers would naturally come around. Some could find nothing better than to urge more dinners for farmers. Even the generally level-headed editors of *The Field* could go on about this as late as 1891. [47] Fortunately for the future of hunting, however, there were many who realized that, useful though dinners might once have been, the unusual times required far stronger measures.

The problem facing hunting people was how to satisfy the farmers without either straining their own finances past the breaking point or putting themselves in the uncomfortable moral position of admitting that the farmers' complaints were justified. The solution seemed to lie in somehow reducing the number of people who hunted, thus reducing the damages caused by the hunt, and at the same time somehow increasing hunt revenues. One convenient scapegoat seemed to offer a place to begin. If the fields were too large, sportsmen argued, who made them that way but the outsiders who were ignorant of local ways and customs, who were probably most responsible for damage, who antagonized the farmers, and who spent not a penny among local people? If the hunt treasury was empty, who was to blame but the outsider, who was unaffected by the depression, who spent huge sums on clothes and horses, but who probably never paid a penny in subscriptions, while the hunt depended upon the support of local men?

This dislike of outsiders was nothing new, of course. We have already seen that in the course of the nineteenth century the city man had moved from being a figure of fun to one receiving grudging recognition as a good sportsman, but that as the railways brought more city men into the field, the older hunting groups had retreated into social exclusiveness. Now this relatively passive reception was being replaced by an active resentment, natural on the part of many countrymen toward those who were not facing the same privations they faced themselves. Beyond this resentment there was at least a modicum of truth. In some counties the field had got out of hand; in the popular and fashionable hunts there were too many people. There were many who took advantage of the reluctance of masters to ask for money from strangers. What percentage of these were city men is impossible to determine. What is certain is that hunting men and farmers alike were convinced that many, if not most, were.

If, therefore, some way were found of keeping most outsiders away and forcing those who still turned out to pay for their sport, great strides could be taken towards solving the problems. The obvious way to accomplish these ends would have been to bar them from the field or to charge a minimum fee for all those who hunted. Both of these, however, flew in the face of the cherished traditions of the sport. To bar anyone from the hunting field made a mockery of the hunting man's proud boast that his sport was open. To ask for a minimum subscription also seemed to violate that tradition, for it imposed an undue hardship on the poorer sportsman and could have the practical result of effectively barring him from the field. It also went against the tradition of foxhunting as a gentlemanly amusement. Gentlemen did not demand money from other gentlemen for the privilege of showing them sport. These considerations were taken quite seriously by hunting men, as we have seen, and it was precisely because of that fact that apparently obvious steps were not taken immediately. That they were taken at all is a sign that the times demanded extraordinary measures.

When it came to limiting the size of the field, an absolute ban had to be ruled out from the start. Some hunts hit on the idea that secrecy might be the best policy. There was some precedent for this. As early as 1869, W. Selby Lowndes of the Whaddon Chase took to not publishing the meetings of his hounds to keep away the London crowds, [48] and in the seventies and eighties other packs followed suit. [49] Most packs, however, were unwilling to take that step. For one thing, it was not very effective. To take the place of the advertisement, cards had to be sent to all those who were held to have a right to know of the meets – members, subscribers, landowners, and tenant farmers. [50] By the time these had been sent out, anyone who wanted to know about the forthcoming meet could easily find out. Besides, even this relatively minor step smacked of keeping the meets private. The imposition of a required minimum subscription, or worse, of 'day money' for those who did not hunt regularly, was a more serious step. It offered greater prospect for success than simply not advertising the meet, but it was also a greater departure from tradition. Even before the depression, some hunting people had become aware of the need to deal with the problem of the man who hunted without paying. [51] Most agreed that the man who hunted regularly ought to subscribe, even if he did not live within a hunting country. *The Field* considered it 'shabby' if one who hunted regularly with a subscription pack did not subscribe at least ten shillings for each time that he and one horse took the field. [52] The man who hunted only occasionally, on the other hand, presented more of a problem, for he could not be expected to contribute a full subscription for the few days that he came out. One solution would have been to pay for the day, but most masters thought it beneath them to accept 'day money'. Various suggestions were made. Some felt that strangers ought to contribute to the damage and poultry funds or to a special fund set up just for them.[53] After the establishment of the Hunt Servants Benefit Society, *Bell's Life in London,* for one, constantly urged non-regular hunting men to contribute to the society in lieu of a subscription.

In 1863, Lord Maldon, master of the Old Berkeley, the hunt that had been involved in *Essex v. Capel,* and that still faced the problem of large crowds, established twenty-five pounds as the smallest subscription he was willing to accept from regular followers and returned all donations of less than that amount, though he made it clear that those who hunted only occasionally were still welcome without subscribing.[54] In 1866, William Selby Lowndes of the Whaddon Chase, who, it will be recalled, was also to be among the first not to advertise, bowed to the complaints of the farmers, many of whom were his own tenants, and became the first master to try to limit his field directly. He announced that henceforth he would restrict his field only to subscribers and tenant farmers, and that if non-subscribers came out he would be compelled to take his hounds home.[55] Selby Lowndes' decision, however, was not welcomed even by those who recognized that there was some need for it. *Baily's Magazine's* columnist 'the Van Driver' wrote:

> Now by all fox-hunting law, as long as he advertises his meets, he can prevent nobody from joining them. And if the subscribers are to suffer for the strangers, they will very soon cease to be subscribers, and the hunt become extinct.[56]

The Quorn, which probably drew more non-subscribers than any hunt in the country, was another pack that tried to deal with the problem, publishing a statement, in 1875, that henceforth 'strangers' would be expected to help defray expenses, though it was explained that the Quorn, too, had no intention of charging occasional visitors for their day's sport, but was just after non-subscribers who came out regularly. In any event, there was no way to enforce the new policy. Five years later, the hunt was meeting to see what could be done about those who still hunted without subscribing.[57]

Nevertheless, it was not until the effects of the depression were becoming felt that the idea that the man who hunted regularly ought somehow to be compelled to subscribe began to gain more than limited acceptance. The first to question publicly the principle behind the old method of subscribing was the 'Country Correspondent' of *Bell's Life*. In his regular preview of the 1879 hunting season, he drew attention to the lamentable conditions in the agricultural world and contrasted them with the great amount of money that still seemed to be available to some people who wished to hunt, especially those from the cities.

> Such men as I am quoting are not affected at all by agricultural depression. Their money is in safe consols, or securities that cannot fluctuate, and whether Hodge dies of want, and his master with him, it can never disturb them in the smallest degree. It has been a want, however, in this hunting world that those who could pay for the contingent expenses of the pastime have escaped by the too close following of custom without any laid down conditions of rule and law. [58]

For a fox hunter to question the sanctity of hunting custom and wish it to be replaced by 'rule and law' was a new departure indeed. The writer was not one to shrink from the implications of this idea. The man who supported a pack of hounds, he went on, was beholden to no one but the land and covert owners and the farmers. Beyond them, everyone had to be considered a visitor, 'and it is a custom to be deplored that the visitors of a hunt are to be allowed greater freedom than visitors to a private house or a private entertainment'.

What, then, did he propose?

> I think it is desirable that subscription packs should fall under ordinary club rule, that they should be confined to members, either honorary members elected so by their positions as landowners, or by paying the usual fees and subscriptions to be entitled to the privileges of members. To be proposed, seconded, and to pay the demand would be no very difficult process in these days, and such a system would tend to keep many hunts in affluence instead of being threatened with a break up, owing to the agricultural depression falling on the landowners who have hitherto shown themselves to be the principal supporters of fox hunting. [59]

Others were quick to seize upon the same idea. 'Whoever keeps a hunter can afford £10', wrote *Baily's* 'Van Driver'. 'If he cannot, let him stay at home and attend to his duties, and not take pleasure at other people's expense'. [60] This was, if anything, an even more remarkable sentiment to come from a hunting man. On the face of it, it expressly contradicted the so often quoted line about the appeal of hunting to 'the peer and the peasant'. But, of course, it must not be taken at face value. It was written in a burst of indignation at the city man who had money at a time when it seemed that neither the peer nor the peasant had any. It was a product of the sudden realization that the locus of economic power was shifting from the old classes to the new. Finally, we must realize that it did not imply that 'the peasant' should no longer be allowed to hunt. His right to follow hounds was never questioned. The city man was the subject of resentment, and it did not really matter that many city men subscribed handsomely or that many defaulters had connections with the land going back many generations.

As a sign of the position that hunting had attained in English society, the problems of hunting men were not considered by the sporting press alone. Even *The Times* tried to come to grips with the financial issues and came to much the same conclusions. Masters of hounds, in the face of 'roving hunting men' and 'wealthy people of business' who hunted without paying, should place hunt finances on 'a more strictly business footing. . . .'

> For it would be nothing short of a national misfortune if the sport that has done far more than any other to promote kindly feelings among all ranks of Englishmen should be suffered to languish because the landed classes are in temporary difficulties. [61]

In the face of mounting opinion in favour of minimum subscriptions and capping, several packs did, in fact, start to adopt one or the other. In 1882, for example, the North Warwickshire voted to collect ten shillings from everyone, not a member or tenant farmer, each time they hunted. In 1890, the South Staffs imposed a five-shilling cap, and in 1892 the Whaddon Chase imposed a one-guinea cap for all strangers except for those staying in the house of a subscriber or mounted by one. [62]

Capping, though, was a less attractive alternative to most hunts, and a minimum subscription was adopted by more of them, with the minimum ranging from three to thirty guineas, though twenty-five pounds was about the average. [63]

Minimum subscriptions did not, however, meet with the approval of every hunting man. There were those who saw minimums as turning hunting from a 'national sport' to a 'class pursuit' [64] – a change that could only hurt the sport. As late as 1920, these doubts lingered. [65] Those who imposed minimums were not immune to these doubts. They imposed them only after great soul-searching, and they attempted to frame the requirements in such a way as to cause the least interference with the old way of life. Almost without exception, the new minimums did not apply to local people; farmers, as always, were exempt from any payment whatever. [66] The theory behind this, of course, was that the local man, who had always been free to follow hounds and who had his own land ridden over, was to be allowed to continue as he always had, while the outsider, who caused all the trouble in the first place, was to be charged for his sport.

Even this liberal interpretation could lead to some problems. The Essex, for example, had exempted officers quartered in the country from paying a subscription. In 1890, however, when officers of the Royal Dragoons turned out in great numbers, they were made to feel unwelcome, and it was suggested to their colonel that they only come out one or two at a time. [67]

The adoption of minimum subscriptions by this minority of packs [68] might seem a small thing. It was, in fact, a symbolic step of the greatest magnitude. It was nothing less than a recognition, though an unconscious one for some, that the tradition that everyone was welcome to hunt, no matter what his means or social status, was, in the words of the editor of *The Field*, 'a pleasant fiction'. [69]

In the absence of detailed accounts for most packs, it is difficult to judge the financial effects of minimum subscriptions. [70] Contemporaries seemed to feel that the rule was working well, [71] but the fact that a minimum subscription was not adopted by most packs would seem to indicate that it was not a panacea for all that ailed hunting.

Another sign of the pressures that hunting men were feeling was that their attitude toward foot followers was also undergoing a change. As we have seen, even in the earlier years of the nineteenth century some masters had had trouble with foot followers. Most masters would have been happier not to have them out at any time, but no one would have suggested that they did not belong there. This accepted attitude never quite underwent a complete change. Partly because foot followers, even the factory operatives who turned out in industrial areas, were local people, partly because many hunting people were becoming sensitive to charges that hunting was becoming a rich man's sport, they had to be encouraged. [72] Nevertheless, during the seventies and eighties we see, for the first time, foxhunters openly expressing the opinion that it would be far better for the sport if the foot people, now referred to not as 'hardy sportsmen', but as 'idle loungers', were to stay at home.[73] The most vocal of them was *Baily's* 'Borderer', who complained in 1887:

> There is another thing that troubles me, and helps to kick the beam adversely to hunting, and that is the increase of foot people and idle loungers that hang about our meets nowadays . . . . They come out of the large towns and villages; a few are sportsmen after their manner, but *men who cannot afford a horse are better at home than in the hunting field.*[74] [Italics mine.]

This would have been anathema twenty-five years earlier, and to most hunting people still was. That it was printed at all, indicates the pressure that hunting people were feeling. Seeking to exonerate sportsmen from the charges that they caused undue damage at a time when farmers could least afford it, 'Borderer' seized upon any scapegoat he could find, and the foot people were closest at hand. It is significant that he chose to portray them as the product of the large towns and villages, rather than as agricultural labourers. As we have seen, villagers and manufacturing hands were not new to the hunting field, though 'Borderer' wrote as though they were.

It is ironic that the attempt to limit the size of the field had been one way to respond to the attacks made by some farmers on the idealized picture of hunting, for it had the effect of destroying one part of that ideal. In their attempt to deal with other aspects of the farmers' complaints, hunting people were far less revolutionary. An attempt was made to restore some validity to the ideal picture of the relations between hunting and farming. Though motivated largely by self-interest, the attempt was highly creditable, but it was also extremely conservative. It was an attempt to restore conditions to what they were believed to have been before the depression.

One of the least successful measures was an attempt to get hunting men to buy directly from farmers. As we have seen, farmers were generally unwilling to raise horses because it did not pay and were unable to provide the services hunting men required when it came to other supplies. When farmers, as a part of their general attack upon hunting conditions, increasingly began to point this out, some foxhunters attempted to remedy the situation. Sportsmen were urged repeatedly by the sporting press to buy directly from farmers whenever they could,[75] and some attempts were made to facilitate this trade. Lord Lonsdale, master of the Quorn from 1893 to 1898, for example, used to fill two pages in the *Melton Mowbray*

Times and Loughborough Advertiser with names of farmers with produce to sell.[76] In the same vein, masters and other hunting men began to make sires available to service farmers' mares free or at nominal fees.[77] Hunting people who could not buy from farmers were urged to contribute money to the Royal Agricultural Benevolent Institution instead, and, following the example set by the Prince of Wales, some did. Several hunts began making regular, though small, contributions to the R.A.B.I.[78]

Where hunting men were able to express their concern for the farmers in this way, relations between them tended to be good. When W. E. Oakeley, master of the Atherstone, for example, announced that he was giving up the hounds in 1883, over a thousand farmers and tradesmen presented him with a petition urging him to reconsider.[79] Oakeley had always bought forage from farmers and kept a horse for their use.[80] There were limitations, however, to how far popularity could be attained in this way. Even so popular a master as Oakeley met with stiff resistance from farmers when he suggested that others beside the hunt should pay for the removal of wire fences.[81] Furthermore, despite the efforts of men like Lonsdale, the factors that had led most foxhunters to buy from dealers did not change. In the Quorn country, for example, Lonsdale's efforts were unsuccessful. Though a few farmers became corn merchants and a few corn merchants began calling themselves farmers, most farmers did not sell. One of them told the author, T. F. Dale, 'I only grow as much straw as I want on the farm, and I make but little hay and grow no oats. No: if hunting does me no harm, it does me little or no good.'[82]

The failure of farmers and foxhunters to come to terms on the question of horses and forage, however, was relatively unimportant. Most farmers had only to look at their accounts to know that they had never sold much to foxhunters. They had only raised the issue to show that hunting offered nothing to offset the damages it caused. It was on this question of damages that all was to depend, for it was precisely upon this question that farmers demanded satisfaction.

The attempts to limit the size of the field indicate that the hunting world was beginning to recognize that the problem of damages was a real one. As we have seen, respect for the rights of farmers, subject of course to the 'exigencies' of the chase, had always formed a part of hunt etiquette, even if that etiquette was often sadly disregarded. The depression and the new hostility of the farmers brought more than a new urgency to the expressions of that etiquette. For the first time we find spokesmen for hunting admitting that perhaps the rights of the farmers might come first.

'In the present depressed state of the agricultural interest', wrote *The Field's* editor in 1883, defending the decision by that paper to accept advertising for a potentially dangerous fence, 'hunting interests can hardly be first attended to.' [83]

In the face of pressure, hunting men were beginning to take a more realistic view of their responsibilities towards the farmers over whose land they rode. Their attitudes did not change completely, of course. It would be too much to expect that they would, but they were changing nonetheless. The attitude toward wire is a good example. It will be recalled that when wire had first made its appearance in the 1860s, the hunting world had united in opposition to the deadly innovation, and the outcome of the first clash had been defeat for the farmers.

Wire did not completely disappear after that, of course. Some landlords allowed their tenants to use it despite pressure from hunting men, [84] and in these cases there was little the hunt could do. On the whole, however, the use of wire was rare in hunting districts. The depression, however, caused a new increase in the use of wire, as farmers found it made the cheapest fencing available, and landlords or their agents reluctantly went along. The first reaction of hunting men was much the same as it had been twenty years earlier. The wire, they felt, had to come down, and they saw no reason to assume the responsibility for taking it down. [85] But for the first time hunting men were also beginning to look at the other side. In 1888, *The Field* published a picture of a notice for marking wire, said to have been designed by a hunting farmer, and urged that it be used in the interests of safety, thus grudgingly admitting that the use of wire was justifiable. [86] In the Atherstone country, W. E. Oakeley was going even further. Barbed wire had made its appearance, and though Oakeley threatened to take the hounds home the first time a hound or horse was injured by the wire, he became the first master of hounds to accept the responsibility of paying to take it down. If local committees were formed to arrange for taking wire down, the hunt would pay the cost. [87] Other masters followed suit. [88]

Not all hunting men were as enlightened, of course. Even those who were willing to pay, like Oakeley or the Duke of Sutherland, master of the North Staffordshire, hoped that wire could be avoided, and paid only as a last resort. [89] Nevertheless, despite these reservations, the idea had gained respectability. [90] It was to take time before it was adopted by the majority of hunts, but it was only a matter of time.

Some hunts made a start at a **more realis**tic attitude toward damages as well. It was perhaps too much to expect that they would admit responsibility for mending fences, though no less an authority than 'Brooksby' had come out in favour of the plan, [91] but poultry and crop damage began to be recompensed on a greater scale. Enlightened masters emulated Lord Lonsdale, who, in addition to his forage listings, the introduction of a 'cap', the buying of huge game orders for farmers, keeping a stallion for them, and making sure that second horsemen stayed on the roads, rather than riding across fields, [92] also vastly increased the amount of money available for damages. In 1891, the Quorn paid £568 in poultry claims and £133 for damages. In 1897-98, Lonsdale had increased that to £1370 in poultry and £692 in damages. [93] There were those who accused him of being a spendthrift, but it had to be admitted that during his mastership there were always plenty of foxes and little wire. [94] Hunts like the Cottesmore, which had had poultry funds, began to set up damage funds as well; [95] perhaps more significantly, the farmers themselves were pressed into service to assess the damages, though judging from a column of 'Brooksby's' in 1890, this innovation had not become general by that date. [96]

This last development was among the most significant of all. For the first time, the hunting world began to admit that farmers had a legitimate role in the management of the sport. As with the other reforms of the depression years, this new development was not generally adopted by the majority of hunts, but, like the others, it was a sign of things to come. The new role of the farmers was not limited to the question of damage alone, but extended to the most basic question of all, by whom and in what way was the country to be hunted. It had always been tacitly recognized that without the cooperation of the farmers no master could hope to hunt a country successfully, and, as we have seen, once appointed, most masters, if they were wise, went out of their way to gain that cooperation. It had even become customary in many packs that a proposed master be presented for approval to a meeting of landowners and farmers. [97] If the farmers were adamant, they were generally listened to. [98]

Farmers did not gain their say in the same way in every pack that extended it to them. In a few they were able to gain it only as a result of conflict, and only because they were willing to threaten the existence of the sport itself. The two most notable cases of this occurred in the Billesdon and Vale of White Horse countries, and in both cases the crisis that brought about the reform was not originally of the farmers' making.

The first controversy began in 1878 out of a dispute over the hunting of what was known as the Billesdon, Harborough, or South Quorn Country.[99] The Billesdon country had been a part of the original Quorn country as hunted by Hugo Meynell, but that country was too vast by nineteenth-century standards to be hunted by one pack, and Quorn masters had lent one part or another of it to different masters from time to time. The Billesdon country had been hunted since 1856 by W. W. Tailby of Carlton Hall. During the early years of his mastership there was some dispute as to whether he had only borrowed it from the Quorn or held it as a separate country, but his twenty years as master had established at least his personal right to hunt it as long as he wished.[100] Upon his resignation in 1878, two claims were made for the country. The first was by J. R. Coupland on behalf of the Quorn, of which he was master, the second by Sir Bache Cunard, of the shipping family, who offered to hunt it as a separate country in the same way that Tailby had.[101]

The problem was complicated by the fact that, on hearing of Tailby's resignation, Coupland did not immediately claim the country as Quorn territory, but, like Cunard, applied to the Billesdon committee for the vacant country, thus appearing to recognize the authority of that committee.[102] Faced with the two offers, Sir Henry Halford, who had been the chairman of Tailby's committee, was unsure of how to proceed, and he wrote to twenty-seven local landowners asking for their advice. Only eighteen of them responded, fifteen favouring Coupland and three favouring Cunard. Still unsure of what to do, he called a public meeting to discuss the matter, to which all 'owners and occupiers, subscribers and others interested' were invited.[103]

Meetings of this sort had become a traditional way of sounding out public opinion, though their authority to make decisions had never been established. At the meeting, opinion seems to have been fairly evenly divided. The farmers, however, were almost all united in favour of Cunard. It was not that they disliked Coupland, but most of them feared that reuniting with the Quorn would bring the huge Quorn fields over their land.[104]

The meeting would probably have decided in favour of Cunard had it been able to put the question to a vote, but Halford, fearing that the wishes of the landowners who had written to him in Coupland's favour but who had not been able to attend, would be overruled by a meeting open to all, refused to let the vote be taken. Instead, a committee composed equally of landowners and farmers was set up, though precisely what the authority of this committee was to be was never settled.[105]

Whatever its authority, the committee met the next day, decided, eleven to three, in favour of Cunard and declared that 'by virtue of that election' Cunard was master of the Billesdon Hunt. [106] Coupland refused to accept the authority of the committee or the validity of its vote and reiterated his claim to the Billesdon as part of the original Quorn country. [107]

The dispute between the two factions excited local opinion through most of the spring of 1878. The local papers were full of correspondence, and the leader writers joined in. The dispute even spilled over into the national sporting press, which reprinted many of the letters that had originally appeared in the local papers. [108] The issue was not clear-cut. Both sides claimed that they had the support of most of the landlords, and Coupland's supporters dismissed the actions of the Billesdon committee as being representative of the farmers alone. [109] The committee also seemed unwilling to claim authority on the basis of the support of the farmers alone. [110] Nevertheless, the dispute took on the character of a conflict between farmers and landowners. [111] Some farmers took the opportunity to claim that farmers had as much right as anyone to decide the future management of the hunt. [112]

With the approach of the new hunting season, Cunard and Coupland agreed to submit the dispute to the M.F.H. committee of Boodle's Club. The Billesdon committee, seeing this as a denial of their authority, was not pleased but had no choice but to accept, having pledged themselves to support whatever decision Cunard made. The M.F.H. committee deliberated the problem for months as the patience of both sides wore thin. Finally, at the end of February, 1879, the committee made its decision, ruling unanimously in favour of Coupland. [113]

The decision was received with shock by the Billesdon farmers. A public meeting was held, largely attended by farmers, though some landowners were also present. The meeting passed three resolutions, protesting against the turning out of Sir Bache Cunard, warning Coupland that if he hunted over their land he would be sued for trespass, and setting up a fund to defray the legal costs of such prosecutions. [114] The farmers' resolutions put a whole new light upon the question. 'Boodle's can decide to whom a country belongs', wrote one of the hunting correspondents of *Baily's Magazine,*

> but can its members say that any number of individuals shall have their land ridden over against their will? Can they stop actions for trespass? Can they cause wire to be removed, and prevent gates being locked and the hinges turned down? Can they prevent foxes being killed? [115]

In the face of this determined opposition, both sides had to reconsider. A compromise was worked out, reaffirming the official control of the Quorn but allowing Sir Bache Cunard to hunt the country, first for a term of two years, and then, after intervention of forty masters of hounds anxious to head off another controversy, for as long as he wished. [116] This last intervention was probably most significant of all. At a meeting of angry Billesdon farmers, Sir Arthur Hazlerigg of the Billesdon committee assured them that if they only accepted the Quorn's legal claim, they would have the support of 'everyone who mattered' in hunting in standing for a separate country for as long as Cunard was prepared to hunt it. [117] At least tacitly, the right of farmers to a voice in the selection of a master had been affirmed. Eight years later, when the mastership of the Quorn itself became vacant, the Quorn farmers were able to claim that they too had a right to a voice, and four of them were named to the Quorn committee. [118]

If the Billesdon dispute were not enough to impress foxhunters with the fact that farmers had the power to bring hunting to its knees and the willingness to use that power, the dispute in the V.W.H. country was. The master of the V.W.H. was C. A. R. Hoare, of the banking family. He was a wealthy man and spent his money freely among the local farmers, who all swore by him, especially since the Vale was among the hardest hit areas of the country. [119] He was, however, carrying on an affair with Beatrice Holme Sumner, the under-age daughter of Arthur Holme Sumner, himself a master of hounds, and, as a result of that affair, relations between Hoare and some members of the hunt grew so bad that in January, 1884, the hunt committee called upon him to resign. The farmers, however, supported him, and a petition in his favour with six hundred signatures was sent to the hunt committee, which, in the face of this determined opposition, reconsidered. [120]

The next year, however, what had been a private embarrassment became a public scandal. Hoare had fathered Miss Sumner's child, and the story came out in an open court trial. [121] The scandalized landowners of the V.W.H. could stand no more. Lord Bathurst, who was chairman of the committee and owner of the kennels, gave Hoare notice that he must vacate the kennels, [122] and on April 25, 1885, a meeting of 'subscribers, members, and owners of coverts' was held at the King's Head Hotel, Cirencester, to consider the future of the hunt. About one hundred people attended, including 'most of the leading farmers of the hunt'. [123] At the meeting a split between the landlords and the farmers developed. Most of the landlords, agreeing that 'a master of hounds is like a member of

Parliament, in a public position', called upon Hoare to resign and indicated that if he refused they would not only forbid him to draw their coverts, but would warn him off their land. The farmers, however, wanted none of it. Mr. Hoare, said one of them,

> had always been a very cheery man and a capital Master: he spent his money in the country, which had never been done before (cheers) the whole of his expenditure for hay, corn, straw, etc. was laid out with the people over whose land he rode, and therefore Mr. Hoare was a class of men they could not afford to lose in these bad times. (Cheers) [124]

Though by buying from farmers, Hoare was only following the best ideals of the sport, he was, as a result of this statement, accused by his opponents of trying to buy the farmers, a charge that did nothing to calm the spirits at the meeting. Hoare was accused by some opponents of fomenting class war by refusing to resign, while others of them objected to the whole question of class being raised and suggested that had times been better they would be glad to see tenant farmers on the committee. It was finally decided that before any further action be taken, the six hundred who had signed the petition in Hoare's favour the year before be allowed to express an opinion, though Hoare himself wished to go further and poll everyone who occupied any land whatever in the hunt. Any man, he said,

> who had a bit of land as big as that room was an occupier, and they had no right to tell such a man that he had no voice in the matter. The loss to a man with a small garden was greater than when some of his [Hoare's] farms in Braydon were ridden over. He had more difficulty in keeping the field from spoiling the small gardens than he had with everything else. [125]

Such egalitarian talk was too much for most of those present, and it was finally decided that circulars be sent only to those who had signed the original petition. Of 686 circulars sent out, 304 drew no reply, but the remaining farmers were found to be overwhelmingly on Hoare's side. He was favoured by 331 men farming 51,731 acres, while only 39 men, farming 16,380 acres, opposed him. [126] Hoare's appeal to the small landholder had been successful.

In the face of this overwhelming support from the farmers, Hoare could not be forced out, though a number of landowners closed their coverts to him, warned him off their land, and took to hunting with other packs, leaving him to take the field followed largely by farmers. [127]

As in the case of Coupland and Cunard, the original issue of the conflict soon lost its importance. What became the central issue was the attitude of the farmers, who were adamant that Hoare not be turned out and who used the conflict to express their discontent at not having a voice in a sport that caused them great damages. [128] Beyond the border of the V.W.H., the case was viewed as setting a dangerous precedent, which threatened the future of the sport. [129]

Like the Coupland–Cunard controversy, this dispute ended peacefully through compromise. [130] But more important, that compromise was only possible because the farmers had stood resolutely for their rights and, in the end, managed to gain much of what they had fought for. The principle that farmers had a right to a say in the management of hunting was not accepted by many, even as a result of these cases. That they had the power to demand such a say, however, was clear to all, and they occasionally used it. [131]

In some countries, however, they had no need to exercise that power, for slowly they were beginning to be admitted into the councils of the hunt. As early as 1873, the Worcestershire hunt had come under the supervision of three committees, appointed by covert owners, subscribers, and farmers respectively. [132] As we have already seen, the Quorn admitted four farmers to their committee in 1887. The Meynell Hunt, whose rules admitted farmers of fifty acres and upwards to hunt meetings equally with landowners, covert owners, and subscribers, considered admitting farmers to their committee in 1881 and finally admitted four in 1889. [133] The Taunton Vale appointed farmers to their committee in 1888 [134] only to have the new members attempt to make all puppy walkers members of the hunt. [135] In 1890, the South Berkshire allotted three seats on their nine-man committee to farmers. [136]

The new role won by farmers was just as significant as the minimum subscription. It, too, may seem a small step. It was to take time to gain general acceptance, but it had enormous symbolic importance. Though the new power of the farmers was, in a sense, the modernizing of one facet of the hunting ideal, while the minimum subscription was a rejection of another facet, they both tended toward the same end, the transformation of the old hunting society that had lasted since the days of Meynell. The old society had been based upon informal, personal relationships. Though farmers had often been treated unjustly and made to bear far more than their share of the burdens imposed by the sport, hunting society was, nevertheless, predicated upon the ideal of a community. Though survivals of that society have lasted, even to the present day, the new society was to be 'business-like'. Those who hunted were to be made to pay. Those who suffered damages were to be paid. Almost at the end of Victoria's reign, hunting society was taking on the connotations of 'Victorian' that we associate with business and industrialization. It was not until after World War I, if ever, that hunting was truly placed on a 'business-like' footing, but, as a result of the depression, a beginning was made.

CONCLUSION

Between the middle of the eighteenth century and the end of the nineteenth, there were three major turning points in the history of fox-hunting. The first was the development of the modern form of the sport by Hugo Meynell and its adoption over most of the country between 1790 and 1820. The second was the coming of the railways. The third was the agricultural depression.

During the years between Meynell and the railways, hunting ceased to be the sport merely of a few country squires and farmers. It was taken up by a segment of fashionable society and by many more ordinary country dwellers, and thus acquired its image as the most aristocratic and the most popular of field sports. It was also during those years that the mystique that set hunting apart from other sports and raised it to the level of a unique social institution developed.

For hunting people, and for many who never hunted at all, the sport became an integral part of country society and a bond among neighbours, irrespective of their social class. This social bond was used, above all else, to justify the demands that hunting made on all who lived within the district, whether they hunted or not. All residents were expected to aid in the preservation of foxes despite the damages they caused. Farmers and landowners were expected to welcome hunting people on their land despite the damages they caused. In return for these sacrifices, it was believed, the country neighbourhood benefited, not only from the presence of country gentlemen on their estates and the money circulated locally by sportsmen, but also from the good fellowship and neighbourliness that hunting encouraged. The sport was, therefore, looked upon as a conservative force, which, by binding landlord, tenant, and labourer together and giving them a sense of belonging to the same community, acted as a counterweight to the forces of radicalism, urbanization, and industrialization that threatened the stability of that community.

Those who believed this – and they were in the majority – were at least partly correct. Foxhunting was, on the whole, a cohesive force in rural society, and in much the way it was believed to be. It did provide the opportunity for the mingling of members of all classes of country people at the meet, in the field, and at those social functions that were open to everyone. But it was able to do so only because the ideals of deference on which the openness of the hunting field depended were accepted by all. Members of all classes could mingle freely only because the hierarchical structure of the neighbourhood was known to everyone and questioned by no one. In that sense, hunting did not prop up the local social structure. It was, on the contrary, supported by that structure. But given this limitation, hunting could do a great deal toward infusing local relations with a certain cordiality and good-will. At its best, hunting could make landlord and tenant alike feel that they had a shared concern and interest. Even farmers and others who did not hunt took an interest in the doings of the local pack and enjoyed the spectacle, the dinners, and the lawn meets.

While we must not underestimate the importance of this, we must also be careful not to exaggerate it. For all the strength that hunting possessed as a social bond, it could exert that strength only when there was basic harmony among the various classes. Where there was conflict over more important issues, or where hunting men were not considerate of the rights of others, the role of hunting as a conciliator could not be decisive. When times were bad, farmers were less friendly to the sport and far less willing to suffer any losses resulting from it. On the whole, however, the essentially local character of most hunting fields and the relatively limited scale of hunting in the pre-railway years, which kept the damage within reasonable bounds, reduced friction to a minimum.

The years between 1850 and 1875 have been called the 'golden age' of foxhunting. It was during those years that the sport achieved its greatest social prestige but still managed to retain its popular character in many rural districts. It is no accident that these are the years marked at one end by the general introduction of railways, and at the other by the great agricultural depression, nor that they coincide with another 'golden age', that of English agriculture. The railways created hunting's golden age. The railways also were responsible for the eventual collapse of that age, for they created a hunting society that, for all its love of tradition, was increasingly alien to the conditions out of which hunting had developed – conditions that were themselves changing.

In these years of its greatest prosperity, foxhunting was a grand survival of an earlier age. The sport had originated in a traditional, pre-industrial, rural society, and though the institutionalization of hunting organization and the increasing presence of outsiders in the field had robbed it of its original character, it nevertheless mirrored and celebrated the values of that earlier society. In the hunting field, the old England of squires and tenants, of mutual dependence and deference lived on unchanged, unmindful of the growth of cities, of the appearance of new men, and of the establishment of new relationships. It was this that constituted hunting's appeal for so many who hunted and others who merely watched. It was this that made hunting so natural a part of the life of a country gentleman, for in the hunting field, as indeed at the rent-day dinner or the agricultural show, he was fulfilling the natural destiny of his order. It was this that made hunting so attractive to the newly-rich city man who saw it as a quick, simple way of entering the life of that old England.

In the years before the agricultural depression, this old England was not dead; it did not even seem to be dying. The tenacity with which the old images were clung to and the confidence with which hunting society followed its pursuits are eloquent testimony to the reality of the old way of life for so many people.

There is, nevertheless, ample indication that this old way of life could not survive indefinitely. Signs of tension between landlord and tenant were beginning to appear in many areas. The hunting field was not immune to these tensions. The farmer could not help but be aware that the field was becoming increasingly crowded and that hounds and horses were crossing his land more often. This was resented all the more at a time when he was trying to produce a greater yield per acre than ever before, and when more and more of those who trampled the crops seemed to be strangers. In the past, he had been willing to accept a small amount of damage in the interests of neighbourliness, but the days when hunting meant only an occasional incursion by the squire and his few friends had passed in many countries.

Conclusion

Only the agricultural prosperity of these 'golden years' kept many farmers from actually opposing the sport. So long as times were good, farmers were willing to accept some damage – though they quietly took steps to ensure that the damage would not be too great – in the interests of local peace, and because they, too, believed that hunting was a natural part of country life. The agricultural depression put an end to that willingness.

The immediate result of the depression was that farmers began to demand compensation for hunting damages. In itself this would not have been greatly significant, but it led, for the first time, to a questioning of the basic ideals of hunting and its place in country society. For the first time, a sizeable number of farmers began to say what had heretofore been unsayable: that abstract ideas about rural community were no substitute for just dealings; that those who had their land ridden over and their fences broken down had as much right to determine how hunting would be carried out as those who rode over them and broke them; that if hunting men expected them to make special arrangements about fences or stock, they had to be prepared to pay for them. The entire deferential basis of hunting was brought into question, and it could no longer be revived, no matter what recovery agriculture might make.

Hunting people were unwilling to accept many of the farmers' complaints, but even in rejecting them, they launched their own attack on aspects of the hunting ideal. By instituting minimum subscriptions, they acknowledged that hunting had ceased to be the informal gentlemanly amusement of legend, even if they refused to acknowledge that the legendary society had never existed or that it had been unjust. In admitting farmers to hunt committees, they acknowledged that the age of deference was passing. This recognition was perhaps the greatest result of the depression. It is not just that hunting people now had to start paying for what they had been accustomed to receive for nothing. It was, rather, that in hunting, as in so many other areas, the days of the hierarchical rural community were going, though they had not yet gone completely.

Old habits of mind die slowly. The reforms instituted to meet the challenge of the depression were not uniformly adopted, and some of them, as we have seen, were of an essentially conservative nature. Nevertheless, a beginning had been made. The society whose values hunting had mirrored was changing irrevocably, and hunting people had no choice but to follow suit.

A Short Glossary of Hunting Terms

For a more extensive glossary, see D. W. E. Brock, *The A.B.C. of Fox-Hunting, A Handbook for Beginners* (London, 1936), pp. 231-247.

Bag fox, bagged fox,
    bagman: A captured fox, turned out for hunting.
Blank day: A day when no foxes are found.
Brush: A fox's tail.
Bye day: A hunting day in addition to the advertised ones. Provided at the expense of the master.
Cast: An attempt to find a lost scent.
Check: A temporary loss of the scent.
Chop: To kill a fox in a covert.
Couple: Two foxhounds.
Country: The territory in which a pack may draw.
Cover, covert: Woodland or undergrowth in which foxes lie up.
Cubhunting: A training period before the start of the regular season, during which the young hounds are taught to hunt and the young foxes learn that safety lies in breaking from the covert.
Earth: A fox's burrow.
Field: The mounted followers of hounds.
Fixture: Advertised meeting of hounds.
Head: To divert the fox from its original path.

Glossary of hunting terms

M.F.H.:	Master of foxhounds.
Mask:	A fox's head.
Over-ride:	To ride too close to the hounds.
Pad:	A fox's foot.
Provinces, Provincial packs:	All hunts but those in the shires.
Shires:	The Midland grass counties of Leicestershire, Northamptonshire, and Rutland; more particularly, the packs that hunt there – the Belvoir, Cottesmore, Fernie, Pytchley, and Quorn.
Trencher-fed:	A pack that is not kept in a kennel. The hounds are cared for by individual members.
Walk:	To keep a foxhound puppy before it is old enough to hunt is to walk him. The place where the puppy is kept is his walk.

Selected Bibliography

1. Manuscripts

A. Public Collections

Bedford County Record Office.
    Barnard MSS.–BD.
    Lee Antonie MSS.–UN.
    Lucas MS.–L30
    Oakley Hunt MSS.–X213
    Whitbread MSS.–W1; ST1 100
Berkshire Record Office.
    T. T. Morland Letters – D/ELs F17; D/EM F2
    Clippings and Printed Correspondence on Gifford-Morland Dispute – D/EM F3.
    Craven Hunt. Correspondence – D/EW E28.
    Robert Lee, Diary – D/EZ 30F1.
    Old Berks Hunt Club. Printed Rules, 1865 – D/EL1 Z24.
Bury St. Edmunds and West Suffolk Record Office.
    Hunting Journals of John Josselyn, 1845-1883 – 1677/6/10-32.
Devon Record Office.
    Fortescue MSS. Groom's Book, 1813-1816 – 1262m/FE90.
    Lord Ebrington's Hunting Journal – 1262m/FZ25.
Durham County Record Office.
    Londonderry MSS. Wynyard Stable Accounts, 1821-1827 – D/Lo/F462-3.
        Wynyard Pack Hunt Reports – D/Lo/E685.

Selected bibliography

South Durham Hunt. Account Book, 1890-1905 – D/BR/142.
Hunt Club Rules, Various Hunts – D/Sa/X 42-4.
East Riding County Record Office.
    William Constable Maxwell, Correspondence – DDEV60/30.
    Darley MSS.–DAR 77.
    Hunting Diaries of Charles Chichester, 1828-1845 – DDCH.
Essex Record Office.
    Arkwright MSS.–D/DAr.
    DuCane MSS. Papers on Election of 1865 – D/DDc E4/11.
    East Essex Foxhounds. Agreement, 1798 – D/DHa F5.
    Essex Union Foxhounds. Draft Notice, c.a. 1800 – D/DHw F9.
    Hunting Diary of R. Y. Bevan, 1877-1887 – D/DU574/2.
    Essex Union Hunt. Accounts, 1848-1871 – D/DU655.
    Copt Hall Estates. Farm Accounts, 1814 – D/Dw A7.
    Noble, W. F. 'A Survey of the Hundred of Rochford in the County of Essex', Vol. V. Unpublished handwritten book, 1869 – T/P 83/5.
Gloucestershire Records Office.
    Hunting Journals of Nigel Kingscote, 1849-1869 – D471/F21.
    Hunting Journal of R. W. Blathwayt, 1888-1894 – D1799/F283.
Kent Archives Office.
    Lord Guilford, Correspondence, 1871-1877 – U471 E40.
    Knatchbull MSS. Records of Provender Hounds, 1786-1790 – U951 E13.
    Hound Book, 1760-1790 – U1127/E15.
Lincolnshire Archives Office.
    Jarvis MSS. Letters on Hunting, 1874 – Jarvis VII/A/6, 11, 13, 14, 18.
    Monson MSS. Papers on Puppy-Walking – Monson 28A/19/2/23-4.
    Hunting Diaries of the Smith Family, 1813-1920 – Yarb 7.
North Riding County Record Office.
    Printed Pamphlets on Bilsdale Hunt–Hurworth Hunt Boundary Dispute, 1898–C. R. 11.
Northamptonshire Record Office.
    Fitzwilliam Hunt Accounts, 1880-1888 – Box 1794.
    Hunting Diaries, Journals, Accounts of Charles King and H. King – YZ 2585-9.
    Farming Woods Journal, 1770-1826 – YZ 4949.
    Hunting Diary of Sir H. Dryden, 1880-1888 – ZA 477.
Northumberland Record Office.
    Sir Matthew White Ridley, Hunting Papers, 1818-1852 – ZRI 51.
    Papers on Vulpicide, 1884 – ZSA 3/25.
Somerset Record Office.
    Hunting Papers of George Luttrell, West Somerset Hounds, Various Dates – DD/L.

Hunting Diaries of W. B. Portman, 1847-1906 – DD/PMN Box 1.
University of Durham, Department of Paleography and Diplomatic.
Baker Baker MSS. Elemore Kennel Book, 1783-1786 – 16/85.
Durham County Hunt Agreement, 1798 – 18/101–102.
Fourth Earl Grey Papers. Miscellaneous Correspondence, Uncatalogued.
Warwickshire County Record Office.
Quarley Hounds. Papers, 1778-1790 – CR114A/355.

B. *In Private Collections*

Braes of Derwent Hunt and Cowen Family MSS.
  Mr G. A. Cowen, Apperley Dene, Stocksfield, Northumberland.
Burton Hunt MSS.
  Dr Robert Fountain, Lincoln.
Hampshire Hunt MSS.
  Mr P. R. H. Elliott, T.D., Ropley, Alresford, Hants., Honorary Secretary, Hampshire Hunt.
Heythrop Hunt MSS.
  Major J. F. Ballard, Middle Barton, Oxon., Honorary Secretary, Heythrop Hunt.
Hicks-Beach MSS.
  The Rt Hon. the Earl St Aldwyn, Coln St Aldwyns, Fairford, Glos.
New Forest Hunt Club MSS.
  Mrs P. Du Pre,, Minstead, Lyndhurst, Hants., Honorary Secretary, New Forest Hunt.
North Cotswold Hunt MSS.
  Mr M. A. McCanlis, Laverton, Broadway, Worcs., Honorary Secretary, North Cotswold Hunt.
Taunton Vale Foxhounds MSS.
  Major J. P. R. Power, Wellington, Somerset, Honorary Secretary, Taunton Vale Foxhounds.

2. Periodicals and Newspapers

Annals of Sporting and Fancy Gazette, 1822-1828.
Baily's Monthly Magazine of Sports and Pastimes, 1860-1895.
Bell's Life in London and Sporting Chronicle, 1822-1886.
Chelmsford Chronicle, 1865.
Daily Telegraph.
Edinburgh Review, 1809, 1927.
Essex Standard, 1865.
Essex Telegraph, 1865.

Essex Weekly News, 1865.
Essex and West Suffolk Gazette, 1865.
The Farmer's Magazine, 1834-1879.
The Field, or Country Gentleman's Newspaper, 1853-1895.
Fortnightly Review, 1869-1870.
Journal of the Household Brigade, 1862.
Leicester Advertiser, 1868, 1878.
Leicester Chronicle and Leicestershire Mercury, 1868, 1878.
Leicester Daily Mercury, 1878.
Leicester Guardian, 1868.
Leicester Journal, 1868, 1878.
Leicester Mail, 1868.
Life in London, 1822.
Mark Lane Express, 1849-1880.
Middlesex and Hertfordshire Notes and Queries, 1897.
Morning Chronicle.
Morning Herald.
Morning Post.
Murray's Magazine, 1887.
New Sporting Magazine, 1831-1846.
New Tom Spring's Life in London and Sporting Times, 1843-1844.
Pall Mall Gazette.
Pierce Egan's Life in London, and Sporting Times, 1824-1827.
Saturday Review, 1869.
Spectator, 1869-1870.
Sporting Magazine: or Monthly Calendar of the Transactions of the Turf, the Chace and Every Other Diversion Interesting to the Man of Pleasure and Enterprize, 1792-1870.
Sporting Repository, 1822.
Sporting Review, A Monthly Chronicle of the Turf, the Chase, and Rural Sports in all their Varieties, 1839-1846.
Sportsman and Veterinary Recorder, 1835.
Standard.
The Times.
Wilts and Gloucestershire Standard, 1884-1885.

3. Government Publications, Reports, Debates

Hansard's Parliamentary Debates.
The Parliamentary History of England, From the Earliest Period to the Year 1803.
Parliamentary Papers.
    1873, Vol. XIV.'Report From the Select Committee of the House of Lords on Horses'.

1874, Vol. LXXII. 'Return of Owners of Land–1873'. ('New Domesday Book').
1888, Vol. XLVIII. 'First Report of the Royal Commission on Horse Breeding'.
1888, Vol. XLVIII. 'Second Report of the Royal Commission on Horse Breeding'.
1890, Vol. XXVII. 'Third Report of the Royal Commission on Horse Breeding'.
1893, Vol. XXXI. 'Fourth Report of the Royal Commission on Horse Breeding'.
1895, Vol. XXXV. 'Fifth Report of the Royal Commission on Horse Breeding'.
1897, Vol. XV. 'Final Report of the Royal Commission on the Agricultural Depression'.

4. Bibliographies, Reference Books, Directories

The Abolition of Certain Field Sports. House of Commons Library. Bibliography No. LXI.
Baily's Fox-Hunting Directory. London, 1897-1971.
Bateman, John. *The Great Landowners of Great Britain and Ireland.* New ed. London, 1879.
Burke's Landed Gentry.
Burke's Peerage, Baronetage, and Knightage.
Debrett's Peerage, Baronetage, Knightage, and Companionage.
Dictionary of National Biography.
Higginson, Alexander Henry. *British and American Sporting Authors, Their Writings and Biographies.* With a Bibliography by Sydney R. Smith. Berryville, Va., 1949. London and New York, 1951.
Kelly's Handbook to the Titled, Landed and Official Classes. London.
Schwerdt, C. F. G. R. *Hunting, Hawking, Shooting. Illustrated in a Catalogue of Books, Manuscripts, Prints, and Drawings.* 4 vols. London, 1928, 1937.
The Victoria History of the Counties of England.
Walford, Edward. *County Families of the United Kingdom.* London, Various editions.

5. Printed Books and Articles

Acton, C. R. *Sport and Sportsmen of the New Forest.* London, 1936.
Aesop [W. N. Heysham.] *Sporting Reminiscences of Hampshire From 1745 to 1862.* London, 1864.
Aflalo, F. G. *Fifty Leaders of British Sport.* London and New York, 1904.

[Andrews, Tom.] *The Fox Hunting Reminiscences of 'Gin and Beer' and Two 'Turpin' Romances of Local Interest*. Worcester, [1930].
Anstruther Thomson, John. *Eighty Years Reminiscences*. 2 vols. London, 1904.
Apperley, Newton Wynne. *A Hunting Diary*. Edited by E. W. Cuming. London, 1926.
Apsley, Lady [Viola Bathurst, Viscountess Apsley.] *Bridleways Through History*. London, 1936.
Arch, Joseph. *Joseph Arch, The Story of his Life Told by Himself*. London, 1898.
Astley, Sir John Dugdale. *Fifty Years of My Life in the World of Sport at Home and Abroad*. 2 vols. London, 1894.
Auden, J. E. *A Short History of the Albrighton Hunt*. London, 1905.
Austin, Philip. *Our Duty Towards Animals: A Question Considered in the Light of Christian Philosophy*. London, 1885.
Bagatelle [A. G. Bagot.] *Men We Meet in the Field, or, The Bullshire Hounds*. London, 1881.
Ball, Richard Francis, and Gilbey, Tresham. *The Essex Foxhounds with Notes upon Hunting in Essex*. London, 1896.
Bathurst, [Seymour Bathurst,] Seventh Earl. *A History of the V. W. H. Country*. London, 1936.
Beaufort, [Henry Somerset,] Eighth Duke of, and Morris, Mowbray. *Hunting*. The Badminton Library of Sports and Pastimes. 2nd Edition. London, 1886.
[Beckford, Peter.] *Thoughts on Hunting. In a Series of Familiar Letters to a Friend*. Sarum, 1781.
Bell, Isaac. *Foxiana*. London, 1929.
Berkeley, Grantley F. *My Life and Recollections*. 4 vols. London, 1865-1866.
Berkeley, Grantley F. *A Pamphlet, Dedicated to the Noblemen, Gentlemen, and Sportsmen of England, Ireland, and Scotland, by the Hon. Grantley Fitzhardinge Berkeley, M.P. in Reply to a Prize Essay by the Rev. John Styles, D.D. On the Claims of the Animal Creation to the Humanity of Man*. London, 1839.
Berkeley, Grantley F. *Reminiscences of a Huntsman*. London, 1854.
The Berkshire Hounds: Correspondence etc. as to the Dispute between Lord Gifford and Mr. Morland. London, 1845.
Blagg, C. J. *A History of the North Staffordshire Hounds and Country*. London, 1902.
Blaine, Delabere P. *An Encyclopaedia of Rural Sports: or, A Complete Account, Historical, Practical, and Descriptive, of Hunting, Shooting, Fishing, Racing, and other Field Sports and Athletic Amusements of the Present Day*. London, 1840.
[Blane, W., ed.] *Essays on Hunting. Containing a Philosophical Enquiry into the Nature and Properties of the Scent; Observations on the Different Kinds of Hounds with the Manner of Training Them. Also Directions for the Choice of a Hunter; the Qualifications Requisite for a Huntsman; And Other General Rules to be Observed in Every Contingency Incident to the Chace*. Southampton, [1781].

Bovill, E. W. *The England of Nimrod and Surtees, 1815-1854*. London, 1959.
Bovill, E. W. *English Country Life, 1780-1830*. London, 1962.
Bradley, Cuthbert. *The Reminiscences of Frank Gillard (Huntsman) with the Belvoir Hounds, 1860 to 1896*. London, 1898.
Bray, William. *Sketch of a Tour into Derbyshire and Yorkshire including Part of Buckingham, Warwick, Leicester, Nottingham, Northampton, Bedford, and Hartford – Shires*. 2nd ed. London, 1783.
Bridges, J. A. *A Sportsman of Limited Income: Recollections of Fifty Years*. London, 1910.
British Blood Sports: 'Let Us Go Out and Kill Something'. London, 1901.
British Hunts and Huntsmen. 4 vols. London, 1908-11.
Brock, D. W. E. *The ABC of Fox-Hunting, A Handbook for Beginners*. London, 1936.
Bromley Davenport, W. 'Fox-Hunting'. *Nineteenth Century*, XIII (June, 1883), 978-991.
Brooksby [E. Pennell–Elmhirst.] *The Best Season on Record*. London and New York, 1884.
Brooksby [E. Pennell–Elmhirst.] *The Cream of Leicestershire*. London and New York, 1883.
Brooksby [E. Pennell–Elmhirst.] *Fox-Hound, Forest, and Prairie*. London, 1892.
Brooksby [E. Pennell–Elmhirst.] *The Hunting Countries of England*. London; 1878.
Bryden, H. A. 'Foxhunting, Past and Present'. *Edinburgh Review*, CCXLVI (October, 1927), 303-319.
Burrows, George T. *Gentleman Charles: A History of Foxhunting*. London, 1951.
Burn, W. L. *The Age of Equipose, A Study of the Mid-Victorian Generation*. New York, 1965.
Byng, Hon. John (later 5th Viscount Torrington). *The Torrington Diaries, Containing the Tours through England and Wales of the Hon. John Byng between the years 1781 and 1794*. Edited by C. Bruyn Andrews. 4 vols. London, 1934.
Butler, E. M., ed. *A Regency Visitor, The English Tour of Prince Pückler-Muskau Described in his Letters, 1826-1828*. London, 1957.
Cecil [Cornelius Tongue.] *Records of the Chase, and Memoirs of Celebrated Sportsmen; Illustrating Some of the Usages of Olden Times, and Comparing Them with Prevailing Customs, Together with an Introduction to Most of the Fashionable Hunting Countries, and Comments*. London, 1854.
Chalmers, Patrick. *The History of Hunting*. The Lonsdale Library, Vol. XXIII. London, [1936].
Chalmers, Thomas. *On Cruelty to Animals: A Sermon, Preached in Edinburgh, on the 5th of March, 1826*. Glasgow, 1826.
Champion de Crespigny, Sir Claude, Bt. *Forty years of a Sportsman's Life*. 2nd ed.

Selected bibliography 189

London, 1910.
[Channing, John.] *Hunting Journal of the Blackmoor Vale Hounds, from 1826 to 1831.* Sherborne, 1831.
Chitty, J. *Continuation of a Treatise on the Law Respecting Game and Fish, with a Copious Collection of Precedents:...* London, 1816.
Chitty, J. *A Treatise on the Game Laws, and on Fisheries.* 2nd ed. London, 1826.
Coaten, Arthur, ed. *British Hunting: A Complete History of the National Sport of Great Britain and Ireland from Earliest Records.* London, [1910].
Cobbett, William. *Rural Rides in the Counties of Surrey, Kent, Sussex, Hampshire, Wiltshire, Gloucestershire, Herefordshire, Worcestershire, Somersetshire, Oxfordshire, Berkshire, Essex, Suffolk, Norfolk, and Hertfordshire:...* London, 1830.
Collins, George E. *Farming and Foxhunting.* London, n.d.
Collins, George E. *History of the Brocklesby Hounds 1700-1901.* London, 1902.
Cook, Colonel [John.] *Observations on Fox-Hunting, and the Management of Hounds in the Kennel and the Field. Addressed to a Young Sportsman, About to Undertake a Hunting Establishment.* London, 1826.
Cooper, Leonard. *R. S. Surtees.* London, 1952.
Corballis, James Henry. *Forty-Five Years of Sport.* Edited by Arthur T. Fisher. London, 1891.
Corbett, Henry. *Tales and Traits of Sporting Life.* London, 1864.
Cowen, G. A. *The Braes of Derwent Hunt: A Hundred Years of Foxhunting in the Derwent Valley.* Gateshead on Tyne, 1955.
Cox, Harding. *Chasing and Racing: Some Sporting Reminiscences.* London and New York, 1922.
Cuming, E. D. *British Sport Past and Present.* London, 1909.
Curtis, J. *A Topographical History of the County of Leicester.* Ashby-De-La-Zouch, 1831.
Dale, T. F. *The Eighth Duke of Beaufort and the Badminton Hunt. With a Sketch of the Rise of the Somerset Family.* Westminster, 1899.
Dale, T. F. *Fox-Hunting in the Shires.* The Hunting Library, Edited by F. G. Aflalo. Vol. II. London, 1903.
Dale, T. F. *The History of the Belvoir Hunt.* Westminster, 1899.
Daniel, Rev. William B. *Rural Sports.* 2 vols. London, 1801.
Darton, F. J. Harvey. *From Surtees to Sassoon: Some English Contrasts (1838-1928).* London, 1931.
Davenport, Henry S. *Memories at Random: Melton and Harborough.* London, 1926.
[Davies, Edward William Lewis.] *A Memoir of the Rev. John Russell, and His Out-of-Door Life.* London, 1878.
de Costobadie, F. Palliser. *Annals of the Billesdon Hunt (Mr. Fernie's) 1856-1913.* London and Leicester, 1914.

Delmé Radcliffe, F. P. *The Noble Science: A Few General Ideas on Fox-Hunting, For the Use of the Rising Generation of Sportsmen, and More Especially those of the Hertfordshire Hunt Club.* London, 1839.
Dixie, Lady Florence. 'The Mercilessness of Sport'. *Humanitarian Essays.* 2nd Ser. London, 1904.
Dixon, Henry Hall. *A Treatise on the Law of the Farm: including the Agricultural Customs of England and Wales.* London, 1858.
Dixon, William Scarth. *A History of the Bramham Moor Hunt.* Leeds, 1898.
Dixon, William Scarth. *A History of the York and Ainsty Hunt.* Leeds, 1899.
Dixon, William Scarth. *In the North Countree: Annals and Anecdotes of Horse, Hound, and Herd.* London, 1900.
Dixon, William Scarth. *The Ledbury and North Ledbury Hunts.* London, 1933.
The Druid [Henry Hall Dixon.] *The Post and the Paddock: with Recollections of George IV, Sam Chifney, and Other Turf Celebrities.* Hunting Edition: London, [1857].
The Druid [Henry Hall Dixon.] *Saddle and Sirloin, or English Farm and Sporting Worthies.* Part North. London, 1870.
The Druid [Henry Hall Dixon.] *Scott and Sebright.* London, 1862.
The Druid [Henry Hall Dixon.] *Silk and Scarlet.* London, 1859.
Drummond, William H. *The Rights of Animals, and Man's Obligation to Treat Them with Humanity.* London and Dublin, 1838.
Durham, J. M. B., and Richardson, R. J. *Melton and Homespun: Nature and Sport in Prose and Verse.* London, 1913.
Eardley-Wilmot, Sir John E. *Reminiscences of the Late Thomas Assheton Smith, Esq., or, the Pursuits of an English Country Gentleman.* London, 1860.
Edwards, Lionel. *Famous Foxhunters.* London, 1938.
Eeles, Henry S. *The Eridge Hunt.* Tunbridge Wells, 1936.
Ellangowan. *Sporting Anecdotes.* London and Glasgow, 1889.
Elliott, John Malsbury Kirby. *Fifty Year's Fox-Hunting with the Grafton and Other Packs of Hounds.* Edited by Edward Kirby Elliott. London, 1900.
Ellis, Colin D. B. *Leicestershire and the Quorn Hunt.* Leicester, 1951.
Ernle, [Rowland E. Prothero,] Lord. *English Farming, Past and Present*, 6th ed. Chicago, 1961.
Faber, Walter. *Wit and Wisdom of the Shires.* Leicester, 1932.
Fairholme, Edward G., and Pain, Wellesley. *A Century of Work for Animals: The History of the R.S.P.C.A., 1824-1934.* 2nd. ed. London, 1934.
Fane, Lady Augusta. *Chit-Chat.* London, 1926.
Farr, M. W. 'Sir Edward Littleton's Fox-Hunting Diary 1774-89'. To be published in *Essays in Staffordshire History.*
Fawcett, William. *Sporting Spectacle: A Cavalcade of Sport in England's Yesteryear.* London, 1939.
Fitt, J. Nevill. *Covert-Side Sketches: or, Thoughts on Hunting Suggested by Many*

Days in Many Countries with Fox, Deer, and Hare. London, 1878.
Fletcher, T. W. 'The Great Depression of English Agriculture, 1873-1896'. *Economic History Review*, 2nd Ser., XIII (April, 1961), 417-432.
Forester, Frank [Henry William Herbert.] *The Quorndon Hounds: or, A Virginian at Melton Mowbray*. Philadelphia, 1852.
Fowler, J. K. *Echoes of Old Country Life, being Recollections of Sport, Politics, and Farming in the Good Old Times*. London, 1892.
'*A Fox's Tale*': *A Sketch of the Hunting-Field*. By the Author of 'The Autobiography of the Late Salmo Salar, Esq.' London, 1867.
Francis, Francis. *Newton Dogvane. A Story of English Country Life*. 3 vols. London, 1859.
Freeman, E. A. 'The Controversy on Field Sports'. *Fortnightly Review*, XIV (December 1, 1870), 674-691.
Freeman, E. A. 'The Morality of Field Sports'. *Fortnightly Review*, XII (October 1, 1869), 353-385.
Frewen, Moreton. *Melton Mowbray and Other Memories*. London, 1924.
'The Future of Hunting'. *Murray's Magazine*, April, 1887, pp. 527-541.
Gèlert. *A Guide to the Foxhounds and Staghounds of England: to which are added the Otter-Hounds and Harriers of Several Counties*. London, 1908.
Godber, Joyce, ed. *The Oakley Hunt*. Publications of the Bedfordshire Historical Record Society, Vol. XLIV. Bedford, 1965.
Gomersall, William. *Hunting in Craven*. Skipton, [1889].
Goodall, Daphne Machin. *Huntsmen of a Golden Age: Stephen Goodall, 1757-1823, William Goodall, 1817-1859*. London, 1956.
Graham, Sir Reginald. *Fox-Hunting Recollections*. London, 1907.
Greaves, Ralph. *Fox Hunting in Hampshire*. London, n.d.
Greaves, Ralph. *Foxhunting in Leicestershire and Northamptonshire*. London, n.d.
Greaves, Ralph. *A Short History of the Oakley Hunt*. London, n.d.
Greaves, Ralph. *Taunton Vale Hunt and Taunton Vale Harriers, Official Handbook*. London, n.d.
Greville, [Violet,] Lady, ed. *Ladies in the Field*. New York, 1894.
Hamilton, Colonel J. P. *Reminiscences of an Old Sportsman*. 2 vols. London, 1860.
The Hare: or, Hunting Incompatible with Humanity: Written as a Stimulus to Youth Towards a Proper Treatment of Animals. London, 1799.
Harewood, Harry. *A Dictionary of Sports: or, Companion to the Field, the Forest, and the Riverside*. London, 1835.
Harrison, Brian. 'Animals and the State in Nineteenth-Century England'. *English Historical Review*, LXXXVIII (October, 1973), pp. 786–820.
Harrison, Brian. 'Religion and Recreation in Nineteenth-Century England'. *Past and Present*, 38 (December, 1967), pp. 98-125.
Hawkes, John. *The Meynellian Science, or Fox-Hunting Upon System*. Leicester, 1932.

[Helps, Sir A.] *Some Talk about Animals and their Masters.* London, 1873.
Hieover, Harry [Charles Bindley.] *The Hunting-Field.* London, 1850.
Hieover, Harry [Charles Bindley.] *Sporting Facts and Sporting Fancies.* London, 1853.
Higginson, Alexander Henry. *'The Meynell of the West': being a Biography of James John Farquharson, Esqre, Master of Fox-Hounds, 1806-1858.* London, 1936.
Higginson, Alexander Henry. *Two Centuries of Foxhunting.* London, 1946.
Hill, J. Woodroffe. *The Relative Positions of the Higher and Lower Creation: or, A Plea for Dumb Animals.* London, 1881.
Hodgson, J. C., ed. *North Country Diaries.* Publications of the Surtees Society, Vols. CXVIII, CXXIV. Durham, 1910, 1915.
Hole, Christina. *English Sports and Pastimes.* London, 1949.
Howitt, William. *The Rural Life of England.* 2 vols. London, 1838.
Humanitarian Essays, 2nd Ser. London, 1904.
Humanitarian League. *Annual Reports.* London.
Hurst, Mrs Victor. *Hunting, Shooting and Fishing.* London, 1953.
Hutchinson, G. T. *The Heythrop Hunt.* London, 1935.
Impecuniosus. *Unasked Advice: A Series of Articles on Horses and Hunting, Reprinted From 'The Field'.* London, 1872.
Johnson, T. B. *The Hunting Directory: Containing a Compendious View of the Ancient and Modern Systems of the Chase, The Method of Breeding and Managing the Various Kinds of Hounds, Particularly Fox Hounds . . . Together with a Variety of Illustrative Observations.* London, 1826.
Jones, Owen. *Ten Years of Game-Keeping.* London, 1910.
Jones, Thomas. *A Diary of the Quorndon Hunt, From the Year 1791 to 1800, Inclusive, in which will be Given a Succinct Detail of Every Day's Sport, etc. To which will be Subjoined, The Celebrated Billesdon Coplow Pamphlet.* Derby, 1816.
Jones, William. *The Diary of the Revd William Jones, 1777-1821.* Edited by O. F. Christie. London, 1929.
K., T. [T. Kemble.] *Sporting Reminiscences of an Old Squire: Being Notes Jotted Down in a Farming Book.* Chelmsford, 1887.
Kendall, S. G. *Farming Memoirs of a West Country Yeoman.* London, 1944.
Kennard, Mrs. Edward. *The Right Sort: A Romance of the Shires.* London and New York, [1886].
Kent, John. *A Few of My Most Favourite Fox Chases in East Sussex.* Lewes, n.d.
Kent, Nathaniel. *Hints to Gentlemen of Landed Property.* London, 1775.
Kingsley, Charles. *Prose Idylls, New and Old.* London and New York. 1907.
Kirby, Chester. *The English Country Gentleman: A Study of Nineteenth Century Types.* London, [1937].
Kitchen, Fred. *Brother to the Ox: The Autobiography of a Farm Labourer.* London,

Selected bibliography

1940.
Kitson Clark, G. *The Making of Victorian England.* Cambridge, Mass., 1962.
Lambert, Uvedale. *Jorrocks' Country.* London, 1961.
Lawrence, John. *A Philosophical and Practical Treatise on Horses, and on the Moral Duties of Man towards the Brute Creation.* 2 vols. London, 1796, 1798.
Lee, J. M. *Social Leaders and Public Persons: A Study of County Government in Cheshire Since 1888.* Oxford, 1963.
Le Marchant, Sir Denis. *Memoir of John Charles, Viscount Althorp, Third Earl Spencer.* London, 1876.
Lennox, Lord William. *Merry England: Its Sports and Pastimes.* London, 1857.
Loder-Symonds, F. C., and Crowdy, E. Percy. *A History of the Old Berks Hunt From 1760 to 1904.* London, 1905.
Londonderry, Edith Stewart, Marchioness of. *Henry Chaplin, A Memoir.* London, 1926.
Lucas, G. F. *Memoirs of an Undistinguished Man.* Kettering, Northants, 1955.
Macaulay, James. *Essay on Cruelty to Animals.* Edinburgh, 1839.
Macaulay, James. *Plea for Mercy to Animals.* London, [1875].
McNeill, C. F. P. *The Unwritten Laws of Foxhunting.* London, [1911].
Malcolmson, Robert W. *Popular Recreations in English Society, 1700-1850.* Cambridge, 1973.
Mason, G. Finch. *Flowers of the Hunt.* London, 1889.
[Maxwell, W. Hamilton.] *The Field Book: or Sports and Pastimes of the British Islands: by the Author of 'Wild Sports of the West'.* London, [1833].
Meysey-Thompson, R. F. *Reminiscences of the Course, the Camp, the Chase.* London, 1898.
[Mills, John.] *D'Horsay: or, The Follies of the Day.* By A Man of Fashion. London, 1844.
Mitford, Nancy, ed. *The Ladies of Alderley: Being the Letters between Maria Josepha, Lady Stanley of Alderley and Her Daughter-in-Law Henrietta Maria Stanley during the Years 1841-1850.* London, 1938.
Moore, D. C. 'Politics of Deference: A Study of the Political Structure, Leadership, and Organization of English County Constituencies in the Nineteenth Century'. Unpublished Ph.D. dissertation, Columbia University, 1958, now published as 'Politics of Deference: a study of the mid-nineteenth century English Political System' by the Harvester Press Ltd., Hassocks, Sussex, 1976.
Moore, Thomas. *The Sin and Folly of Cruelty to Brute Animals: A Sermon.* Birmingham, 1810.
Mordaunt, Sir Charles, and Verney, Hon. and Rev. W. R. *Annals of the Warwickshire Hunt, 1795-1895, From Authentic Documents.* 2 vols. London, 1896.
Nelson, William. *The Laws Concerning Game, etc.* 6th ed. London, 1762.

Nethercote, H. O. *The Pytchley Hunt: Past and Present.* London, 1888.
Nevill, Ralph. *English County House Life.* London, 1925.
Newsome, David. *Godliness and Good Learning: Four Studies on a Victorian Ideal.* London, 1961.
Nicholson, Edward Byron. *The Rights of an Animal: A New Essay in Ethics.* London, 1879.
Nimrod [C. J. Apperley.] *The Chace, The Turf, and The Road.* London, 1837.
Nimrod [C. J. Apperley.] *The Life of John Mytton, Esq.* New ed., Revised and Enlarged. London, [1871].
Nimrod [C. J. Apperley.] *The Life of a Sportsman.* London, 1842.
Nimrod [C. J. Apperley.] *My Life and Times.* Edited with additions by E. D. Cuming. Edinburgh, London, and New York, 1927.
(Nimrod [C. J. Apperley.]) *Nimrod's Hunting Reminiscences. Comprising Memoirs of Masters of Hounds, Notices of the Crack Riders, and Characteristics of the Hunting Countries of England.* London, [1926].
(Nimrod [C. J. Apperley.]) *Nimrod's Hunting Tours Interspersed with Characteristic Anecdotes, Sayings, and Doings of Sporting Men....* London, 1903.
Nimrod [C. J. Apperley]. *Nimrod's Hunting Tour in Scotland and the North of England.* London, [1874].
Noakes, Aubrey. *Horses, Hounds and Humans: Being the Dramatized Story of R. S. Surtees.* [London, 1957].
The Oakley Club. Bedford, 1901.
Orchard, Vincent. *Tattersalls, – Two Hundred Years of Sporting History.* London, 1953.
[Ord, Richard.] *The Sedgefield Country in the Seventies and Eighties, with the Reminiscences of a First Whipper-in.* Written and Compiled by the Author of the Fox-Hunter's 'Vade Mecum'. Darlington, 1904.
Osbaldeston, George. *Squire Osbaldeston: His Autobiography.* Edited, with commentary by E. D. Cuming. London, [1927].
Oswald, John. *The Cry of Nature: or, An Appeal to Mercy and to Justice, on behalf of the Persecuted Animals.* London, 1791.
Paget, Guy. *The History of the Althorp and Pytchley Hunt, 1634-1920.* London, 1937.
Paget, Guy. *The Melton Mowbray of John Ferneley, 1782-1860.* Leicester and New York, 1931.
Paget, Guy, and Irvine, Lionel, eds. *The Flying Parson and Dick Christian.* Leicester, 1934.
Pease, A. E. *The Cleveland Hounds as a Trencher-Fed Pack.* London, 1887.
Pell, Albert. *The Reminiscences of Albert Pell, Sometime M.P. for South Leicestershire.* Edited with an introduction by Thomas Mackay. London, 1908.
Primatt, Humphrey. *A Dissertation on the Duty of Mercy and Sin of Cruelty to*

Selected bibliography 195

Brute Animals. London, 1776.
Quarrell, Thomas Read. *The Worcestershire Hunt.* Worcester, 1929.
Randall, J. L. *A History of the Meynell Hounds and Country, 1780 to 1901.* 2 vols. London, 1901.
Reynard, Frank H. *Hunting Notes From Holderness.* [London, 1914].
Rose, R. N. *The Field, 1853-1953: A Centenary Volume.* London, 1953.
Rumbold, C.E.A.L. 'The Development of Fox-Hunting'. *Badminton Magazine*, VIII(January, 1899), 104-111.
Russell, Fox. *Cross Country Reminiscences.* London, 1887.
[Savile, Albany.] *Thirty-Six Hints to Sportsmen.* Okehampton, [c. 1825].
Scott, J. Robson. *My Life as Soldier and Sportsman.* London, 1921.
Scott, William Henry. *British Field Sports: Embracing Practical Instructions in Shooting – Hunting – Coursing, etc.* London, 1818.
Scrutator [K. W. Horlock.] *The Master of Hounds.* 3 vols. London, 1859.
Scrutator [K. W. Horlock.] *Recollections of a Fox-Hunter.* 2nd ed. London, 1925.
Shee, William Archer. *My Contemporaries, 1830-1870.* London, 1893.
Shenstone, J. C. 'A Yeoman's Common-Place Book at the Commencement of the Nineteenth Century'. *Essex Review*, XVI(April, 1907), 73-89.
Simond, Louis. *Journal of a Tour and Residence in Great Britain, during the years 1810 and 1811.* 2 vols. 2nd ed. Edinburgh, 1817.
Simpson, Charles. *Trencher and Kennel: Some Famous Yorkshire Packs.* London, 1927.
[Smith, Sydney.] 'Proceedings of the Society for the Suppression of Vice'. *Edinburgh Review*, XIII(January, 1809), 333-343.
Smith, Thomas, *Extracts from the Diary of a Huntsman.* London, 1838.
Smith, Thomas. *The Life of a Fox and Extracts from the Diary of a Huntsman.* London, 1897.
Sporting Incidents in the Life of Another Tom Smith. London, 1867.
The Sportsman's Dictionary: or, The Country Gentleman's Companion, in All Rural Recreations. . . . Extracted from the Most Celebrated English and French Authors, Ancient, and Modern . . . Illustrated with Near Thirty Copper-Plates . . . 2 vols. London, 1735.
Stanley, Maria Josepha, Lady. *The Early Married Life of Maria Josepha Lady Stanley, with Extracts from Sir John Stanley's 'Praeterita'.* Edited by Jane H. Adeane. London, 1899.
Steel, Anthony. *Jorrock's England.* London, 1932.
Stephens, W. R. W. *The Life and Letters of Edward A. Freeman D.C.L., LL.D.* 2 vols. London, 1895.
Stillingfleet, Edward, Bishop of Worcester [William Gilpin.] *On the Amusements of Clergymen, and Christians in General: Three Dialogues between a Dean and a Curate.* London, 1820.

Stonehenge [J. H. Walsh.] *Manual of British Rural Sports: Comprising Shooting, Hunting, Coursing, Fishing, Hawking, Racing, Boating, Pedestrianism, and the Various Rural Games and Amusements of Great Britain.* London, 1856.
Stretton, Charles. *Memoires of a Chequered Life.* 3 vols. London, 1862.
Stretton, Charles. *Sport and Sportsmen: A Book of Recollections.* London, 1866.
Styles, Rev. John. *The Animal Creation: Its Claims on Our Humanity Stated and Enforced.* London, [1839].
[Surtees, R. S.] *The Analysis of the Hunting Field: Being a Series of Sketches of the Principal Characters that Compose One. The Whole Forming a Slight Souvenir of the Season, 1845-6.* London, 1846.
Surtees. R. S. *Mr. Facey Romford's Hounds.* Westminster, 1952.
Surtees, R. S. *Handley Cross.* London, 1951.
Surtees, R. S. *Hawbuck Grange, or, The Sporting Adventures of Thomas Scott, Esq.* London, 1847.
Surtees, R. S. *Hillingdon Hall, or, The Cockney Squire.* London, 1888.
[Surtees, R. S.] *The Hunting Tours of Surtees (Creator of Jorrocks).* Edited by E. D. Cuming. Edinburgh, London, and New York, 1927.
Surtees, R. S. *Jorrocks Jaunts and Jollities.* London, [1901].
Surtees, R. S. *Mr Sponge's Sporting Tour.* London, 1852.
Sutherland, Douglas. *The Yellow Earl: The Life of Hugh Lowther, 5th Earl of Lonsdale, K.G., G.C.V.O., 1857-1944.* London, 1965.
Symonds, Henry. *Runs and Sporting Notes from Dorsetshire.* Blandford, 1899.
Tawke, Miss [Augusta S.] *Hunting Recollections.* Rochford, 1911.
Taylor, Helen. 'A Few Words on Mr Trollope's Defence of Fox Hunting'. *Fortnightly Review*, XIII(January 1, 1870), 63-68.
Taylor, Humphrey R. *The Old Surrey Fox Hounds: A History of the Hunt from Its Earliest Days to the Present Time.* Edited by G. G. – H. G. Harper. London, 1906.
Thomas, Joseph B. *Hounds and Hunting Through the Ages.* London, 1928.
Thomas, Sir William Beach. *Hunting England: A Survey of the Sport, and of Its Chief Grounds.* London, 1936.
Thompson, F. M. L. *English Landed Society in the Nineteenth Century.* London and Toronto, 1963.
Thormanby [Wilmot W. Dixon.] *Kings of the Hunting-Field.* London, 1899.
Tozer, Edward J. F. *The South Devon Hunt.* Teignmouth, 1916.
Trollope, Anthony, *The American Senator.* The World's Classics, No. 139. London, [1962].
Trollope, Anthony, *Hunting Sketches.* London, 1865.
Trollope, Anthony. 'Mr Freeman on the Morality of Hunting'. *Fortnightly Review*, XII(December 1, 1869), 616-625.
Underhill, George F. *Hunting and Practical Hints for Hunting Men.* London, 1897.

Underhill, George F. *In at the Death: A Tale of Society*. London, 1888.
Underhill, George F. *The Master of Hounds*. The Hunting Library, Edited by F. G. Aflalo. Vol. III. London, 1903.
Venator [John Cooper]. *The Warwickshire Hunt, from 1795 to 1836: Describing Many of the Most Splendid Runs*. . . . London and Warwick, 1837.
Vyner, Robert T. *Notitia Venatica: A Treatise on Fox-Hunting. To Which is Added, A Compendious Kennel Stud Book*. London, 1841.
Vyner, Robert T. *Notitia Venatica: A Treatise on Fox-Hunting. Embracing the General Management of Hounds and the Diseases of Dogs: Including Distemper and Rabies: Also Kennel Lameness, Its Cause and Cure*. 6th ed. Revised, corrected, and enlarged, with appendix. London, [1871].
Vyner, Robert T. *Notitia Venatica: A Treatise on Fox-Hunting, Embracing the General Management of Hounds*. A new edition. Revised, corrected, and enlarged by William C. A. Blew. London, 1892.
Vyner, Robert T. *Notitia Venatica. A Treatise on Fox-Hunting, Embracing the General Management of Hounds*. 2 vols. A new edition. Revised, corrected, and enlarged by William C. A. Blew. Revised and brought down to date by Cuthbert Bradley. London, 1910.
Watson, Alfred E. T., ed. *The Year's Sport: A Review of British Sports and Pastimes for the Year 1885*. London, 1886.
Watson, Frederick. *Robert Smith Surtees, A Critical Study*. London, 1933.
Webster, B. G. E. *The Badsworth Hunt: Official Handbook*. London, n.d.
[Whyte, Melville, George John.] *Market Harborough: or, How Mr. Sawyer Went to the Shires*. London, 1861.
Wilkins, John. *The Autobiography of an English Gamekeeper*. Edited by Arthur H. Byng and Stephen M. Stephens. 2nd ed., revised. London, 1892.
Willoughby de Broke, Richard Greville Verney, Nineteenth Lord, ed. *The Sport of Our Ancestors, Being a Collection of Prose and Verse Setting Forth the Sport of Fox-Hunting As They Knew It*. London, 1921.
Wilson, Harriette, *Memoirs of Harriette Wilson*. 4 vols. London, 1825.
Wilson, William. *Green Peas at Christmas: Hunting Reminiscences*. Edited by the Rt. Hon. Sir Guy Fleetwood Wilson. London, 1924.
Wingfield-Stratford, Esmé. *The Squire and His Relations*. London, 1956.
Woodforde, Rev. James. *The Diary of a Country Parson*. Edited by John Beresford. 5 vols. Oxford, 1968.
Yerbergh, H. Beauchamp. *Leaves from a Hunting Diary in Essex*. 2 vols. London, 1900.
Youatt, W. *The Obligation and Extent of Humanity to Brutes. Principally Considered with Reference to the Domesticated Animals*. London, 1839.

NOTES TO TEXT

Introduction

[1] The techniques of foxhunting have been treated by many authors, beginning with Peter Beckford in 1781. A good modern introduction is D.W.E. Brock, *The A.B.C. of Foxhunting* (London and New York, 1936).
[2] *Baily's Mag.*, XXII (January, 1872), pp. 90-94.
[3] I have met children who were blooded with the Burton Hunt in Lincolnshire.

Chapter one

[1] 8 Eliz. I, c.15.
[2] Edward, Earl of Clarendon, *The History of the Rebellion and Civil Wars in England* (8vols.; Oxford, 1826), I, p. 407.
[3] For the claims of several hunts to be the first in the country to hunt foxes, see Robert Vyner, *Notitia Venatica: A Treatise on Fox-Hunting Embracing the General Management of Hounds...* (6th ed. rev.; London [1871]), p. 45; *ibid.* (New Edition; London, 1892), pp. 23 n.1, 84 n.1; A. Henry Higginson, *Two Centuries of Foxhunting* (London, 1946), p.43.
[4] The Nationality of Great Britain depends upon his [the fox's] existence. *Sp.Mag.*, CXI (May, 1849), p. 347.
[5] F.M.L. Thompson, *English Landed Society in the Nineteenth Century* (London and Toronto, 1963), p. 150.
[6] See, for example, M.W. Farr, 'Sir Edward Littleton's Fox-Hunting Diary, 1774-89' in *Essays in Staffordshire History*. Mr Farr kindly showed me a proof of this article before publication.

⁷*Sp. Mag.*, XVII (January, 1801), p. 176; XXIV (March, 1804), p. 296. Colonel [John] Cook *Observations on Fox-Hunting, and the Management of Hounds in the Kennel and the Field, Addressed to a Young Sportsman, About to Undertake a Hunting Establishment* (London, 1826), p. 143.

⁸[Peter Beckford], *Thoughts on Hunting. In a Series of Familiar Letters to a Friend* (Sarum, 1781), p. 178.

⁹*Sp. Mag.*, VII (November, 1795), p. 69.

¹⁰Cook, *Observations on Fox-Hunting*, p. 139.

¹¹Meynell was heir to a large fortune founded in the seventeenth century by a banker and Sheriff of the City of London. The fortune was increased by Meynell's father, an inveterate gambler and friend of Frederick, Prince of Wales. In addition to his sporting activities, Hugo Meynell was well-known in fashionable London circles, served as M.P. in the Grafton interest from 1762 to 1780, and was High Sheriff of Derbyshire. For details of his life, see Colin D.B. Ellis, *Leicestershire and the Quorn Hunt* (Leicester, 1951), pp. 8-13; 'Thormanby' Wilmot W. Dixon, *Kings of the Hunting Field* (London, 1899), pp. 58-67; and Sir Lewis Namier and John Brooke, *The House of Commons 1754-1790* (3 vols.; London, 1964), III, pp. 134-135. Much of my discussion of Meynell is taken from Ellis' book which is one of the few reliable hunt histories.

¹²It is significant that the farm on which Bakewell conducted his famous animal breeding experiments is less than six miles from Quorn Hall. Ellis, *Leicestershire and the Quorn*, p. 14.

¹³*Ibid.*, pp. 23-24.

¹⁴*Ibid.*, pp. 24-26.

¹⁵'Cecil' [Cornelius Tongue], *Records of the Chase, and Memoirs of Celebrated Sportsmen; illustrating some of the Usages of Olden Times...*(London, 1854), p. 120. Ellis, *Leicestershire and the Quorn*, p. 12.

¹⁶MS. letter, Bedford County Record Office, L30/11/151/16. Also see William Bray, *Sketch of a Tour into Derbyshire and Yorkshire...*(2nd ed.; London, 1783), p. 98.

¹⁷Bray, *Sketch of a Tour*, p. 98.

¹⁸Hon. John Byng (later 5th Viscount Torrington), *The Torrington Diaries: containing the tours through England and Wales of the Hon. John Byng between the years 1781 and 1794*, ed. by C. Bruyn Andrews (4 vols.; London, 1934), II, p. 85. Ellis, *Leicstershire and the Quorn*, p. 16.

¹⁹Ellis, *Leicestershire and the Quorn*, pp. 18, 19.

²⁰When Nimrod first visited Melton in 1802, 'there was only one inn, and that a very bad one; not one bank, and but a few houses with which a well-breeched Meltonian would be satisfied.' Quoted in *Ibid.*, p. 18. In John Nichol's history of Leicestershire, published in 1800, there was no reference to hunting under 'Melton Mowbray'. *Ibid.*, p. 3.

²¹See, for example, the famous poem, 'The Billesdon Coplow Run,' written in

1800 to celebrate one of the greatest runs of the Quorn under Meynell, in *Sp. Mag.*, XVI (April, 1800), pp. 45-52, and since reprinted many times. The footnotes already speak of the pre-eminence of Melton, and the feeling of the Meltonians of their own superiority.

[22] For hunting people, 'the shires' refers to the great grasslands of the Midland counties of Leicestershire, Northamptonshire, and Rutland, but more particularly, to the fashionable packs that hunt there — the Quorn, Belvoir, Cottesmore, and Pytchley, and later, to the Billesdon, or Fernie, a country that split off from the Quorn in the mid-nineteenth century. Some have also included several other packs, notably the Atherstone and the Warwickshire, but strictly speaking only the first group are 'shire' packs. All others, from the greatest to the smallest, are 'provincial' packs.

[23] Ellis, *Leicestershire and the Quorn*, p. 16.

[24] *Sp. Mag.*, XV (December, 1799), p. 109.

[25] Questions of chonology here must be extremely loose. Over the country as a whole there was wide regional variation, and practices that had died out in Leicestershire by 1780, for example, may have survived in some of the more remote sections of Yorkshire as late as the 1880s. Nor was this variation solely the result of geographical distance, for neighbouring hunts might differ widely. This is not to say, however, that there were not certain definite accepted practices that could generally be found in all parts of the country, and the railways lessened regional variations as the nineteenth century progressed. Nevertheless, backwaters did exist where it was possible, as late as 1880, to see hunting much as it had existed one hundred years earlier.

[26] J.S. Gardiner, 'Six Letters on Hunting' (1750) in [W. Blane, ed.], *Essays on Hunting. Containing a Philosophical Enquiry into the Nature and Properties of Scent... And Other General Rules to be Observed in Every Contingency Incident to the Chace.* (Southampton, [1781]), pp. 52-53.

[27] See *Sp. Mag.*, I (December, 1792), p. 170; X (May, 1796), p. 98; XVII (December, 1800), p. 139, for accounts of foxhunts with harriers.

[28] Richard Francis Ball and Tresham Gilbey, *The Essex Foxhounds: With Notes upon Hunting in Essex* (London, 1896), p. 47; *Sp. Mag.*, LXXI (December, 1827), p. 124; Vyner, *Notitia Venatica* (New edition, 1892), p. 28 n.2.

[29] MS letter, Richard Orlebar to the Duke of Bedford, March 21, 1796. Bedford County Record Office, BS 460/3.

[30] *Sp. Mag.*, III (March, 1794), p. 337.

[31] *Ibid.*, VII (October, 1795), p. 50.

[32] Beckford, *Thoughts on Hunting*, p. 275.

[33] MS letter, Alex Hume Campbell to Countess de Grey, April 14, 1780. Bedford County Record Office, L30/11/151/57.

[34] Beckford, *Thoughts on Hunting*, p. 177.

[35] In 1751, Lord Chesterfield had characterized English hunting as fit only for

'bumpkins and boobies'. Charles Strachey, ed., *The Letters of the Earl of Chesterfield to his Son* (2 vols.; New York and London, 1925), II, p. 176.

[36] *Sp. Mag.*, I (February, 1793), p. 305.

[37] *Ibid.*, X (September, 1797), p. 325.

[38] MS letter, Amabel Hume-Campbell to Marchioness Grey, November 4, 1780. Bedford County Record Office, L30/9/60/251.

[39] For some examples, see: *Sp. Mag.*, XXVIII (April, 1806), p. 3; XLIII (November, 1813), p. 101; LI (December, 1817), p. 147; LIII (December, 1818), p. 144; LXV (November, 1824), pp. 110, 139; LXXI (December, 1827), p. 103; [Edward William Lewis Davies,] *A Memoir of the Rev. John Russell, and his Out-of-Door Life* (London, 1878), p. 97.

[40] *Sp. Mag.*, LXI (January, 1823), p. 210. For a similar complaint, see *ibid.*, LXIII (March, 1824), p. 284.

[41] Nimrod, in *Sp. Mag.*, LX (September, 1822), p. 275.

[42] *Ibid.*, LXXII (August, 1828), p. 307.

[43] In 1845, the Heythrop Hunt sent a letter to a local master of harriers 'stating to him that this country has never been considered capable of admitting the regular hunting of a pack of Harriers over the whole of it as well as a pack of Foxhounds and representing to him the inconvenience which has arisen from the manner in which he has hunted it.' Heythrop Hunt. MS minute book, December 4, 1845; see too, MS letter, J. Foljambe to G. E. Jarvis, April 25, 1875 in which the master of the Burton Hunt stated that 'according to the unwritten law of foxhunting *all* coverts in a hunting country are *fox coverts* subject to the owners rights.' Lincolnshire Archives Office, Jarvis VII/A/18.

[44] Precisely how many packs there were is hard to determine. During the nineteenth century it was generally believed that there were between twenty-five and thirty packs in 1800. *Baily's Mag.*, XLV (December, 1885), p. 101. This estimate is much too low, and I have been able to account for sixty-three packs in that year through references in the press and hunt histories. Many of these accounts are probably inaccurate, and some of the packs referred to probably did not last for very long. The tax returns which show that the number of packs of hounds in Britain grew from sixty-nine in 1812 to ninety-one in 1835, Thompson, *English Landed Society in the Nineteenth Century*, p. 146, are unsatisfactory because they do not distinguish between foxhounds and other types, and because some of the more informal packs probably avoided paying the tax. All contemporary observers, however, agreed that there was a great increase in the popularity of the sport.

[45] *Sp. Mag.*, LXII (May, 1823), p. 85; also see *ibid.*, LXV (November, 1824), p. 137 on the number of packs in Devon, another poor country for hunting, and *ibid.*, LXVIII (May, 1826), p. 47.

[46] George Rudé, *Wilkes and Liberty* (Oxford, 1965), pp. 156-158.

[47] One of their first efforts on hunting, for example, was a long series of articles

by a writer calling himself 'Acastus', which began in 1792 and stretched into 1796. Much of the material on foxhunting was taken word for word from Beckford.

[48] *Sp. Mag.*, III (February, 1794), p. 268.

[49] *Bell's Life in London*, founded in 1822, was the next periodical to deal with the sport, but it was a weekly newspaper, and not in direct competition with the *Sporting Magazine*. It, too, was far more interested in boxing, cockfighting, and horseracing in its earlier years.

[50] *Sp. Mag.*, LIX (January, 1822), p. 177.

[51] Because Apperley was so well known by his pseudonym, I shall use it hereafter without enclosing it in quotation marks.

[52] For accounts of his life, see his posthumously discovered memoirs, *My Life and Times*, ed. with additions by E. D. Cuming (Edinburgh, London, and New York, 1927); *DNB*, vol. XXII; E.W. Bovill, *The England of Nimrod and Surtees, 1815-1854* (London, 1959), pp.14-23.

[53] Nimrod, *My Life and Times*, p. 194.

[54] *Ibid.*, p. 197.

[55] Robert Smith Surtees, *Handley Cross* (London, 1951), p. 258.

[56] For the effect of his visit on a pack, see 'The Pomponious Ego Day', *ibid.*, chapters xlii-xliv.

[57] Nimrod, *My Life and Times*, p. 208; Bovill, *The England of Nimrod and Surtees*, p. 16.

[58] Nimrod, *My Life and Times*, pp. 206-207.

[59] *Quarterly Review*, XLVII (March, 1832), pp. 216-243; XLVIII (December, 1832), pp. 346-375; XLIX (July, 1833), pp. 381-449. They were later reprinted as *The Chace, The Turf, and The Road* (London, 1837).

[60] Some of these borrowed more than his style. Among them were men writing under the pseudonyms: 'Dormin', 'Nim North', and 'Nim South'.

Chapter two

[1] Quoted in T.B. Johnson, *The Hunting Directory* (London, 1826), p. 209.

[2] *Gundry v. Feltham*. Charles Durnford, and Edward Hyde East, *Reports of Cases Argued and Determined in the Court of King's Bench* (London) I, p. 334. Usually cited *I T.R. 334*. See chapter V.

[3] Blane, *Essays on Hunting*, p. viii.

[4] Beckford, *Thoughts on Hunting*, p. 323.

[5] *Ibid.*, p. 9.

[6] See *Sp.Mag.*, XI (November, 1797), pp. 107-108, for a song, 'The Country Life', comparing the comforts of town and country. One verse ran:
'In the Country you're nailed, like a pale in your park, / To some stick of a neighbour cramm'd into the ark; / Or if you are sick, or in fields tumble down, /

You reach Death ere the Doctor can reach you from town.' It was answered the following month by a similar poem, stressing the advantages of country life. *Sp. Mag.*, XI (December, 1797), pp. 171-172.

[7] The Torrington Diaries, III, 73; see also, Cook, *Observations on Fox-Hunting*, p. 80.

[8] Sir C. Sykes to T. Grimston, December 5, 1792. Quoted in Thompson, *English Landed Society in the Nineteenth Century*, p. 149.

[9] Vyner, *Notitia Venatica* (1st ed., 1841), p. 2.

[10] Quoted in *Sp. Mag.*, IV (April, 1794), p. 15.

[11] MS letter, James Yorke to Countess de Grey, August 25, [1802], Bedford County Record Office, L30/11/332/2.

[12] Daphne Machin Goodall, *Huntsmen of a Golden Age: Stephen Goodall, 1757-1823, William Goodall, 1817-1859* (London, 1956), pp. 95-96.

[13] Lowder-Symonds and Crowdy, *History of the Old Berks Hunt*, pp.1-2.

[14] For the testimony of one commanding officer who, during the thirteen years that he commanded a regiment, always gave general leave to all officers who wished to hunt, see J. Anstruther Thomson, *Eighty Years Reminiscences* (2 vols.; London, 1904) II, p. 9. Also see Sir Reginald Graham, Bt., *Fox-Hunting Recollections* (London, 1907), p. 6; and *Field*, LXXV (January 4, 1890), p. 6; (January 18, 1890), p. 76.

[15] Douglas Sutherland, *The Yellow Earl: The Life of Hugh Lowther, 5th Earl of Lonsdale, K.G., G.C.V.O., 1857-1944* (London, 1965), p. 189.

[16] As was done by J. Anstruther Thomson. 'Thormanby', *Kings of the Hunting Field*, p. 281.

[17] Esmé Wingfield-Stratford, *The Squire and his Relations* (London, 1956), p. 283. For an obituary of Cardigan by the novelist George Whyte-Melville, see *Baily's Mag.*, XV (June, 1868), pp.55-60. Also see *Sp. Mag.*, CXXVII (March, 1856), p. 180; CLVI (November, 1870), p. 354; *Field*, IV (November 25, 1854), p. 1108; *Bell's Life*, February 15, 1856, March 23, 1856.

[18] For a fuller discussion of the ideal of manliness as understood in the nineteenth century, see David Newsome, *Godliness and Good Learning: Four Studies on a Victorian Ideal* (London, 1961), pp. 195-239. Newsome contrasts the meaning of the term 'manly' – i.e., 'mature' – for people in the early nineteenth century like S.T. Coleridge, with its meaning – i.e., 'energetic', 'courageous', 'physically vital' – for such later men as Charles Kingsley and Thomas Hughes. *Ibid.*, pp. 196-197. Foxhunters used the term in its second meaning from the beginning of the century. See, for example, Cook, *Observations on Fox-Hunting*, pp. 2, 145.

[19] Delabere P. Blaine, *An Encyclopaedia of Rural Sports*. (London, 1840), pp. 152-155.

[20] Lionel Edwards, *Famous Foxhunters* (London, 1938), pp. 59-60. For Kingsley's role as apostle of manliness, see Newsome, *Godliness and Good*

Learning, pp. 198-199ff. Also see Charles Kingsley, 'My Winter Garden' in his *Prose Idylls, New and Old* (London and New York, 1907), pp. 142-151.

[21] *Saturday Review*, January 29, 1859, p. 122.

[22] Foxhunting was primarily an English sport, though there were packs in Scotland and Wales. Hunting writers, however, often used the term 'British' to describe the national character moulded by hunting.

[23] Ball and Gilbey, *The Essex Foxhounds*, p. 97.

[24] *Sp. Mag.*, LXVII (January, 1826), p. 121. For two more examples, see Sir John E. Eardley-Wilmot, *Reminiscences of the Late Thomas Assheton Smith, Esq., or, the Pursuits of an English Country Gentleman* (London, 1860), p. 2 (hereinafter cited as *Assheton Smith.*), and J. Robson Scott, *My Life as Soldier and Sportsman* (London, 1921), p. 81. The list of examples is almost endless.

[25] *Sp.Mag.*, LXXII (July, 1828), p. 244n.

[26] New Forest Hunt Club. MS Secretary's notebook, January 20, 1864. See, too, *Sp. Mag.*, XCI (February, 1838), p. 257, and *Field*, LXIV (November 1, 1884), p. 595.

[27] See, for example, Cook, *Observations on Fox-Hunting*, p. 144.

[28] Louis Simond, *Journal of a Tour and Residence in Great Britain, during the Years 1810 and 1811* (2 vols., 2nd ed.; Edinburgh, 1817), II, 202.

[29] See 'Report From the Select Committee of the House of Lords on Horses, 1873' in *Parliamentary Papers*, 1873, Vol. XIV; and the Reports of the Royal Commission on Horse Breeding in *Parliamentary Papers*, 1888, Vol. XLVIII; 1890, Vol. XXVII; 1893, Vol. XXXI; 1895, Vol. XXXV.

[30] John Hawkes, *The Meynellian Science, or, Fox-Hunting upon System* With Notes upon Fox-Hunting in 1912, a Comparative Study, by The Right Hon. The Earl of Lonsdale, K.G., with some Notes on Present-day Fox-Hunting, by Major Algernon Burnaby, D.L., now re-edited by L.H. Irvine (Leicester, 1932), p. 48.

[31] *Sp. Mag.*, LVIII (May, 1821), p. 101.

[32] *Bell's Life*, December 18, 1836.

[33] Ball and Gilbey, *The Essex Foxhounds*, p. 101.

[34] George F. Underhill, *In at the Death. A Tale of Society* (London, 1888), p. vi.

[35] William Cobbett, *Rural Rides* (London, 1830), pp. 269-270.

[36] 'Cecil', in *Sp. Mag.*, CXIII (February, 1849), p. 147.

[37] *Bell's Life*, December 18, 1836.

[38] *The Times*, September 22, 1858.

[39] *Bell's Life*, October 10, 1858.

[40] See Loder-Symonds and Crowdy, *History of the Old Berks Hunt*, p. 96; 'Scrutator', *Recollections of a Fox-Hunter*, p.65; *Baily's Mag.*, XXXV (April, 1880), pp. 222-226.

[41] This choice of vocabulary is, itself, significant. For foxhunters, the old was

always to be preferred to the new.

⁴²'Venator' [John Cooper], *The Warwickshire Hunt, from 1795 to 1836;* ... (London, 1837), pp. 270 n.1. and 279.

⁴³*Field*, XIII (January 8, 1859), p. 24. See, too, Thompson, *English Landed Society in the Nineteenth Century*, pp. 148-149.

⁴⁴'Harry Hieover', *Sporting Facts and Sporting Fancies*, (London, 1853), p. 379.

⁴⁵*Field*, XX (August 16, 1862), p. 149.

Chapter three

¹See below.

²'Cecil', *Records of the Chase*, pp. 127-128.

³'The Druid' [Henry Hall Dixon], *The Post and the Paddock* (Hunting edition; London, [1857]), p. 278.

⁴For some horse prices, see *Sp. Mag.*, LXIII (November, 1823), p. 89; XCIV (May, 1839), p. 61; William Wilson, *Green Peas at Christmas* (London, 1924), p. 36; *Field*, VI (September 15, 1855), p. 164; XXXIV (November 20, 1869), p. 433; XXXVII (February 4, 1871), p. 87; L (October 6, 1877), p. 391.

⁵R.S. Surtees, *The Analysis of the Hunting Field* (London, 1846), p. 183.

⁶*Field*, I (January 22, 1853), p. 56; *Baily's Mag.*, XXII (November, 1872), p. 322; The Eighth Duke of Beaufort and Mowbray Morris, *Hunting*, The Badminton Library of Sports and Pastimes (2nd edition; London, 1886), p. 281.

⁷In the 1870s and 1880s, the Braes of Derwent Hunt in Northumberland regularly received subscriptions of one pound. Braes of Derwent Hunt MSS. Printed Subscription Lists. The Duke of Bedford subscribed £800 to the Oakley Hunt in 1880, Bedford County Record Office, X 213/61, p. 38.

⁸*Saturday Review*, December 23, 1876, p 777.

⁹Nimrod, *The Life of a Sportsman* (London, 1847), p. 107.

¹⁰George E. Collins, *History of the Brocklesby Hounds* (London, 1902) p. viii.

¹¹*Sp. Mag.*, XXVII (December, 1805), p. 157.

¹²*Ibid.*, XXVIII (April, 1806), p. 4.

¹³Bovill, *England of Nimrod and Surtees*, p. 39.

¹⁴Surtees, *Analysis of the Hunting Field*, p. 178; *Sp. Mag.*, LXI (October, 1822), p. 5; Vyner, *Notitia Venatica* (1st ed.), p. 166. There is a good deal of correspondence on the subject in the papers of the North Cotswold Hunt, in the possession of M. A. McCanlis, Hon. Sec.

¹⁵Nimrod, in *Sp. Mag.*, LXVI (July, 1825), p. 338; Surtees, in *Analysis of the Hunting Field*, pp. 218-219. Cf. *Sp. Mag.*, LXVI (October, 1825), pp. 414-415.

[16] September 2, 1826.
[17] 'Shelton Gorse', an 1839 hunting poem, in Bedford County Record Office, HY947; also see Bedford County Record Office, UN574 p. 10.
[18] J.C. Shenstone, 'A Yeoman's Common-Place Book at the Commencement of the Nineteenth Century', *Essex Review* (Chelmsford), XVI (April, 1907), p. 85.
[19] E.g., *Morning Herald*, September 2, 1826. Surtees went so far as to use the number of farmers in the hunting field as a barometer of economic and agricultural conditions. *Analysis of the Hunting Field*, p. 181.
[20] *Sp. Mag.*, LXV (December, 1824), p. 216. 'The Druid', *Silk and Scarlet*, p. 13. Cf. *Sp. Mag.*, LXXVI (July, 1830), p. 236.
[21] Collins, *History of the Brocklesby Hounds*, p. 244.
[22] 'The Druid', *Post and Paddock*, pp. 237, 242.
[23] *Sp. Mag.*, LXV (November, 1824), p. 66.
[24] *Sp. Mag.*, XVI (April, 1800), pp. 45-52, and since reprinted many times.
[25] Hunting songs by the Rev. J.W. Hawksley, Rector of Souldrop, Beds., 1792-1801, are in the Bedford County Record Office, UN 316, 317, and 324; songs by the Rev. John King, Vicar of Cotcombe, Somerset, in the 1820s are in the Somerset Record Office, DD/L.
[26] Russell kept hounds in North Devon on a small clerical income during the 1820s, 30s, and 40s. For an account of his life, see [Edward William Lewis Davies], *A Memoir of the Rev. John Russell, and His Out-of-Door Life* (London, 1878).
[27] *Ibid.*, pp. 215-216, 218-220.
[28] *Ibid.*, p. 214. Clergymen, of course, hunted in black, and those who belonged to hunt clubs attended the club dinners dressed in black, which the club rules generally permitted only for clergymen or men in mourning. See the rules of several hunt clubs in Durham County Record Office, D/Sa/X/42, 43, and 44.
[29] E. M. Butler, ed., *A Regency Visitor, The English Tour of Prince Pückler-Muskau Described in his Letters, 1826-28* (London, 1957), pp. 292-293.
[30] *Gentleman's Magazine*, July, 1802, p. 621.
[31] September 9, 1803. *The Diary of the Rev. William Jones 1777-1821*, ed. by O. F. Christie (London, 1929), p. 158.
[32] 'The Druid', *Scott and Sebright* (London, 1862), p. 363.
[33] Edward Stillingfleet, Ld Bishop of Worcester [William Gilpin], *On the Amusements of Clergymen, and Christians in General, Three Dialogues between a Dean and a Curate* (London, 1820), p. 19.
[34] *Ibid.*, p. 35.
[35] *Ibid.*, p. 33.
[36] Quoted in Seventh Earl Bathurst, *A History of the V. W. H. Country* (London, 1936), p. 13.
[37] See *Nimrod's Hunting Tours*, p. 73, for the distinction between the 'hunting

Notes to Chapter Three   207

parson', and the 'parson who hunts'.

[38] See Byng, *Torrington Diaries*, IV, 130, for a reference to the sporting butcher and baker.

[39] See 'Venator', *The Warwickshire Hunt*, p. 123n, and Loder-Symonds and Crowdy, *History of the Old Berks Hunt*, pp. 172-176 for accounts of well-known dealers.

[40] Surtees, *Analysis of the Hunting Field*, pp. 157-169. See 'Venator', *The Warwickshire Hunt*, p. 12, and J. E. Auden, *Short History of the Albrighton Hunt* (London, 1905), p. 44, for accounts of real-life counterparts to Peter.

[41] *Sp. Mag.*, LXV (February, 1825), p. 357.

[42] *Bell's Life*, December 18, 1836.

[43] Watson, *Robert Smith Surtees*, p. 39.

[44] See *Sp. Mag.*, LVII (November, 1820), p. 88, for an account of the annual Cock-Bridge Hunt, near Carlisle. The hunt, probably for hare, was followed by a sumptuous dinner of the kind for which unreformed municipal corporations were famous.

[45] *Ibid.*, I (November, 1792), pp. 91-92.

[46] *Ibid.*, XXI (October, 1802), p. 2; Bovill, *English Country Life*, pp 121-122; Watson, *Robert Smith Surtees*, p. 39.

[47] *Sp. Mag.*, VIII (August, 1796), p. 262.

[48] *Ibid.*, XI (December, 1797), p. 112; Watson, *Robert Smith Surtees*, pp. 38-39.

[49] *Life in London*, April 21, 1822, p. 20; *Sp. Mag.*, LXXVI (October, 1830), p. 412.

[50] See *Sp. Mag.*, III (March, 1794), pp. 327-328, for a typical example.

[51] The Surrey tried it in 1823, the Old Berkeley, two years later. *Sp. Mag.*, LXIII (December, 1823), p. 110; LXVI (May, 1825), p. 76.

[52] See chapter V. For the landowners' resolutions, see *Middlesex and Hertfordshire Notes and Queries*, III (1897), pp. 75-77.

[53] Colonel John Cook, who had been master in Essex, wrote: 'Should you happen to keep hounds at no great distance from London, you will find many of the inhabitants of that capital (cockneys if you please), *good sportsmen* well mounted, and riding well to hounds; they never interfere with the management of them when in the field, contribute liberally to the expense, and pay their subscriptions regularly.' *Observations on Fox-Hunting*, pp. 148-149. Cf. MS letter, H. J. Conyers to John Nesbitt, June 30, 1826. Essex Record Office, D/DAr C1.

[54] R.S. Surtees, *Jorrocks' Jaunts and Jollities* (London, [1901]), p. 22.

[55] *Bell's Life*, November 15, 1835.

[56] *Sp. Mag.*, LXXVI (September, 1830), pp. 360-362. Ten years later his prices had not changed. Blaine, *Encyclopaedia of Rural Sports*, p. 459.

[57] *Baily's Mag.*, X (December, 1865), p. 346.

[58] *Ibid.*, LXIII (December, 1823), p. 102.

[59] Ellis, *Leicestershire and the Quorn*, p. 93.
[60] *Sp. Mag.*, X (April, 1797), p. 6.
[61] Ellis, *Leicestershire and the Quorn*, p. 34.
[62] *Sp. Mag.*, LXVI (June, 1825), p. 152.
[63] See the bibliography for the books of Nimrod, Surtees, and 'The Druid'.
[64] Goodall, *Huntsmen of a Golden Age*, p. 67.
[65] 'The Druid', *Silk and Scarlet*, pp. 26-27.
[66] See Ellis, *Leicestershire and the Quorn*, pp. 26-28 for a description o% the different types of fence to be met with.
[67] *Nimrod's Hunting Tours* (London, 1903), p. 6.
[68] Bovill, *England of Nimrod and Surtees*, p. 87 n.1.
[69] Ellis, *Leicestershire and the Quorn*, p. 47.
[70] 'The Druid', *Scott and Sebright*, pp. 389-390.
[71] Wilson, *Green Peas at Christmas*, p. 36.
[72] *Sp. Mag.*, LXVII (February, 1826), p. 276; *Bell's Life*, March 10, 1822, April 2, 1826.
[73] Harriette Wilson, *Memoirs of Harriette Wilson* (4 vols.; London, 1825), III, 391. See Bedford County Record Office, W1/6219, for some verses describing Melton as the town where 'strumpets notorious' abound.
[74] *Bell's Life*, February 22, 1825.
[75] *Sp. Mag.*, LXXX (June, 1832), p. 85.
[76] *Ibid.*, (July, 1830), p. 189.
[77] Of the Meltonians listed in the 'first flight' by the Rev. J. Empson in 1817, most were between the ages of twenty-three and thirty-four. Guy Paget and Lionel Irvine, eds., *The Flying Parson and Dick Christian* (Leicester, 1934), pp. 16-63.
[78] For lists of Meltonians and their horses, see: *Bell's Life*, February 10, 1828, March 3, 1833; *Sp. Mag.*, LXXI (March, 1828), p. 363.
[79] Nimrod, *Life of a Sportsman*, p. 281; Nimrod, *The Chace, The Turf, and The Road*, p. 14.
[80] 'Cecil', *Records of the Chase*, p. 133. This was slightly higher than the average price over the rest of the country, which varied from twenty to twenty-four shillings per week.
[81] *Sp. Mag.*, LXIV (September, 1824), p. 345.
[82] Paget and Irvine, *The Flying Parson and Dick Christian*, p. 5. Paget claims that only five, the Manners and the Lowthers, were local landowners, but he seems to have omitted Lord Rancliffe and Sir Francis Burdett, both of whom owned land in the country. Ellis, *Leicestershire and the Quorn*.
[83] *Sp. Mag.*, LXVI (July, 1825), p. 226; Wilson, *Green Peas at Christmas*, p. 42; Ellis, *Leicestershire and the Quorn*, pp. 41-42.
[84] One notable exception was the second Earl of Wilton, who first came to the town in the 1820s, hunted from there until his death in 1882, and was known as

the 'King of Melton'. *Ibid.*, p. 40 n.3.

[85] George Osbaldeston, *Squire Osbaldeston: His Autobiography*, ed. by E.D. Cuming (London, [1927]), p. 40.

[86] Ellis, *Leicestershire and the Quorn*, p. 52.

[87] Nimrod, *The Chace, The Turf, and The Road*, p. 63.

[88] Eardley-Wilmot, *Assheton Smith*, p. 27.

[89] Nimrod, *The Chace, The Turf, and The Road*, p. 64.

[90] 'The Druid', *Silk and Scarlet*, p. 13.

[91] Ellis, *Leicestershire and the Quorn*, p. 47.

[92] *Ibid.*, p. 56.

[93] Byng, *Torrington Diaries*, I, 320.

[94] *Sp. Mag.*, LXXXIV (October, 1834), p. 434; XCIII (March, 1839), p. 358; CIX (February, 1847), p. 147.

[95] *Ibid.*, LXIII (December, 1823), p. 110.

[96] Osbaldeston, *Autobiography*, p. 10.

[97] Edith Stewart, Marchioness of Londonderry, *Henry Chaplin, a Memoir* (London, 1926), p. 21. Chaplin (1840-1923), later first Viscount Chaplin, was one of the last of the old style country gentlemen who combined landed wealth, sporting pursuits, and an active political career. A Lincolnshire squire, he was master of two packs of hounds, active on the turf, and a Member of Parliament from 1868 to 1906, and again from 1907 to 1916, when he became a peer. He was a follower of Disraeli, an avid protectionist, and served as Chancellor of the Duchy of Lancaster, President of the Board of Agriculture, and President of the Local Government Board.

[98] *Sp. Mag.*, VII (December, 1795), p. 120.

[99] 'Harry Hieover' [Charles Bindley], *The Hunting-Field* (London, 1850), pp. 28-29; *Sp. Mag.*, VII (January, 1796), p. 176.

Chapter four

[1] *Sp. Mag.*, LXXI (November, 1827), p. 31.

[2] See Thompson, *English Landed Society in the Nineteenth Century*, p. 259; Heythrop Hunt MSS, Minutes, December 4, 1845.

[3] *HMC 24, Rutland MSS*, III, 199.

[4] *Sp. Mag.*, CII (October, 1843), p. 213.

[5] Quoted in Bovill, *England of Nimrod and Surtees*, p. 36.

[6] Foxes seemed to have little fear of crossing the lines and it was the hounds that were occasionally killed by trains. See the hunting diaries of John Josselyn for cases of this. Bury St Edmunds and West Suffolk Record Office, 1677/6/12, December 2, 1851; 1677/6/16, January 7, 1862.

[7] Reynard, *Hunting Notes from Holderness*, p. 86; Ball and Gilbey, *The Essex Foxhounds*, p. 21; Vyner, *Notitia Venatica* (New edition, 1892), p. 299 n.1.

Notes to Chapter Four

[8] Ellis, *Leicestershire and the Quorn*, p. 71.
[9] *Bell's Life*, November 29, 1879.
[10] *Field*, I (April 23, 1853), p. 292.
[11] For some early examples, see *Field*, II (November 19, 1853), p. 482; *Sp. Mag.*, CXXVII (March, 1856), pp. 197-205; *Baily's Mag.*, II (December, 1860), p. 116.
[12] *Baily's Mag.*, XI (July, 1866), p. 344; *Bell's Life*, January 27, 1877; *The Times*, February 14, 1881.
[13] 'Cecil', *Records of the Chase*, p. 331.
[14] *Ibid.*, pp. 330-335.
[15] 'Cecil', *Records of the Chase*, p. 341.
[16] *Bell's Life*, October 2, 1853; *Field*, VI (November 10, 1855), p. 291.
[17] 'Cecil', *Records of the Chase*, p. 334.
[18] See *Bell's Life*, October 14, 1855, November 14, 1868. There is a copy of a railway company circular advising sportsmen about hunting trains in the Bedford County Record Office, AD 3238/7.
[19] Marchioness of Londonderry, *Henry Chaplin*, p. 225.
[20] 'The Druid', *Silk and Scarlet*, p. 59; *Bell's Life*, November 11, 1871; *Baily's Mag.*, VII (November, 1863), p. 116; *Sp. Mag.*, CXXXVII (February, 1861), p. 91.
[21] *Parliamentary Papers*, 1873, XIV, 'Report of the Select Committee of the House of Lords on Horses', p. 119, Testimony of Thomas Parrington.
[22] Bovill, *The England of Nimrod and Surtees*, pp. 177-179; *Baily's Mag.*, XLVII (November, 1887), p. 255-256.
[23] Surtees, *Analysis of the Hunting Field*, p. 214.
[24] 'Harry Hieover', quoted in Ellis, *Leicestershire and the Quorn*, p. 95.
[25] Surtees, *Analysis of the Hunting Field*, p. 317. *Sp. Mag.*, CVI (November, 1845), p. 309.
[26] *Baily's Mag.*, XVI (February, 1869), p. 108.
[27] *Saturday Review*, December 23, 1876, p. 776.
[28] For a description of the year of a fashionable young man, see Moreton Frewen, *Melton Mowbray and Other Memories* (London, 1924), p. 98.
[29] [George John Whyte Melville,] *Market Harborough: or, How Mr. Sawyer Went to the Shires* (London, 1861), p. 6.
[30] By 'Scrutator', published in 1859. For another example, see Mrs Edward Kennard, *The Right Sort: A Romance of the Shires* (London and New York, [1886]).
[31] See, for example, *Bell's Life*, December 29, 1877, March 11, 1882.
[32] *Baily's Mag.*, VII (November, 1863), p. 117.
[33] *Baily's Mag.*, VII (November, 1863), p. 117; XIX (October, 1870), p. 59; T. F. Dale, *Fox-Hunting in the Shires* The Hunting Library, ed. by F. G. Aflalo, Vol. II (London, 1903), p. 18.

Notes to Chapter Four 211

[34] Dale, *Fox-Hunting in the Shires*, p. 13.
[35] *Sp. Mag.* CXXXVII (April, 1861), p. 239.
[36] *Ibid.*, (March, 1861), p. 146.
[37] *Field*, LVIII (December 10, 1881), p. 836.
[38] Wilson, *Green Peas at Christmas*, p. 76; Lennox, *Merry England*, p. 86.
[39] *Baily's Mag.*, IV (January, 1862), p. 84; *Bell's Life*, October 28, 1876, February 10, 1883.
[40] *Bell's Life*, December 7, 1851. This called forth an angry reply from the lady concerned. *Ibid.*, December 14, 1851.
[41] Surtees, *Analysis of the Hunting Field*, p. 295; Trollope, *Hunting Sketches*, p. 30. For the arguments against women hunting, see the letter from 'Foxhunter', in *Field*, III (April 15, 1854), p. 342.
[42] *Field*, X (September 12, 1857), p. 180.
[43] *Bell's Life*, January 2, 1864; *Sp. Mag.*, CXXXVII (March, 1861), p. 147; *Bell's Life*, November 9, 1872; *Baily's Mag.*, XXIII (February, 1873), p. 121.
[44] *Baily's Mag.*, XV (May, 1868), p. 11. Whyte Melville had beaten them to it in *Market Harborough*.
[45] *Field*, XXXVI (October 22, 1870), p. 356.
[46] Guy Paget, *The History of the Althorp and Pytchley Hunt 1634-1920* (London, 1937), p. 206.
[47] Quoted in Ellis, *Leicestershire and the Quorn*, p. 106.
[48] Osbaldeston, *Autobiography*, pp. 66-67.
[49] For the story and implications of the Cheshire Difficulty, see chapter VI.
[50] On the whole, Lord Stamford was successful in getting his wife accepted despite her sordid past. Ellis, *Leicestershire and the Quorn*, p. 83 n.1. The whole episode, of course, has its echoes in Surtees' *Mr. Facey Romford's Hounds*, published four years later.
[51] For the main points of the debate, see *Field*, XVI (December 1, 1860), p. 452; *Baily's Mag.*, II (January, 1861), pp. 174-182; and *Field*, XVII (January 12, 1861), p. 29; (January 26, 1861), p. 69.
[52] *Baily's Mag.*, II (January, 1861), p. 174.
[53] *Field*, XVI (December 1, 1860), p. 452.
[54] F. Palliser deCostobadie, *Annals of the Billesdon Hunt (Mr. Fernie's) 1856-1913* (London and Leicester, 1914), pp. 23-24.
[55] *Sp. Mag.*, CX (July, 1847), p. 50; CXXXIII (January, 1859), p. 1.
[56] Wilson, *Green Peas at Christmas*, p. 76.
[57] *Field*, VIII (December 6, 1856), p. 358; XXIX (January 5, 1867), p. 9.
[58] *Baily's Mag.*, XII (November, 1866), p. 214.
[59] See, for example, 'Bagatelle' [A.G. Bagot], *Men We Meet in the Field, or, The Bullshire Hounds* (London, 1881), p. 87, for a story in which the local horse dealer takes advantage of a 'cotton lord'.
[60] See, for example, *Sp. Mag.*, CVI (October, 1845), p. 244, for 'The

Sportsman's Resources Through the Principal Countries of England'; CVIII (July, 1846), p. 1, for 'The Handbook of the Chase', the first in a series of articles written to instruct the new sportsman 'where the most agreeable and the most negotiable fields are to be met with.'

[61] Some of the new books included: 'Harry Hieover', *The Hunting-Field* (London, 1850); Delabere P. Blaine, *An Encyclopaedia of Rural Sports* (London, 1840); 'Stonehenge' [J. H. Walsh], *Manual of British Rural Sports* (London, 1856); 'Scrutator', *Recollections of a Fox-Hunter* (London, 1861).

[62] R. N. Rose, *The Field, 1853-1953: A Centenary Volume* (London, 1953), pp. 17-18.

[63] *Sp. Mag.*, CXXXII (November, 1858), p. 317.

[64] C. J. Blagg, *A History of the North Staffordshire Hounds and Country* (London, 1902), p. 189.

[65] For some complaints about this, see: *Field*, XXII (December 26, 1863), p. 621; XLV (March 20, 1875), p. 290; *Baily's Mag.*, XI (July, 1866), p. 344; XXII (November, 1872), p. 344.

[66] *Baily's Mag.*, LI (May, 1889), p. 308.

[67] For a fuller discussion of hunt finance, see chapter V.

[68] *Baily's Mag.*, XI (July, 1866), p. 345.

[69] *Ibid.*, XLI (December, 1883), p. 314.

[70] 'Harry Hieover', *Sporting Facts and Sporting Fancies*, p. 382.

[71] Surtees, *Analysis of the Hunting Field*, p. 218.

[72] *Sp. Mag.*, CXXIV (November, 1854), p. 369.

[73] *Bell's Life*, October 30, 1880.

[74] *Field*, LII (November 30, 1878), p. 69.

[75] *Ibid.*, LXXIV (1889). 'G.F.M.W.P.'s' letter was published December 7, p. 802. There were several letters in reply, December 14, p. 838. *The Field*'s reply appeared December 28, p. 903.

[76] 'The Future of Hunting', *Murray's Magazine* (London), April, 1887, pp. 527-541, was a survey of masters taken as a response to the depression. Their answers reveal that in many countries the old hunting classes continued to dominate.

[77] *Bell's Life*, January 17, 1874.

[78] For some adverse reactions to this, see Trollope, *Hunting Sketches*, p. 49; Surtees, *Mr. Facey Romford's Hounds*, p. 40.

[79] [Richard Ord], *The Sedgefield Country in the Seventies and Eighties* (Darlington, 1904), p. 82. But cf. Bedford Record Office, X213/61, X213/120, and North Cotswold Hunt MSS for cases where farmers did subscribe.

[80] George E. Collins ('Nimrod Junior'), *Farming and Foxhunting* (London, n.d.), pp. 340-341; Sir John Dugdale Astley, Bart., *Fifty years of my Life in the World of Sport At Home and Abroad* (2 vols.; London, 1894), II, 5; Patrick

Notes to Chapter Five 213

Chalmers, *The History of Hunting* The Lonsdale Library, Vol. XXIII (London, [1936]), p. 373.

[81] Ball and Gilbey, *The Essex Foxhounds*, pp. 272, 297; *Baily's Mag.*, XXIV (December, 1873), p. 267; 'Brooksby' [E. Pennell-Elmhirst], *The Hunting Countries of England* (London, 1878), Part IV, p. 16.

[82] These included two labourers and four others who could only sign with a mark. A printed copy of the statements, *Bilsdale and Hurworth Hunts – Case for the Decision of the Committee of the Master of Fox-Hounds Association, June 1898* is in the North Riding County Record Office, C.R.11.

[83] See *Field*, IV (November 4, 1854), p. 1036, and Trollope's description of a hunting breakfast in *The American Senator*, chapter X.

[84] For some examples, see Ord, *The Sedgefield Country*, p. 200.

[85] Quoted in Edwards, *Famous Foxhunters*, p. 60.

[86] *Saturday Review*, January 29, 1859, p. 122.

[87] Reynard, *Hunting Notes from Holderness*, p. 112; deCostobadie, *Annals of the Billesdon Hunt*, Preface, p. [ii].

[88] *Baily's Mag.*, XXXI (February, 1878), p. 357; XLVII (April, 1887), p. 231; Blagg, *History of the North Staffordshire Hounds*, p. 47.

Chapter five

[1] *T.R.*, 334.

[2] MS letter, Lord Euston to Marchioness de Grey. February 6, 1791. Bedford County Record Office, L30/9/37. For another example, see MS letter, W. H. Lambton to ?, October 29, 1793. East Riding County Record Office, Dar 77.

[3] Hertford Summer Assizes, 1809.

[4] *Sp. Mag.*, XXXIV (July, 1809), p. 157.

[5] *Ibid.*, pp. 157-158; Joseph Chitty, *A Treatise on the Game Laws, and on Fisheries* (2nd ed.; London, 1826), p. 32.

[6] See Henry Hall Dixon, *A Treatise on the Law of the Farm; including the Agricultural Customs of England and Wales* (London, 1858), p. 257.

[7] For some examples see MS letter sent by Sir Matthew White Ridley to twenty-six landowners in 1818. Northumberland Record Office, ZRI 51/8; *Sp. Mag.*, LIX (December, 1821), p. 142, for a letter sent out by Sir Bellingham Graham.

[8] See, for example, MS letter, Duke of Grafton to Sir Henry Dryden, December 2, 182?. Northamptonshire Record Office, D(CA) 406.

[9] See chapters VII, VIII, and IX.

[10] Cook, *Observations on Fox-Hunting*, p. 47. Cook was writing about the drawing of coverts, but the same sentiment applied to the crossing of land.

[11] Hunting law has nothing to do with the law of England, and may even

come into conflict with it. It was developed entirely by hunting people for hunting people, and depended for its enforcement solely on their consent.

[12] *Sp. Mag.*, CXXXI (May, 1858), p. 327.

[13] This was to be the prime consideration of those who arbitrated nineteenth century hunting disputes. The pack which could establish the earliest claim to a covert was awarded the covert. See, for example, the Takely Forest Award of 1854. Ball and Gilbey, *The Essex Foxhounds*, pp. 345-347.

[14] Northamptonshire Record Office, YZ 4949. See, too, MS draft letter, Ca. 1779. Warwickshire County Record Office, CR 114/355.

[15] Loder-Symonds and Crowdy, *History of the Old Berks Hunt*, p. 28.

[16] *Ibid.*

[17] See, for example, a printed circular sent by the Committee of the Oakley Hunt on behalf of the master to covert owners in 1834. Bedford County Record Office, X213/92.

[18] Though as late as 1850, the position was still unclear. Cf. *Sp. Mag.*, CXV (June, 1850), p. 396, and *Bell's Life*, March 2 and November 2, 1851.

[19] Loder-Symonds and Crowdy, *History of the Old Berks Hunt*, p. 106.

[20] See *ibid.*, pp. 128-129.

[21] For several of these disputes, see *Sp. Mag.*, LXXXIII (February, 1834), p. 287; *Bell's Life*, January 15, 1843; Ball and Gilbey, *The Essex Foxhounds*, p. 302.

[22] Loder-Symonds and Crowdy, *History of the Old Berks Hunt*, pp. 129-170; *The Berkshire Hounds: Correspondence etc. as to the Dispute between Lord Gifford and Mr. Morland* (London, 1845); Berkshire Record Office, D/ELs F17, D/EM F2, D/EM F3.

[23] *Sp. Mag.*, LXXXIX (December, 1836), pp. 166-167.

[24] In 1833, for example, two masters arbitrated the dispute between Sir John Cope and the Craven. Berkshire Record Office, D/EW E28.

[25] Vyner, *Notitia Venatica* (6th ed., [1871]), pp. 38-39.

[26] See T. T. Morland to James Dutton, June 11, 1844, *The Berkshire Hounds*, p. 22; MS letter, T. T. Drake to T. T. Morland, June 21, 1844, Berkshire Record Office, D/ELs F17.

[27] *Sp. Mag.*, XCI (March, 1838), p. 391; 'Cecil', *Records of the Chase*, pp. 46, 57; *Bell's Life*, January 15, 1843, November 16, 1851.

[28] The Duke of Beaufort, Lords Southampton and Redesdale, Sir Bellingham Graham, and Henry Greene.

[29] *Bell's Life*, August 10, 1856.

[30] *Ibid.*

[31] See chapter IV for an account of the 'Cheshire Difficulty'.

[32] For some examples of Committee decisions, see *Baily's Mag.*, XVII (July, 1869), p. 4, and (August, 1869) pp. 60-66. For an example of the evidence see *Bilsdale and Hurworth Hunts – Case for the Decision of the Committee of the Master*

of Fox-Hounds Association, June 1898, a printed pamphlet in the North Riding County Record Office, C.R.11.

[33] A copy of the association's rules, dated June 20, 1881, is among the Luttrell papers in the Somerset Record Office, DD/L.

[34] 'Cecil', *Records of the Chase,* pp. 48-49. Also see *Sp. Mag.,* CXV (June, 1850), p. 401; and Vyner, *Notitia Venatica* (1st ed.) pp. 26-29 for nineteenth century hunting law.

[35] This was, in part, a heritage of foxhunting's early association with hare hunting. Since the hare generally ran in rings and stayed in a relatively confined space, a man could often hunt hares without leaving his own property.

[36] Farr, 'Sir Edward Littleton's Fox-Hunting Diary', p. 11ff.

[37] *Sp. Mag.,* LIX (December, 1821), p. 141.

[38] Ellis, *Leicestershire and the Quorn,* pp. 10-11.

[39] A draft copy of their agreement is in the Warwickshire County Record Office, CR114A/355.

[40] MS letter, Duke of Beford to S. Whitbread, April 4, 1809. Bedford County Record Office, W1/2462.

[41] *Sp. Mag.,* CVI (October, 1845), p. 245.

[42] At least three more masters, J. J. Farquharson in Dorset, J. F. Giles of the Ledbury, and William Davenport of the North Staffs took no subscription.

[43] Vyner, *Notitia Venatica* (1st ed.), p. 6.

[44] The Selby-Lowndes family of Whaddon Hall, Bucks., and the Lane Fox family of Bramham Park, Yorkshire hunted, respectively, the Whaddon Chase and the Bramham Moor for centuries. Both were considerable local magnates though each had to ask for a subscription from time to time. *Baily's Hunting Directory, 1970-1971* (London, 1970), pp. 17, 121; John Bateman, *The Great Landowners of Great Britain and Ireland* (new edition; London, 1879), pp. 168, 273.

[45] University of Durham, Department of Paleography and Diplomatic, Baker Baker Papers, 18/101.

[46] Typed copy of letter, R. J. Lambton to W. Lee Antonie, December 17, 1812, Bedford County Record Office, UN 570.

[47] Cf. Essex Record Office, D/DHa F5f1, and Paget, *History of the Althorp and Pytchley Hunt,* p. 99, for two agreements, contemporary with Baker's, which are less restrictive. The former specified only that the master hunt every Monday and Friday during the season, and only once in each week within ten miles of Colchester. The latter specified only that hounds meet three times per week.

[48] Ellis, *Leicestershire and the Quorn,* p. 33.

[49] Auden, *History of the Albrighton Hunt,* p. 31.

[50] *Ibid.,* p. 56.

[51] *Sp. Mag.,* LXVI (May, 1825), p. 97.

[52] For example at a meeting of the East Kent Hunt in 1871, Kent Archives

Office, U471 E40; or the Pytchley, *Field,* XLIII (March 28, 1874), p. 294. See chapters VIII, X.

[53]Cook, *Observations on Fox-Hunting,* pp. 188-190. Some of his estimates are reproduced in Bovill, *The England of Nimrod and Surtees,* p. 53. But cf. *Sp. Mag.,* LXIX(February, 1827), p. 252; *ibid.,* CII(November, 1843), p. 314.

[54]George F. Underhill, *The Master of Hounds* The Hunting Library, ed. by F. G. Aflalo, Vol. III(London, 1903), pp. 97-132.

[55]Pease, *The Cleveland Hounds,* p. 82.

[56]MS notebook of James Bell. Somerset Record Office, DD/L.

[57]Northumberland Record Office, ZRI 51/3.

[58]Ellis, *Leicestershire and the Quorn,* p. 39.

[59]*Ibid.,* p. 129 n.2.

[60]Thomas Read Quarrell, *The Worcestershire Hunt* (Worcester, 1929), p. 23; North Cotswold Hunt. MS records.

[61]See, for example, the minute books of the Hampshire and Heythrop Hunts; also Bedford County Record Office, X213/176, for a circular, dated May, 1887, appealing for a special subscription for the Oakley Hunt.

[62]*Bell's Life,* March 12, 1843; *Sp. Mag.,* CI(April, 1843), p. 314.

Chapter six

[1]Surtees, *Analysis of the Hunting Field,* p. 4.

[2]*Ibid.,* p. 21.

[3]There were several London dealers who specialized in the fox trade, and there were men in most countries from whom foxes could be obtained. In theory, these foxes all came from Scotland, Wales, and the continent, but many were poached from other hunt countries. Osbaldeston, *Autobiography,* p. 244; 'The Druid', *Silk and Scarlet,* p. 391; *Field,* LXV(February 28, 1888), p. 250.

[4]Lord Stamford of the Quorn, for example, was once threatened with vulpicide for evicting a farmer who refused to drink the health of Lady Stamford, a former circus equestrienne. Ellis, *Leicestershire and the Quorn,* p. 83 n.1; *Sp. Mag.,* CXXX(November, 1857), pp. 315-316; CXXXI(January, 1858), p. 68.

[5]*Baily's Mag.,* II(February, 1861), pp. 236-237.

[6]In 1835, the master of the Nottinghamshire was faced with a subscribers' revolt as a result of poor hunting, which was the fault of the weather. *Bell's Life,* February 15, 1835.

[7]Surtees, *Analysis of the Hunting Field,* p. 30.

[8]See, for example, Vyner, *Notitia Venatica* (New ed.; 1892), p. 42 n.1.; 'Venator', *The Warwickshire Hunt,* p. 97.

[9]*Sp. Mag.,* CLV(May, 1870), p. 372.

[10]'Scrutator', *Recollections of a Fox-Hunter,* pp. 141-152.

[11]Wilson, *Green Peas at Christmas,* pp. 88-89.

[12] Edwards, *Famous Foxhunters*, p. 42.
[13] Cowen, *The Braes of Derwent Hunt*, p. 172.
[14] *Field*, XXVII (January 6, 1866), p. 12.
[15] *Ibid.*, LXIV (November 8, 1884), p. 635.
[16] Fitzwilliam Hunt. MS cash book, Northamptonshire Record Office, Box 1794.
[17] G. T. Hutchinson, *The Heythrop Hunt* (London, 1935). p. 87.
[18] Sir Denis Le Marchant, Bt., *Memoir of John Charles, Viscount Althrop, Third Earl Spencer* (London, 1876), p. 145.
[19] Typed copy of letter, Lord Annaly to Duke of Northumberland, November 11, 1900. University of Durham, Department of Paleography and Diplomatic, 4th Earl Grey Papers.
[20] Hampshire Hunt. MS minute book, p. 142.
[21] Quoted in H. J. Hanham, *Elections and Party Management: Politics in the Time of Disraeli and Gladstone* (London, 1959), pp. 3-4.
[22] Ball and Gilbey, *The Essex Foxhounds*, pp. 48-50.
[23] See chapter I for a note on the source of these figures. The number of masters is not the same as the number of packs because several packs had more than one master, while several of the trencher-fed packs of the North had no real master at all.
[24] Humphrey R. Taylor, *The Old Surrey Fox Hounds: A History of the Hunt from its Earliest Days to the Present Time* ed. by 'G.G.' – H. G. Harper (London, 1906), p. 13.
[25] *Nimrod's Hunting Tours*, p. 81; Bovill, *The England of Nimrod and Surtees*, pp. 11 n.1, 68-69.
[26] For his life see Eardley-Wilmot, *Assheton Smith*. He is also listed in the *DNB*, and most of this account of his life is taken from these two sources.
[27] *Sp. Mag.*, CXXXII (December, 1858), p. 413; Bateman, *Great Landowners*, p. 404.
[28] Osbaldeston, *Autobiography*, p. ix, from the introduction by Sir Theodore Cook.
[29] Ellis, *Leicestershire and the Quorn*, p. 37.
[30] Vyner, *Notitia Venatica* (new ed.; 1892), p. 370 n.1; *British Hunts and Huntsmen* (4 vols.; London, 1908-1911), II, 96-99; *Sp. Mag.*, CXV (January, 1850), pp. 15-25.
[31] Osbaldeston, *Autobiography*; *Baily's Mag.*, XII (September, 1866), pp. 86-90.
[32] There is an account of a run with them in *Sp. Mag.*, XXXIII (February, 1809), p. 249.
[33] *Baily's Mag.*, XII (September, 1866), p. 90.
[34] Ellis, *Leicestershire and the Quorn*, p. 37.
[35] Osbaldeston, *Autobiography*, pp. 40-42.

[36] *Ibid.*, pp. 66-67.
[37] *Sp. Mag.*, LXXI(November, 1827), p. 23.
[38] *Ibid.*, LXVIII(June, 1826), p. 95.
[39] Heythrop Hunt, MS minute book, 1837-1850.
[40] See *Bell's Life*, March 13, 1842.
[41] New Forest Hunt. MS notebook, 1849-1851.
[42] New Forest Hunt. MS minute book, 1866-1901.
[43] Ellis, *Leicestershire and the Quorn*, p. 43.
[44] See *Sp. Mag.*, LXXVIII (July, 1831), p. 146; Ball and Gilbey, *The Essex Foxhounds*, pp. 114, 145.
[45] E. Walford, *The County Families of the United Kingdom, 1865* (London, 1865); University of Durham, Department of Paleography and Diplomatic, Baker Baker, 18/101. These figures were calculated from lists of masters in the press, hunt histories, and *Baily's Hunting Directory*, some of which are not totally reliable. They were checked against local directories, histories, *Burke's Landed Gentry*, Walford's *County Families*, Bateman's *Great Landowners*, and the 'New Domesday Book'.
[46] See note above. I have been unable to find anything about three masters: E. R. Sworder, of the East Kent; W. T. Summers, of the Wheatland; and J. M. King, of the Suffolk.
[47] *Baily's Hunting Directory, 1970-71* (London, 1970); *Baily's Mag.*, LIV (November, 1890), pp. 338-341.
[48] Essex Record Office, D/DArC1.
[49] New Forest Hunt Club. MS records. For the ownership of the hounds see Notebook, 1851-1853, for arrangements made in 1851. For the kennel rent see Minute Book, 1866-1901.
[50] See *Sp. Mag.*, LXXVIII (May, 1831), p. 17; see also Surtees, *Analysis of the Hunting Field*, pp. 31-32.
[51] Altogether there seems to have been a very sad lack of discretion on the part of all concerned. Though attempts were made to pretend that no one really knew the facts of the case, *The Field* had published the story in 1857, and copies of the letter had fairly widespread circulation in the county. *Sp. Mag.*, CXXXI (January, 1858), p. 25, (February, 1858), p. 80; *Field*, IX(January 3, 1857), p. 3.
[52] *Field*, IX(January 3, 1857), p. 3.
[53] *Bell's Life*, March 1, 1857.
[54] *Ibid.; Sp. Mag.*, CXXIX(April, 1857), p. 240.
[55] New Forest Hunt Club. MS records.
[56] MS agreement between T. Butt Miller and the Committee, January 22, 1886. Bedford Record Office, X213/61, pp. 72-73.
[57] Trollope, *Hunting Sketches*, p. 91; but cf., *Baily's Mag.*, XII (September, 1866), pp. 70-71.
[58] Henry S. Davenport, *Memories at Random: Melton and Harborough*

(London, 1926), p. 11.

[59] H. W. Selby Lowndes to W. Forbes, December 9, 1897, *Bilsdale and Hurworth Hunts — Case for the Decision of the Committee of the Master of Fox-Hounds Association*, p. 3, North Riding County Record Office, C.R.11.

[60] *Field*, LVIII(December 17, 1881), p. 871.

[61] A. Audrey Locke, *The Hanbury Family* (2 vols.; London, 1916), II, 254, 263.

[62] For the establishment of the pack see Essex Record Office, D/DHaF5fl. For Hanbury, see Locke, *The Hanbury Family*, II, 277.

[63] Taylor, *The Old Surrey Fox Hounds*, p. 13.

[64] *Sp. Mag.*, LXXXII(July, 1833), p. 164, for his biography; Ball and Gilbey, *The Essex Foxhounds*, pp. 53-55; Chalmers, *The History of Hunting*, pp. 327-328.

[65] Esme Wingfield-Stratford, *The Squire and his Relations* (London, 1956), p. 254.

[66] Thompson, *English Landed Society in the Nineteenth Century*, p. 129; *British Hunts and Huntsmen*, III, 219.

[67] Alexander Henry Higginson, *'The Meynell of The West': being a Biography of James John Farquharson Esq" Master of Fox-Hounds 1806-1858* (London, 1936), p. 7.

[68] Loder-Symonds and Crowdy, *A History of the Old Berks Hunt*, pp. 77-78; *Public Characters of 1806* (London, 1806), p. 616.

[69] *Sp. Mag.*, CXVI(July, 1850), p. 32.

[70] Loder-Symonds and Crowdy, *A History of the Old Berks Hunt*, p. 193.

[71] *Nimrod's Hunting Tours*, p. 109; *British Hunts and Huntsmen*, I, 134; *Sp. Mag.*, CXVIII(August, 1851).

[72] J. C. Thackwell of the Ledbury, James Hall of the Holderness, and Carrington Nunn of the Essex and Suffolk. *Field*, LXXIX(January 23, 1892), p. 103; Frank H. Reynard, *Hunting Notes from Holderness* ([London, 1914]); *British Hunts and Huntsmen*, II, 371.

[73] William Davenport of the North Staffs. *Staffordshire Advertiser*, June 12, 1869.

[74] H. G. Hoare of the Burstow, C. A. R. Hoare of the V.W.H., Robert Gosling of the Puckeridge, Ellis Gosling of the Chiddingfold, W. E. Rigden of the Tickham, A. P. Heywood Lonsdale of the Shropshire, and John Hargreaves of the South Berkshire.

[75] Sir Bache Cunard of the Billesdon and Arthur Wilson of the Holderness.

[76] William Wilson of the Barlow and Merthyr Guest of the Blackmore Vale.

[77] John Cowen of the Braes of Derwent, John Straker of the Tynedale, and G. W. Elliot of the Bedale.

[78] P. G. Barthropp of the Essex and Suffolk.

[79] Harding Cox of the Old Berkeley.

[80] T. B. and T. R. Bolitho of the Western.

[81] E. Jesser Coope of the East Essex.
[82] Albert Brassey of the Heythrop.
[83] Frederick Swindell of the Puckeridge.
[84] John Straker owned 12,000 acres; Albert Brassey owned 4000 acres. Merthyr Guest's father, who made his money from the great Dowlais iron works, bought land in 1845, and in 1873 owned over 83,000 acres. Bateman, *Great Landowners*; Parliamentary Papers, *1874*, LXXII, 'Return of Owners of Land, 1872-1873' ('New Domesday Book').
[85] Quarrell, *The Worcestershire Hunt*, pp. 12-13; *VCH, Worcestershire*, II, 323.
[86] See Ball and Gilbey, *The Essex Foxhounds*, pp. 272, 277.
[87] *Baily's Mag.*, LVI(August, 1891), pp. 73-78 for his biography.
[88] Pease, *The Cleveland Hounds as a Trencher-Fed Pack*; J. W. Ord, *The History and Antiquities of Cleveland* (London, 1846), p. 263.
[89] *Bilsdale and Hurworth Hunts — Case for the Decision of the Committee of the Master of Fox-Hounds Association, June, 1898*, North Riding County Record Office, C.R.11, p. 3; *Baily's Hunting Directory, 1970-1971*, p. 13.
[90] *British Hunts and Huntsmen*; *Baily's Hunting Directory*.
[91] *Sp. Mag.*, CXXXIX(May, 1862), p. 387; *ibid.*, CXLIII(March, 1864), p. 198.
[92] 'Aesop' [W. N. Heysham], *Sporting Reminiscences of Hampshire: From 1745 to 1862* (London, 1864), pp. 338-339.
[93] *Baily's Mag.* XL(January, 1883), p. 94.
[94] See W. O. Aydelotte, 'The Business Interests of Gentry in the Parliament of 1841-47' in G. Kitson Clark, *The Making of Victorian England* (Cambridge, Massachusetts, 1962), pp. 290-305.
[95] 'New Domesday Book'; Bateman, *Great Landowners*.
[96] *Baily's Mag.*, L(October, 1888), p. 33; Goodall, *Huntsmen of a Golden Age*.
[97] *Sp. Mag.*, CXIII(February, 1849), p. 148.
[98] See for example MS diary, Will Smith, August, 1847-March, 1848, Lincolnshire Archives Office, Yarb 7.
[99] 'Stonehenge', *Manual of British Rural Sports*, p. 102.
[100] *Bell's Life*, December 26, 1863; *ibid.*, April 23, 1864; *Sp. Mag.*, CXLIV (August, 1864), pp. 80-81; Loder-Symonds and Crowdy, *A History of the Old Berks Hunt*, p. 232.
[101] Underhill, *The Master of Hounds*, p. 211.
[102] Bradley, *The Reminiscences of Frank Gillard*, p. 67.
[103] Johnson, *The Hunting Directory*, p. 147.
[104] George E. Collins ('Nimrod Junior'), *History of the Brocklesby Hounds 1700-1901* (London, 1902), p. 67; *Baily's Mag.*, VI(February, 1863), p. 38.
[105] University of Durham, Department of Paleography and Diplomatic, Baker Baker, 18/102a; Northumberland Record Office, ZRI 51/7 and 51/8.

[106]The Atherstone huntsman received £100 in 1850, Wilson, *Green Peas at Christmas*, pp. 88-89. Charles Payne at the Pytchley received £130 wages plus another £28 in allowances in the 1860s, but this was considered high. Thomson, *Eighty Years Reminiscences*, I, 325. Also see 'Stonehenge', *Manual of British Rural Sports*, p. 115; *Baily's Mag.*, XI(June, 1866), pp. 342-343.

[107]*Bailey's Mag.*, XI (June, 1866), pp. 342-343; 'Stonehenge', *Manual of British Rural Sports*, p. 115.

[108]*Sp. Mag.*, LXXXVII (December, 1835), p. 100; Thomas Smith, *Extracts from the Diary of a Huntsman* (London, 1838), p. 120; Blaine, *An Encyclopaedia of Rural Sports*, p. 485; Harry Hieover, *The Hunting-Field*, p. 145; *Field*, XXIX (January 27, 1872), p. 88.

[109]At the end of the century the custom was to give the huntsman one pound for the brush, the first whipper-in, ten shillings for the mask, and the second whipper-in, five shillings for a pad. George F. Underhill, *Hunting and Practical Hints for Hunting Men* (London, 1897), p. 48.

[110][Tom Andrews], *The Fox Hunting Reminiscences of 'Gin and Beer'* ... (Worcester, [1930]), p. 63.

[111]Ord, *The Sedgefield Country in the Seventies and Eighties*, p. 15.

[112]Heythrop Hunt. MS minute book, 1850-1873.

[113]Davies, *Memoir of the Rev. John Russell*, p. 51.

[114]*Bell's Life*, January 22, 1848; *Sp. Mag.*, CXI(February, 1848), p. 149; *Sp. Mag.*, LXXXV(January, 1835), p. 268.

[115]*Bell's Life*, November 19, 1848.

[116]Blaine, *An Encyclopaedia of Rural Sports*, p. 485.

[117]*Rules of the Hunt Servants Benefit Society* (1872). A copy is in the Somerset Record Office, DD/L. Later, the premiums and benefits were changed slightly. *Bell's Life*, November 11, 1876.

[118]*Bailey's Mag.*, XXXIII(March, 1879), p. 306.

[119]*Ibid.*, XXVIII(January, 1876), p. 120.

[120]The officers of the 60th Rifles gave a performance in 1874. *Field*, XLIII (February 28, 1874), p. 197. See *Bell's Life*, December 20, 1879.

[121]*Baily's Mag.*, XXX(July, 1877), p. 367.

[122]*Ibid.*, XVII(July, 1869), p. 33.

[123]Vyner, *Notitia Venatica* (New ed.; 1892), p. 224 n.2. For the rules of the North Staffordshire Hunt on earthstopping c. 1890, see Blagg, *History of the North Staffordshire Hounds*, p. 184.

[124]"The Druid', *The Post and Paddock*, p. 353. Also see Nimrod, *The Chace, The Turf and The Road*, p. 56.

[125]"The Druid', *The Post and Paddock*, p. 359.

[126]"The Druid', *Silk and Scarlet*, p. 2.

Notes to Chapter Seven

Chapter seven

[1] There is no way of telling precisely how many people hunted. Taking an average of 150 riders on a given day with approximately 150 packs, the number in 1885, yields a total of 22,500 riders, which may be doubled to account for the number of people who did not hunt every day. No figure, however, is more than a guess.

[2] Cobbett, *Rural Rides,* p. 277. See, too, J. C. Hodgson, ed., *North Country Diaries* Publications of the Surtees Society, Vol. CXVIII (Durham, 1910), pp. 230-233.

[3] Fred Kitchen, *Brother to the Ox: The Autobiography of a Farm Labourer* (London, 1940), p. 10.

[4] See *Bell's Life,* December 18, 1836, and 'Cecil', *Records of the Chase,* pp. 196-197, for descriptions of this event in the 1830s and 1850s.

[5] 'Cecil', in *Sp. Mag.,* CXIII(May, 1849), p. 319.

[6] *Bell's Life,* April 7, 1861.

[7] The tradition of St Stephen's Day persisted in Yorkshire at least into the 1840s. Pease, *The Cleveland Hounds as a Trencher-Fed Pack,* pp. 81, 108.

[8] MS hunting diary of Sir Henry Dryden, December 27, 1841. Northamptonshire Record Office, ZA 477.

[9] Cobbett, *Rural Rides,* p. 17.

[10] See *Bilsdale and Hurworth Hunts — Case for the Decision of the Committee of the Master of Fox-Hounds Association June 1898,* p. 10, North Riding County Record Office, C.R.11, for a 74 year old labourer, who claimed to have followed the Bilsdale 'scores of times'.

[11] A labourer in the Quorn country, for example, was given a sovereign to retrieve the corpse of a fox that the hounds had killed in a river. Davenport, *Memories at Random,* p. 15. Also see Pease, *The Cleveland Hounds as a Trencher-Fed Pack,* p. 171.

[12] Frank Edson, a weaver of Monk Bretton, near Barnsley, used to turn out with the Badsworth two or three times per week in the 1850s. He would often work at night in order to be able to hunt during the day. *Field,* VII (March 22, 1856), p. 185.

[13] 'Cecil', *Records of the Chase,* pp. 221-222.

[14] For one example among many, see MS hunting journal of John Josselyn, January 23, 1849, for an account of a fox being lost because there were 200 foot people at a check. Bury St Edmunds and West Suffolk Record Office, 1677/6/11.

[15] 'Cecil' quoted a shepherd in the Vine country in 1849: 'They'd be like halloo if they saw a gentleman in a red coat, or may-be they'd only halloo just to get the hounds back to them if they zeed 'um going another way; they be fond a zeeing the hounds'. *Sp. Mag.,* CXIII(January, 1849), p. 57. Cf. MS hunting diary

of John Josselyn, January 23, 1851. Bury St Edmunds and West Suffolk Record Office, 1677/6/11.

[16]'The Druid', *Silk and Scarlet*, p. 378.

[17]Paget, *History of the Althorp and Pytchley Hunt*, p. 132; Paget and Irvine, *The Flying Parson and Dick Christian*, p. 96; Osbaldeston, *Autobiography*, pp. 123-127, 160-162.

[18]'The Druid', *Silk and Scarlet*, p. 64.

[19]Surtees, *Mr. Facey Romford's Hounds*, p. 89.

[20]*Bell's Life*, November 14, 1874; Davies, *Memoir of the Rev. John Russell*, p. 251; Higginson, *'The Meynell of the West'*, p. 29.

[21]For the rules of several hunt clubs see: Berkshire Record Office, D/EM F2 bundle 1; Bury St Edmunds and West Suffolk Record Office, 1677/6/37; Durham County Record Office, D/Sa/X/42, 43, 44; *The Oakley Club* (Bedford, 1901); *Sp. Mag.*, LXV(January, 1825), p. 292.

[22]Berkshire Record Office, D/EL1 Z24, Printed rules of the Old Berks Hunt Club, 1865; New Forest Hunt Club. MS Minute Book.

[23]See *Sp. Mag.*, XI(November, 1797), p. 100, for a description of some.

[24]*Ibid.*, LXVIII(June, 1826), pp. 113-114.

[25]For example, the Heythrop supper and ball at Christmas, 1837, *Bell's Life*, January 1, 1838.

[26]*Ibid.*, December 14, 1872.

[27]Higginson, *'The Meynell of the West'*, pp. 248-270; *Bell's Life*, January 12, 1840.

[28]Higginson, *'The Meynell of the West'*, p. 214.

[29]Surtees, *Handley Cross*, p. 494.

[30]*The Meets of the Suffolk Pack, 1851*. There is a copy in the Bury St Edmunds and West Suffolk Record Office, 1677/6/36.

[31]For the Hampshire Hunt Races of 1794, see 'Aesop', *Sporting Reminiscences of Hampshire*, p. 38. *Sp. Mag.*, XI(November, 1797), p. 100 describes another.

[32]Sir Reginald Graham, *Fox-Hunting Recollections* (London, 1907), p. 35.

[33]*Bell's Life*, February 1, 1879.

[34]*Ibid.*, March 4, 1860; March 25, 1860, supplement; September 16, 1860; October 14, 1860; November 18, 1860.

[35]For a history of Farquharson's mastership, see Higginson, *'The Meynell of the West'*.

[36]Higginson, *'The Meynell of the West'*, p. 235.

[37]Loder-Symonds and Crowdy, *History of the Old Berks Hunt*, p. 116; *Sp. Mag.*, XXXIX(November, 1811), p. 87.

[38]*The Times*, May 31, 1851.

[39]See *Bell's Life*, December 7, 1851, December 14, 1851, January 11, 1852.

[40]For a third example, taken from the Cambridgeshire election of 1868, see D. C. Moore, 'Politics of Deference: A Study of the Political Structure,

Leadership, and Organization of English County Constituencies in the Nineteenth Century' (unpublished Ph.D. dissertation, Columbia University, 1958), pp. 226-228. Now published (1976) as 'The Politics of Deference: A Study of the Mid-nineteenth Century English Political System' by the Harvester Press, Hassocks, Sussex, England and Barnes & Noble, New York.

[41] *VCH Essex*, II, 249; Walford, *County Families, 1883*.

[42] *Parliamentary Debates*, 3d Ser., Vol. 150 (June 10, 1858), cols. 1860-1871.

[43] MS letter, February 11, 1865, T. G. G. White to C. DuCane. Essex Record Office, D/Dc E4/11.

[44] Letter from 'A Tenant Farmer', *Essex Telegraph* (Colchester), February 14, 1865.

[45] February 18, 1865. Essex Record Office, D/Dc E4/11.

[46] Published in *Essex and West Suffolk Gazette, Essex Standard*, and *Chelmsford Chronicle*, February 17, 1865, and *Essex Weekly News*, February 24, 1865. The originals are in Essex Record Office, D/Dc E4/11.

[47] *Essex and West Suffolk Gazette* and *Chelmsford Chronicle*, February 24, 1865; *Essex Telegraph*, February 28, 1865.

[48] *Essex and West Suffolk Gazette*, February 24, 1865, leading article. It was based on a draft in DuCane's handwriting in Essex Record Office, D/Dc E4/11. Other letters filed under the same shelfmark indicate the close ties between DuCane and the paper.

[49] Letter of Charles Cottee, *Chelmsford Chronicle* and *Essex and West Suffolk Gazette*, March 3, 1865; *Essex Standard*, March 8, 1865. See Essex Record Office, D/DC E4/11, for a draft of the letter in DuCane's hand on Carleton Club stationery, and a letter from DuCane to his solicitor I. H. Blood, February 28, 1865 suggesting that Cottee be given the letter to write.

[50] *Essex Standard*, March 3, 1865.

[51] March 7, 1865.

[52] Leading article, written by DuCane, February 24, 1865.

[53] MS letters, J. G. Chamberlain to C. DuCane, February 25, 1865, and F. Pearse to C. DuCane, March 4, 1865, suggest that DuCane was unpopular with some of his tenants because of his strict preservation of game. Essex Record Office, D/Dc E4/11.

[54] *Essex and West Suffolk Gazette*, March 10, 1865.

[55] *Bell's Life*, March 11, 1865.

[56] *Chelmsford Chronicle*, February 11, 1876, February 18, 1876, February 25, 1876, March 3, 1876; *Bell's Life*, March 4, 1876.

[57] *Leicester Journal*, August 14, 1868; *VCH Leicestershire*, II, pp. 133-134.

[58] *Churton v. Frewen*, *Leicester Advertiser*, May 12, 1866.

[59] *Leicester Advertiser*, leading article, September 19, 1868.

[60] *Leicester Advertiser*, November 14, 1868. A truncated version of the letter is in *Bell's Life*, November 28, 1868, and parts of it are in Ellis, *Leicestershire and*

Notes to Chapter Eight

the Quorn, pp. 104-105.

[61] *Leicester Mail*, November 7, 1868.

[62] *Leicester Journal*, November 20, 1868.

[63] In Loughborough and Shepshed, the radical strongholds, he was first; in all other polling districts, he was last. *Leicester Advertiser*, November 21, 1868.

[64] *Leicester Journal*, November 20, 1868; *Leicester Advertiser*, November 21, 1868.

[65] *Leicester Mail*, November 28, 1868.

[66] *Leicester Journal*, November 20, 1868.

[67] *Leicester Advertiser*, November 28, 1868.

[68] *Leicester Journal*, November 27, 1868; *Leicester Mail*, November 28, 1868.

[69] See chapters VIII and X.

[70] *Leicester Journal*, November 27, 1868.

[71] *Leicester Mail*, November 21, 1868.

[72] *Ibid.*, November 28, 1868.

[73] *Leicester Journal*, December 4, 1868.

[74] *Eleanor Frewen Turner v. W. W. Tailby*, Oakham County Court, February 9, 1869. *Bell's Life*, February 10, 1869.

Chapter eight

[1] See any of the collections of sketches of 'hunting types', which were published at various times throughout the nineteenth century. Among them are: Surtees, *Analysis of the Hunting Field;* Trollope, *Hunting Sketches;* 'Bagatelle', *Men We Meet in the Field;* G. Finch Mason, *Flowers of the Hunt* (London, 1889).

[2] Cook, *Observations on Fox-Hunting*, p. 126.

[3] *Sp. Mag.*, LIX(January, 1822), p. 180.

[4] See, for example, *Bell's Life*, January 28, 1849; *Baily's Mag.*, XLVII (April, 1887), p. 225.

[5] Nimrod, in *Sp. Mag.*, LXV(February, 1825), p. 329.

[6] Surtees, *Analysis of the Hunting Field*, p. 177.

[7] *Sp. Mag.*, I(March, 1793), pp. 319-320.

[8] See letters sent out by Sir Matthew White Ridley in 1818, Northumberland Record Office, ZRI 51/8; Lord Charles FitzRoy in 1839, Northamptonshire Record Office, YZ 9623; and the Duke of Wellington, 'Aesop', *Sporting Reminiscences of Hampshire*, p. 194.

[9] MS letter, F. J. Snowball to Thomas Sample, April 9, 1884. Northumberland Record Office, ZSA 3/25. For other examples, see Somerset Record Office, DD/L; *Evesham Journal*, April 30, 1881.

[10] Lincolnshire Archives Office, Yarb 7.

[11] See Northumberland Record Office, ZSA 3/25.

[12] Blaine, *Encyclopaedia of Rural Sports*, p. 484.

[13] Wilson, *Green Peas at Christmas*, p. 88; *Field*, XLV (April 17, 1875), p. 378; typed copy of letter, Lord Annaly to Duke of Northumberland, November 11, 1900. University of Durham, Department of Paleography and Diplomatic, 4th Earl Grey Papers.

[14] *Field*, LXXV(April 19, 1890), p. 557.

[15] See Byng, *Torrington Diaries*, II, 314-315.

[16] MS letter, H. Magniac to W. B. Higgins, c. 1836, Bedford County Record Office, X213/105.

[17] Thomas Johnson in *The Hunting Directory*, p. 304, claimed that farmers in foxhunting districts sustained no more than one pound annual losses as a result of fox damages, and that the average figure was probably no more than five shillings. Also see Thomas Smith, *Extracts from the Diary of a Huntsman* (London, 1838), p. 164; 'Cecil', *Records of the Chase*, p. 84; Beaufort and Morris, *Hunting*, p. 72.

[18] See North Cotswold Hunt. MS poultry receipts, 1871; MS hunting diary of R. W. Blathwayt, 1888-1894, Gloucestershire Records Office, D1799/F28, for the New Forest Hunt poultry claims, 1889-1890. Both show the hunt paying less than was claimed. Typically, £2 would be paid for a claim of £2. 17s. 6d. Bagot, *Men We Meet in the Field*.

[19] Burton Hunt. MS minute book, committee meeting, April 23, 1875.

[20] Taunton Vale Foxhounds. MS minute book, November 1, 1890.

[21] In the early nineteenth century, it cost £1000 per year. Nimrod, *The Chace, The Turf, and The Road*, p. 21. In 1865, the Pytchley paid £1500, *Field*, XXVI (November 11, 1865), p. 349.

[22] See MS letter, William Coldicott to Cregoe Colmore, February 3, 1864, North Cotswold Hunt MSS. Also see, L. Loraine to M. Milbanke, March 28, 1818, Northumberland Record Office, ZRI 51/8.

[23] See the correspondence over the covert at Kirkheaton, in Sir Matthew White Ridley's country in 1820. Northumberland Record Office, ZRI 51/8.

[24] Beaufort and Morris, *Hunting*, p. 124.

[25] The puppies were generally sent back from their walks by the end of March, for few farmers could be prevailed upon to keep them longer because of the danger to their young lambs and poultry. Vyner, *Notitia Venatica* (1st ed.), p. 113.

[26] The Duke of Grafton gave prizes in the 1860s, others may have done so earlier. John Malsbury Kirby Elliott, *Fifty Year's Fox-Hunting with the Grafton and Other Packs of Hounds* ed. by Edward Kirby Elliott (London, 1900), p. 89.

[27] Ord, *The Sedgefield Country*, p. 209.

[28] Berkeley, *Reminiscences of a Huntsman*, p. 150; Lincolnshire Archives Office, Monson 28A/19/2/23-24; *Bell's Life*, February 4, 1871.

[29] *Field*, LXXII(October 13, 1888), p. 544.

[30] *Field*, LIX(February 4, 1882), p. 135.

[31] Surtees, *Analysis of the Hunting Field*, p. 174.
[32] See Henry Hall Dixon, *A Treatise on the Law of the Farm: including the Agricultural Customs of England and Wales* (London, 1858), pp. 267, 439-451.
[33] Surtees, *Analysis of the Hunting Field*, p. 174.
[34] MS diary of Will Smith I, 1816. Lincolnshire Archives Office, Yarb 7.
[35] *Baily's Mag.*, XVI(May, 1869), p. 317.
[36] See, for example, *Sp. Mag.*, CXLII(November, 1863), pp. 387-388.
[37] Lady Augusta Fane, *Chit-Chat* (London, 1926), p. 122.
[38] *Baily's Mag.*, XIII(March, 1867), p. 4.
[39] *Sp. Mag.*, LXV(February, 1825), p. 363.
[40] *Field*, XV(January 14, 1860), p. 24.
[41] *Field*, XIX(January 25, 1862), p. 69.
[42] *Ibid.* (February 1, 1862), p. 93.
[43] *Ibid.*, XX(December 6, 1862), p. 517.
[44] See the letter from 'South Leicestershire', *ibid.*, XIX (March 22, 1862), p. 247.
[45] *Ibid.*, XXII (October 24, 1863), p. 401.
[46] *Ibid.*
[47] *Ibid.* (October 31, 1863), p. 425.
[48] *Ibid.* (November 7, 1863), p. 453.
[49] *Ibid.* (November 14, 1863), p. 473.
[50] *Baily's Mag.*, VII(November, 1863), p. 124.
[51] *Mark Lane Express*, November 23, 1863.
[52] October 31, 1863.
[53] *Sp. Mag.*, CXLII(October, 1863), p. 400.
[54] *Ibid.*; *Bell's Life*, November 21, 1863.
[55] *Field*, XXIII(April 2, 1864), p. 241; (April 9, 1864), p. 251.
[56] *Ibid.*, XXXVIII(November 25, 1871), p. 460; XXXV (January 1, 1870), p. 13; LXXXI(February 4, 1893), p. 108.
[57] *Ibid.*, XXII(November 14, 1863), p. 473.
[58] See *Mark Lane Express*, November 23, 1863.
[59] *Sp. Mag.*, CXLII(December, 1863), pp. 399-400.
[60] Leading article, November 23, 1863.
[61] MS letter, J. Lee to the Oakley Committee, December, 1834. Bedford County Record Office, X213/100.
[62] *Field*, XXXVIII(December 2, 1871), p. 484.
[63] For versions of the story, see: *Sp. Mag.*, LXVIII(May, 1826), p. 32; LXXI (March, 1828), p. 334; LXXVII (February, 1831), p. 295; *Bell's Life*, November 15, 1857; *Baily's Mag.*, LIII(February, 1890), p. 139; Elliott, *Fifty Year's Fox-Hunting*, p. 113; Collins, *History of the Brocklesby Hounds*, pp. 306-307.
[64] Surtees, *Handley Cross*, pp. 298-299.

[65] Letter from 'X', *Field*, XXVII(January 6, 1866), p. 11.
[66] *Parliamentary Debates*, 3rd Series, Vol. 181 (February 20, 1866), col. 863.
[67] *Field*, XXVII (February 24, 1866), p. 147. Reprinted in *The Times*, February 26, 1866.
[68] *Baily's Mag.*, XI(February, 1866), p. 106.
[69] See *The Times*, January 26, 1866; *Field*, XXVII(February 3, 1866), p. 91.
[70] *Field*, XXVII(February 10, 1866), p. 116; (March 24, 1866), p. 240.
[71] *Ibid.* (March 31, 1866), p. 255.
[72] *Ibid.* (March 3, 1866), p. 184.
[73] *Parliamentary Debates*, 3rd Series, Vol. 181 (February 16, 1866), cols. 595-596; *The Times*, March 7, 1866.
[74] On March 3, 1866, ninety-three of the approximately 115 packs advertised their meets in *The Field*. Also see, *Sp. Mag.*, CXLVII(April, 1866), p. 293.
[75] Goodall, *Huntsmen of a Golden Age*, p. 151; MS letter, Cregoe Colmore to J. Wilson Wilson, February 3, 1866. North Cotswold Hunt MSS.
[76] See, for example, *Mark Lane Express*, October 14, 1850, p. 6; November 23, 1863, p. 8; *The Farmer's Magazine*, September, 1834, p. 335; June, 1835, pp. 387-392; January, 1849, p. 89.
[77] Paget and Irvine, *The Flying Parson and Dick Christian*, p. 76. Also see *Life in London*, April 21, 1822; *Bell's Life*, December 6, 1840; 'The Druid', *Saddle and Sirloin* (London, 1870), p. 454.
[78] *Sp. Mag.*, CXXX(November, 1857), pp. 315-316; CXXXI(January, 1858), p. 68.
[79] *Field*, LXXVII(February 14, 1891), p. 203.
[80] *Sp. Mag.*, LXIX(April, 1827), pp. 351-353; *Bell's Life*, January 24, 1836.
[81] Vyner, *Notitia Venatica* (1st ed.), p. 166.
[82] See *Bell's Life*, January and February, 1851, where the increased vulpicide was blamed on hard times.
[83] Letter from 'Loxias', *Field*, XXXIV(October 16, 1869), p. 325.
[84] *Middlesex and Hertfordshire Notes and Queries*, III(1897), pp. 75-77.
[85] *Bell's Life*, November 14, 1841, February 2, 1862; *Field*, XXVII(April 14, 1866), p. 307.
[86] *Bell's Life*, February 2, 1862.
[87] 'The Druid', *Scott and Sebright*, p. 395.
[88] Graham, *Fox-Hunting Recollections*, p. 183.
[89] MS diary of Sir Charles Chichester, November 18, 1829. East Riding County Record Office, DDCH A26.
[90] *Ibid.*, November 27, 1829.
[91] See 'Aesop', *Sporting Reminiscences of Hampshire*, p. 38, for a dinner in 1794.
[92] For the dinner given by Richardson Gardner, M.P., for two hundred Cotswold farmers, see *Baily's Mag.*, XXVIII(December, 1875), p. 57.
[93] *Sp. Mag.*, LXV(November, 1824), p. 66.

[94] *Bell's Life*, March 21, 1841.
[95] Elliott, *Fifty Year's Fox-Hunting*, p. 87.
[96] *Bell's Life*, December 28, 1828.
[97] Bathurst, *History of the V.W.H. Country*, pp. 121-125.
[98] Essex Record Office, D/DW A7.
[99] Surtees, *Analysis of the Hunting Field*, p. 177.
[100] *Sp. Mag.*, LXV (February, 1825), p. 329; (March, 1825), p. 423.
[101] *Ibid.*, LXVI (June, 1825), pp. 237-238.
[102] 'Harry Hieover', *The Hunting-Field*, p. 11; *Sp. Mag.*, CX (August, 1847), p. 109.
[103] *Baily's Mag.*, VII (February, 1864), p. 279; *Field*, XLII (September 27, 1873), p. 330, among others.
[104] *Parliamentary Papers*, 1873, Vol. XIV, 'Report From the Select Committee of the House of Lords on Horses', pp. 38, 88, 116.
[105] Some did, of course. Lord Suffield, master of the Quorn in the 1830s, bought corn directly from farmers. *Sp. Mag.*, XCII (October, 1838), p. 474. C. A. R. Hoare, master of the V.W.H., bought from local farmers, and was accused of trying to buy popularity. See chapter X.
[106] *Field*, LXXV (January 11, 1890), p. 42.

Chapter nine

[1] 'Conversation', line 405.
[2] Charles Strachey, ed., *The Letters of the Earl of Chesterfield to his Son* (2 vols.; New York and London, 1925), II, 176.
[3] Wingfield-Stratford, *The Squire and his Relations*, p. 187.
[4] Rev. J. Curtis, *A Topographical History of the County of Leicester* (Ashby-de-la-Zouch, 1831), p. xliv; Stillingfleet, *On the Amusements of Clergymen*, p. 19; Thomas Chalmers, *On Cruelty to Animals: A Sermon, Preached in Edinburgh, on the 5th of March, 1826* (Glasgow, 1826), p. 29.
[5] Stillingfleet, *On the Amusements of Clergymen*, p. 19.
[6] When Mr Jorrocks first came to Handley Cross, the 'religious Freedom Society', placarded the town with 'Foxhunters Will All Go To – .' Surtees, *Handley Cross*, p. 84. Sir Francis Holyoke-Goodricke, Master of the Quorn, 1833-35, and of the Pytchley, 1842-44, and known as one of the hardest riding Meltonians, gave up hunting 'under the influence of deep and very sincere religious impressions', though his new wife may have also played a part. J. E. Auden, *A Short History of the Albrighton Hunt* (London, 1905), p. 41n.
[7] *Sp. Mag.*, LXV (January, 1825), p. 258.
[8] *Ibid.*, LXXXIII (November, 1833), p. 23; CVIII (August, 1846), p.89; CXII (October, 1848), pp. 251-252.
[9] *Punch*, XXXVIII (April 28, 1860), p. 169, supported the popular view of

hunting as a sport which imparted 'a healthy tone and cheerful temper to the mind'.

[10] See Nimrod, *The Chace, The Turf, and The Road*, p. 64.

[11] E.g., *Morning Herald*, September 2, 1826; *Joseph Arch, The Story of his Life Told by Himself* (London, 1898), p. 30.

[12] Ellis, *Leicestershire and the Quorn*, p. 100.

[13] Skinner Philippo, *Thoughts on Hunting*, quoted in *Sp. Mag.*, CXXXII (August, 1858), p. 83. For a more detailed account of the attack on popular amusements in general by those who wished to promote 'industry' among the working classes, see Robert W. Malcolmson, *Popular Recreations in English Society, 1700-1850* (Cambridge, 1973), pp. 89-100.

[14] *The Times*, September 17, 1858.

[15] *The Times*, September 22, 1858. Letters from John Drummond and Robert Pritchard.

[16] See *Bell's Life*, October 10, 1858, for an article by 'Scrutator'.

[17] *The Times*, September 22, 1858.

[18] The Radical *Leicester Mail*, for example, criticized hunting magistrates for neglecting their judicial duties for the diversions of the hunting field. November 7, 1868.

[19] Cobbett defended one sportsman from the charge that he had squandered his money on hunting by asserting that it was his perfect right to do so. Cobbett, *Rural Rides*, pp. *76-*77.

[20] *Bell's Life*, December 25, 1869, January 1, 1870, November 27, 1880, January 14, 1882; Vyner, *Notitia Venatica* (6th ed.) p. 9; Beaufort and Morris, *Hunting*, p. 2.

[21] This opinion was held as late as 1862. See the letter from 'Cynic' in *Field*, XX(October 11, 1862), p. 330.

[22] Humphrey Primatt, *A Dissertation on the Duty of Mercy and Sin of Cruelty to Brute Animals* (London, 1776), p. 62.

[23] 'The Task', Book III, 'The Garden', lines 326-329.

[24] See, for example, letter from 'Constant Subscriber' in *Sp. Mag.*, VII (October, 1795), pp. 40-42; John Oswald, *The Cry of Nature; or, An Appeal to Mercy and to Justice, on behalf of the Persecuted Animals* (London, 1791), a vegetarian tract by an English Jacobin.

[25] For some examples see *Sp. Mag.*, III(December, 1793), pp. 155, 157-158; IV(July, 1794), pp. 130-131, 188, 199; V(October, 1794), pp. 40-41.

[26] Wingfield-Stratford, *The Squire and his Relations*, p. 198.

[27] See Surtees, *Analysis of the Hunting Field*, p. 68; Blaine, *Encyclopaedia of Rural Sports*, p. 478. According to 'Cecil', the system of harsh punishment for hounds was obsolete by 1853. *Sp. Mag.*, CXXI(June, 1853), p. 445.

[28] John Lawrence, *A Philosophical and Practical Treatise on Horses* (2 vols.; London, 1796, 1798), II, 14.

[29] London, 1799.
[30] By Thomas Day, published in parts, 1783-1789.
[31] *The Parliamentary History of England*, Vol. 35 (April 18, 1800), p. 207. Sydney Smith attacked the Society for the Suppression of Vice, which had opposed bull-baiting, on these same grounds. *Edinburgh Review*, XIII (January, 1809), pp. 333-343. See Malcolmson, *Popular Recreations*, pp. 118-138, for an account of the movement against bull-baiting and similar sports.
[32] Beckford, *Thoughts on Hunting*, pp. 179, 286.
[33] *Sp. Mag.*, LXXX (July, 1832), pp. 175-176, See, too, *ibid.*, LXXXV (January, 1835), p. 261. *ibid.*, XCIV (May, 1839), p. 14.
[34] See *Field*, IX (June 6, 1857), p. 397.
[35] *Bell's Life*, March 13, 1859. For the story of Marsh-Walker see 'Aesop', *Sporting Reminiscences of Hampshire*, pp. 338-339.
[36] Berkeley, *Reminiscences of a Huntsman*, p. v.
[37] The major concern of the R.S.P.C.A. may be seen in such actions as its unsuccessful prosecution of Lord Middleton's whippers-in for riding their horses too hard. *Baily's Mag.*, XIX (February, 1871), pp. 343-344. For accounts of the R.S.P.C.A. and its relationship to the anti-cruel sports movement, see Malcolmson, *Popular Recreations*, pp. 118-138, 152-157, and 172-173, and two articles by Brian Harrison, 'Religion and Recreation in Nineteenth-Century England', *Past and Present* no. 38 (December, 1967), pp. 98-125, and 'Animals and the State in Nineteenth-Century England', *English Historical Review*, LXXXVIII (October, 1973), pp. 786-820. Malcolmson's contention that it was class bias that kept the R.S.P.C.A. from attacking hunting is overstated. Certainly the desire to attract the support of the upper-classes was an important element in determining their programme, but the egalitarian tradition of hunting, as well as the belief that it was less cruel than many other sports, were, I believe, of greater importance.
[38] John Styles, *The Animal Creation: Its Claims on our Humanity Stated and Enforced* (London, [1839]), p. 23. For the answer of the sporting community, see Grantley Fitzhardinge Berkeley, *A Pamphlet . . . in Reply to . . . the Rev. John Styles, D.D.* (London, 1839).
[39] Styles, *The Animal Creation*; James Macaulay, *Essay on Cruelty to Animals* (Edinburgh, 1839).
[40] William H. Drummond, *The Rights of Animals, and Man's Obligation to Treat Them with Humanity* (London and Dublin, 1838).
[41] W. Youatt, *The Obligation and Extent of Humanity to Brutes, Principally Considered with Reference to the Domesticated Animals* (London, 1839), p. 109.
[42] Blaine, *Encyclopaedia of Rural Sports*, pp. 150-152, 478; Nimrod, *Life of a Sportsman*, p. 13, where cruelty to animals is called 'a vice the very reverse of the characteristic of the thorough English sportsman'. See *Bell's Life*, February 2, 1840; *Field*, IX (June 6, 1857), p. 397; XIII (January 29, 1859), p. 80.

[43] The exchange continued throughout September and October, 1862.
[44] *Sp. Mag.*, CXLVI (December, 1865), p. 424.
[45] Freeman (1823-92), a prolific writer, a magistrate in Somerset, and an unsuccessful political candidate, was later (1884) Regius Professor of Modern History at Oxford. *DNB*, Vol. XXII.
[46] E. A. Freeman, 'The Morality of Field Sports', *Fortnightly Review*, October 1, 1869, p. 354.
[47] *Ibid.*, p. 379.
[48] Anthony Trollope, 'Mr Freeman on the Morality of Hunting', *Fortnightly Review*, December 1, 1869, p. 619.
[49] *Ibid.*, pp. 622-623.
[50] *Ibid.*, p. 624.
[51] See, for example, *Bell's Life*, December 25, 1869, January 1, 1870, January 5, 1870; *Spectator*, December 4, 1869, pp. 1421-1422; *Fortnightly Review*, December 1, 1870, pp. 674-691, January 1, 1870, pp. 63-68; *Saturday Review*, December 11, 1869, pp. 760-761; *Pall Mall Gazette*, January 4, 1870; *Sp. Mag.*, CLV (February, 1870), p. 106; *Macmillan's Magazine*, February, 1870, pp. 341-342.
[52] *Bell's Life*, January 14, 1871, letter from 'Fox': 'For what purpose does he think the fox, deer, and hare have such a strong scent, and why does he think dogs of chase were created?'
[53] See, for example, the letter from Lord Winchelsea in the *Pall Mall Gazette*, January 4, 1870, quoted in *Bell's Life*, January 5, 1870. Foxes, he claimed, would soon be exterminated were it not for hunting. To this argument, Freeman had a ready answer: '... the fox like the wolf, is a beast which must and ought to die out before the advance of civilization.... We have a perfect right to kill them; we have no right to seek amusement in their death or suffering'. Freeman, 'The Controversy on Field Sports', p. 684.
[54] *Spectator*, December 4, 1869, pp. 1421-1422.
[55] *Saturday Review*, December 11, 1869, pp. 760-761.
[56] See, for example, [Sir A. Helps], *Some Talk about Animals and their Masters* (London, 1873); J. Woodroffe Hill, *The Relative Positions of the Higher and Lower Creation; or A Plea for Dumb Animals* (London, 1881); James Macaulay, *Plea for Mercy to Animals* (London, [1875]); Edward Byron Nicholson, *The Rights of an Animal: A New Essay in Ethics* (London, 1879).
[57] See, for example, Vyner, *Notitia Venatica* (6th ed.), p. 5; *Bell's Life*, January 22, 1870; J. Nevill Fitt, *Covert-Side Sketches: or, Thoughts on Hunting Suggested by Many Days in Many Countries with Fox, Deer, and Hare* (London, 1878), p. 56; Beaufort and Morris, *Hunting*, pp. 1-2, 64; Kennard, *The Right Sort*, p. 114; Fox Russell, *Cross Country Reminiscences* (London, 1887), pp. 26-27.
[58] Humanitarian League. *Annual Reports* (London, 1892, 1896, 1897);

Notes to Chapter Nine 233

British Blood Sports: 'Let Us Go Out and Kill Something'. (London, 1901).
[59] See *Parliamentary Debates*, 3rd Series, Vol. 276 (March 7, 1883), col. 1670; *Baily's Mag.*, XLI(September, 1883), p. 184.
[60] *Field*, LXIII(February 16, 1884), p. 203.
[61] *Field*, LXVI(July 11, 1885), p. 39; *Baily's Mag.*, XLIV (August, 1885), p. 324.
[62] W. Bromley Davenport, 'Fox-Hunting', *Nineteenth Century*, June, 1883, p. 989. Cf. *Baily's Mag.*, XLI(July, 1883), p. 58.
[63] See, for example, Thomas Smith, *Extracts from the Diary of a Huntsman*, p. 213; letter from 'V', *The Times*, November 24, 1840; 'Stonehenge', *Manual of British Rural Sports*, p. 8; and virtually every other book on hunting.
[64] Owen Jones, *Ten Years of Game-Keeping* (London, 1910), p. 169; *Field*, XX (July 5, 1862), p. 8, for letter from 'Fair Play'.
[65] See, for example, the diaries of John Josselyn, master of the Suffolk, October 16, 1849, Bury St Edmunds and West Suffolk Record Office, 1677/6/11; October 16, 1879, *ibid.*, 1677/6/28.
[66] Ellis, *Leicestershire and the Quorn*, p. 103. Others who did the same included Lord Hardwicke in Cambridgeshire, *Bell's Life*, December 13, 1840; and Lord Ashburnham in Sussex, *Field*, XXXII(December 26, 1868), p. 526.
[67] See, for example, *Field*, XIV(December 17, 1859), p. 507, for an account of dog spears in the East Riding, or Ball and Gilbey, *The Essex Foxhounds*, p. 83, for their use in Essex.
[68] *Sp. Mag.*, LXVI(May, 1825), p. 79.
[69] *Bell's Life*, April 25, 1841.
[70] *Sp. Mag.*, CLIII(March, 1869), p. 163.
[71] MS letter, T. J. Lloyd Baker to Colonel Berkeley, June 18, 1822, Gloucestershire Records Office, D471 C1; MS letter, Lord Hotham to Thomas Hodgson, April 4, 1838, East Riding Record Office, DDEV 60/30 xi.
[72] *Bell's Life*, December 29, 1844; Cook, *Observations on Fox-Hunting*, p. 52. It will be recalled that this was the accusation against Charles DuCane in the 1865 North Essex election.
[73] See, for example, the preview of the coming season in *Field*, XXXIV (November 6, 1869), p. 386.
[74] See *Bell's Life*, January 25, 1857; Underhill, *Hunting*, p. 11.
[75] This was especially common in extensively preserved counties like those of East Anglia. The hunting journals of John Josselyn, which cover the sport of the Suffolk hounds from 1845 to 1883, contain numerous references to three-legged foxes. Bury St Edmunds and West Suffolk Record Office, 1677/6/10-32; *Sp. Mag.*, CXLII(December, 1863), p. 398.
[76] *Sp. Mag.*, XLVII(March, 1816), p. 301.
[77] *Field*, V(January 20, 1855), p. 36.
[78] 26 and 27 Vict., c. 113.

[79] 27 and 28 Vict., c. 115.
[80] See *Parliamentary Debates*, 3rd Series, Vol. 172 (July 8, 1863), cols. 385-386.
[81] *Ibid.*, Vol. 176 (July 14, 1864), col. 1435.
[82] In 1870, the *Sporting Magazine* reported they were on the increase. *Sp. Mag.*, CLV(April, 1870), p. 266. Within the space of one week, three packs lost hounds. *Ibid.*, p. 298. Also see *Baily's Mag.*, XVIII (February, 1870), p. 54; (May, 1870), p. 189; *Field*, XXXVII (February 25, 1871), p. 148; XLIII (February 28, 1874), p. 197; (April 4, 1874), p. 329.
[83] Ironically, one case involved the keepers of a master of the York and Ainsty, Sir George Wombwell, *Bell's Life*, January 29, 1876; while the other involved the keepers of a member of the Quorn Committee, E. B. Hartopp of Little Dalby, *Bell's Life*, March 27, 1875; *Field*, XLV(March 27, 1875), p. 316.
[84] *Field*, V(February 3, 1855), p. 69; XXXIX(January 6, 1872), p. 1.
[85] *Sp. Mag.*, CXXXI (January, 1858), p. 5. The Holderness farmers were supposed to have done just that.
[86] The poisoning of a few of the Essex Union hounds in 1874, for example, was thought to be deliberate, though there was never any indication of who was guilty. *Field*, XLIII(April 4, 1874), p. 329.
[87] *Sp. Mag.*, LXXII(July, 1828), pp. 244-247.
[88] *Bell's Life*, February 27, 1842, January 26, 1851; *Baily's Mag.*, XVI (January, 1869), p. 96. One account of vulpicide was headed TREASON. *Bell's Life*, March 24, 1833.

Chapter ten

[1] For some of these, see Kitson Clark, *The Making of Victorian England*, pp. 244-247.
[2] See, for example, the leading article in *The Standard*, November 2, 1875, and the letters in reply in succeeding issues.
[3] *Pall Mall Gazette*, November 19, 1875.
[4] For some contemporary opinion on the depression, see *Parliamentary Papers*, 1897, Vol. XV, 'Final Report of the Royal Commission on the Agricultural Depression'. More modern opinion may be found in T. W. Fletcher, 'The Great Depression of English Agriculture, 1873-1896', *Economic History Review*, 2d Ser. XIII (April, 1961), pp. 417-432. For the way in which non-landed wealth was gaining increased status in one English county even before the depression, see J. M. Lee, *Social Leaders and Public Persons: A Study of County Government in Cheshire Since 1888* (Oxford, 1963), pp. 14-43.
[5] *Evesham Journal*, April 30, 1881.
[6] *Field*, LXVII(May 1, 1886), p. 569.
[7] Andrews, *Fox Hunting Reminiscences of 'Gin and Beer'*, pp. 36-37.

[8] Letter from A. Whitehouse, *Field*, LXIX (January 8, 1887), p. 35.
[9] *Ibid.*, LXVII (May 1, 1886), p. 569.
[10] *Ibid.*, XXXIX (February 24, 1872), p. 171. For the spread of wire, also see: *ibid.*, LXI (January 27, 1883), p. 107; *Baily's Mag.*, XLIX (April, 1888), p. 73; L (November, 1888), p. 70.
[11] Barbed wire fencing was advertised in *The Field* in 1883. *Field*, LXI (January 27, 1883), p. 107. Hunting men began to note its presence in the hunting field by 1887. *Baily's Mag.*, XLVIII (December, 1887), p. 287; XLIX (April, 1888), p. 73.
[12] *The Field*, for example, published letters on the subject in every issue during the 1889-90 season.
[13] For a few out of many see: *Field*, LI (February 16, 1878), p. 188; LXIII (February 16, 1884), p. 214; LXXIV (December 21, 1889), p. 890; *Chelmsford Chronicle*, January 25, 1884.
[14] *Field*, LXXIV (December 21, 1889), pp. 865-866).
[15] *Parliamentary Debates*, 3rd Series, Vol. 341 (February 17, 1890), cols. 437-439.
[16] Randall, *History of the Meynell Hounds*, II, 367.
[17] 'The Future of Hunting', *Murray's Magazine*, April, 1887, p. 529.
[18] *Field*, LXVIII (October 30, 1886), p. 623; *Baily's Mag.*, XLVII (January, 1887), pp. 31-32.
[19] See 'The Future of Hunting', pp. 527-541 for a symposium of thirty-five English and Welsh masters. Those who reported the least trouble were those in whose countries the crowds were smallest and damages slight.
[20] *Field*, LIV, (October 4, 1879), p. 441.
[21] *Field*, LV (February 21, 1880), p. 208; LXV (February 21, 1885), p. 223; *Bell's Life*, February 24, 1880; *Baily's Hunting Directory, 1970-1971*, p. 88.
[22] *VCH Berkshire*, II, 336; *VCH Hertfordshire*, II, 134.
[23] *VCH Lincolnshire*, II, 398-399.
[24] Burton Hunt. MS minute books, notebooks, accounts; *Field*, LXXII (October 20, 1888), p. 557.
[25] *Field*, XLIX (January 27, 1877), p. 83.
[26] Bradley, *Reminiscences of Frank Gillard*, pp. 82-83.
[27] *Ibid.*, p. 243.
[28] MS letter, Alexander Acland Hood to George Luttrell, December 9, 1881. Somerset Record Office, DD/L.
[29] Collins, *History of the Brocklesby Hounds*, p. 139.
[30] *Field*, LXVI (October 24, 1885), p. 577; LXXIII (March 23, 1889), p. 391.
[31] In 1870, 25% of the hunts in England and Wales were hunted by amateurs. As late as 1881, this percentage had only risen to 26%, but in 1886, 38%, and in 1887, 41% of packs had amateur huntsmen. *Baily's Mag.*, XIX (November, 1870), pp. 156-165; XXXVIII (November, 1881), pp. 109-117; XLVIII

(November, 1887), pp. 255-256.

[32] For accounts of members who had to give up maintaining coverts, see Burton Hunt MS minute book; and a printed case submitted to the M.F.H. Association, Berkshire Record Office, D/EW E28.

[33] There were 135 in 1875, 138 in 1878, 141 in 1881, 151 in 1886, and 158 in 1893 according to the annual lists in *The Field*.

[34] Randall, *History of the Meynell Hounds*, II, 18-19, 367; *VCH Derbyshire*, II, 286, 318-319. Between 1877 and 1907, rents depreciated between twenty and thirty per cent.

[35] *Field*, II (January 12, 1877), p. 38; LVII (March 26, 1881), p. 406; Randall, *History of the Meynell Hounds*, II, 64.

[36] Heythrop Hunt. MS accounts book.

[37] Hutchinson, *The Heythrop Hunt*, p. 87.

[38] *VCH Bedfordshire*, II, 134, 137.

[39] Bedford County Record Office, X213/61 pp. 38-40, 63-64; X213/136; X213/140.

[40] *Field*, XXXVII (March 11, 1871), p. 189; *Baily's Mag.*, XXVI (November, 1874), p. 81; *Field*, LXIII (March 8, 1884), p. 320; LXVII (January 30, 1886), p. 121; LXXI (March 24, 1888), p. 397.

[41] Ball and Gilbey, *The Essex Foxhounds*, p. 219.

[42] *Ibid.*, p. 203; *Field*, LXXI (March 24, 1888), p. 397.

[43] Blagg, *History of the North Staffordshire Hounds*, pp. 189, 156; *Field*, XXXV (March 26, 1870), p. 273.

[44] *Bell's Life*, December 13, 1879; Fitt, *Covert-Side Sketches*, pp. 29-30; R. F. Meysey-Thompson, *Reminiscences of the Course, the Camp, the Chase* (London, 1898), p. 312.

[45] 'The Future of Hunting', pp. 531, 534, 537, 540.

[46] *Bell's Life*, November 1, 1879, October 22, 1881.

[47] *Field*, LXXXVIII (December 12, 1891), p. 890.

[48] *Bell's Life*, January 13, 1869.

[49] *Field*, XXXIV (November 20, 1869), p. 434; XLIV (October 31, 1874), p. 455; XLIX (February 17, 1877), p. 169; XLVIII (November 5, 1881), p. 652.

[50] *Ibid.*, LVIII (November 5, 1881), p. 652.

[51] See *Field*, XXII (December 26, 1863), p. 621; *Baily's Mag.*, XI (July, 1866), p. 344.

[52] *Field*, XLIX (January 27, 1877), p. 83. By this reckoning, the man who hunted once a week should have subscribed ten to fifteen pounds per year.

[53] *Baily's Mag.*, XI (July, 1866), p. 345; *Field*, LXIX (January 22, 1887); p. 98.

[54] *Field*, XXII (December 26, 1863), p. 621.

[55] *Bell's Life*, December 22, 1866. Also see the letter from F. W. Bignell, *ibid.*, January 12, 1867.

Notes to Chapter Ten   237

⁵⁶*Baily's Mag.*, XII(January, 1867), p. 311.
⁵⁷*Field*, XLV(February 27, 1875), p. 215; (March 6, 1875), pp. 234-235; *Baily's Mag.*, XXVI(March, 1875), p. 364; XXXV(February, 1880), p. 112.
⁵⁸*Bell's Life*, November 1, 1879.
⁵⁹*Ibid.*
⁶⁰*Baily's Mag.*, XXXV(February, 1880), p. 112.
⁶¹*The Times*, February 14, 1881.
⁶²*Field*, LIX(January 21, 1882), p. 79; LXXVI(November 8, 1890), p. 681; LXXXII(October 28, 1893), p. 644.
⁶³*Ibid.*, LIX(March 4, 1882), p. 277; LXIV(November 8, 1884), p. 632; LXXII(October 27, 1888), p. 599; LXXIII(March 23, 1889), p. 391; LXXVI (November 8, 1890), p. 681, (November 22, 1890), p. 755; Ball and Gilbey, *The Essex Foxhounds*, p. 203; Edward J. F. Tozer, *The South Devon Hunt* (Teignmouth, 1916), p. 196.
⁶⁴Words used in a slightly different context by a writer in *Field*, LXIII (February 23, 1884), p. 241.
⁶⁵*Baily's Hunting Directory, 1918-1920*, p. 4.
⁶⁶See Ball and Gilbey, *The Essex Foxhounds*, p. 203; *Field*, LXXIII(March 23, 1889), p. 391.
⁶⁷*Ibid.*, LXXV(January 4, 1890), p. 6.
⁶⁸By 1897, only slightly more than one-fourth of the packs in the country had imposed a minimum subscription, and only one-tenth collected a cap. *Baily's Fox-Hunting Directory, 1897-98.* As late as 1920, these figures had only increased to slightly more than one-third and one-fifth, respectively. *Ibid., 1918-20.*
⁶⁹*Field*, LXXXII(September 9, 1893), p. 395.
⁷⁰The Pytchley subscriptions jumped by almost £400 the first year the minimum ws instituted, but this was offset by a drop of £290 in subscriptions to the covert and poultry funds as some people presumably switched their contributions from one fund to the other. The subscription remained at the new higher level, however, for only two seasons. Paget, *History of the Althorp and Pytchley Hunt*, pp. 296-300, 316.
⁷¹*Field*, LXXI(March 24, 1888), p. 397.
⁷²*Bell's Life*, January 28, 1865, January 1, 1876.
⁷³For one example, see *Field*, XLII(November 29, 1873), p. 550.
⁷⁴*Baily's Mag.*, XLVII(April, 1887), p. 228.
⁷⁵E.g., *Baily's Mag.*, XLV(December, 1885), p. 100; *Field*, LXV(March 28, 1885), p. 394; LXIX(January 15, 1887), p. 59.
⁷⁶Underhill, *Hunting*, pp. 26-27. For another example, see *Baily's Mag.*, LI (February, 1889), p. 116.
⁷⁷For a list of ten who did, see *Field*, LXXII(December 22, 1888), p. 891. Also see *Baily's Mag.*, LII(January, 1890), p. 60, for an account of one country

Notes to Chapter Ten

in which a fund for this purpose was seen as an alternative to capping.

[78] *Field*, LXVIII (November 20, 1886), p. 737; LXXVII (January 3, 1891), p. 7.

[79] *Ibid.*, LXI (March 24, 1883), p. 379.

[80] Bromley Davenport, 'Fox-Hunting', p. 989.

[81] *Field*, LXXII (December 22, 1888), p. 895; LXXIV (December 11, 1889), p. 890.

[82] Ellis, *Leicestershire and the Quorn*, p. 130 n. 2.

[83] *Field*, LXI (January 27, 1883), p. 107.

[84] *Ibid.*, XXXV (January 1, 1870), p. 13; XXXVIII (November 25, 1871), p. 460.

[85] Blagg, *History of the North Staffordshire Hounds*, p. 139; *Baily's Mag.*, L (November, 1888), p. 70; *Field*, LXXIV (December 28, 1889), p. 924.

[86] *Field*, LXXI (March 10, 1888), p. 320.

[87] *Ibid.*, LXXII (December 8, 1888), p. 815.

[88] *Field*, LXXXIV (November 23, 1889), p. 723; LXXX (November 5, 1892), p. 691.

[89] *Ibid*, LXXX (November 5, 1892), p. 691.

[90] 'Brooksby' endorsed it in 1890, *Baily's Mag.*, LIV (November, 1890), pp. 318-320.

[91] *Ibid.*, p. 319.

[92] Ellis, *Leicestershire and the Quorn*, p. 130; *Baily's Fox-Hunting Directory 1897-98*, p. 135; *Field*, LXXXII (November 11, 1893), p. 724.

[93] Ellis, *Leicestershire and the Quorn*, p. 129 n.1.

[94] *Ibid.*, p. 130.

[95] *Bell's Life*, November 5, 1881.

[96] The Heythrop turned poultry claims over to farmers in 1877. Heythrop Hunt. MS minutes, April 3, 1877. The North Cotswold followed suit around 1886. MS letter, Francis Smith [?] to? November 15, 1895. North Cotswold Hunt MSS. For 'Brooksby', see *Baily's Mag.*, LIV (November, 1890), p. 320.

[97] In 1871, for example, when Lord Guilford proposed to take the East Kent Hounds he called a meeting of landowners and occupiers to get their approval. Kent Archives Office, U471 E40.

[98] See, for example, *Bell's Life*, February 17, 1861.

[99] For the detailed story of the dispute from the vantage point of the respective hunts, see: Ellis, *Leicestershire and the Quorn* and de Costobadie, *Annals of the Billesdon Hunt*.

[100] Ellis, *Leicestershire and the Quorn*, p. 135.

[101] By a strange coincidence, Coupland was also a Liverpool shipping man. It has been suggested that he was so adamant on the subject of the country because he did not want it said in Liverpool that he had knuckled under to the Cunards. *Ibid.*, p. 143.

Notes to Chapter Ten

[102] *Field*, LI(April 20, 1878), p. 457.
[103] Ellis, *Leicestershire and the Quorn*, p. 137.
[104] *Ibid.*, p. 137 n.2. The meeting was fully reported in the *Leicester Advertiser*, March 2, 1878. For the fear of the farmers see the letter from 'H' in *Leicester Journal*, March 29, 1878, and the letter from 'A Tenant Farmer', in *Leicester Daily Mercury*, April 12, 1878, reprinted in *Leicester Journal*, April 12, 1878 and *Leicester Chronicle*, April 13, 1878. But cf. letters from, 'Common Sense' and 'All for one Pack, and that one the far-famed Quorn', *Leicester Journal*, April 5, 1878, for the opposing view.
[105] Ellis, *Leicestershire and the Quorn*, p. 138. See the letter from 'Fact', claiming the committee was not representative of the covert owners. *Field*, LI (April 27, 1878), p. 508.
[106] *Leicester Journal*, April 12, 1878. It would appear that the farmers on the committee were unanimously in favour of Cunard and the landowners were split. Ellis, *Leicestershire and the Quorn*, p. 138.
[107] Ellis, *Leicestershire and the Quorn*, p. 138.
[108] E.g., *Field*, LI(April 13, 1878), p. 434; (April 20, 1878), p. 457; (April 27, 1878), pp. 508, 511; (May 4, 1878), pp. 518-519.
[109] Cf. letter from 'A Tenant Farmer', *Leicester Daily Mercury*, April 12, 1878, reprinted in *Leicester Journal*, April 12, 1878; *Leicester Advertiser*, leading article, April 13, 1878; letter from 'Fact', *Field*, LI (April 27, 1878), p. 508; Letter from A. H. Baillie, secretary of the Billesdon committee, *Leicester Advertiser*, April 27, 1878.
[110] Letter from Sir Arthur Hazlerigg, *Field*, LI (April 6, 1878), p. 403; letter from A. H. Baillie, *Leicester Advertiser*, April 27, 1878.
[111] *Leicester Journal*, April 12, 1878.
[112] Letter from 'A Tenant Farmer', *ibid.*; letter from G. V. Braithwaite, *Field*, LI(May 4, 1878), p. 518.
[113] *Ibid.*, LIII(February 22, 1879), p. 202.
[114] *Ibid.*, LII(March 22, 1879), p. 320.
[115] *Baily's Mag.*, XXXIII(June, 1879), pp. 26-27.
[116] Ellis, *Leicestershire and the Quorn*, pp. 141-142. In the end the countries were never reunited and the Billesdon is now known as the Fernie Hunt, in honour of the man who succeeded Cunard.
[117] *Ibid.*, p. 142 n.3.
[118] *Ibid.*, pp. 145-147.
[119] *VCH Berkshire*, II, 336.
[120] Bathurst, *History of the V.W.H. Country*, p. 161; *Wilts and Gloucestershire Standard*, May 2, 1885.
[121] *Summer v. Kingscote*, *Wilts and Gloucestershire Standard*, March 21, 1885.
[122] *Ibid.*, April 11, 1885; Bathurst, *History of the V.W.H. Country*, p. 163.
[123] Detailed minutes of the meeting are in *Wilts and Gloucestershire Standard*,

May 2, 1885.
[124] *Ibid.*
[125] *Ibid.*
[126] Bathurst, *History of the V.W.H. Country*, p. 168.
[127] *Ibid.*, p. 169.
[128] Letter from W. Garne, *Wilts and Gloucestershire Standard*, September 26, 1885; letter from George Beake, *ibid.*, October 24, 1885.
[129] E.g., by 'Borderer', *Baily's Mag.*, XLV (January, 1886), pp. 138-139.
[130] Bathurst, *History of the V.W.H. Country*, pp. 172-173. The country was divided, Hoare keeping enough for two days' hunting, and Lord Bathurst the rest.
[131] In 1886, for example, H. H. Langham resigned as master of the Pytchley when the hunt was in financial trouble. At a meeting to select his successor, the farmers were able to insist that he remain. He was popular for buying horses and forage from local farmers. Paget, *History of the Althorp and Pytchley Hunt*, p. 209.
[132] Quarrell, *The Worcestershire Hunt*, p. 129.
[133] Randall, *History of the Meynell Hounds and Country*, II, 67, 152, 369.
[134] Taunton Vale Foxhounds. MS minutes, January 28, 1888.
[135] *Ibid.*, September 22, 1888.
[136] *Field*, LXXVI (December 13, 1890), p. 862.

Index

"Acastus" (pseud.): 7
agricultural depression: 88, 92, 113, 118–119, 130, 149, 152–175, 176, 178, 179; masters give up hounds: 157–158
Albrighton Hunt: see hunts
Althorpe, Lord, M.F.H.: 75, 83
American Senator, The (Trollope): 22
Andrew, John, M.F.H.: 93
animals, attitude of foxhunters toward domestic: 141–142; cruelty to: see cruelty to animals
Annaly, Lord, M.F.H.: 83
Apperley, Charles James: see Nimrod
Arkwright family, M.F.H.: 88
army officers, avid foxhunters: 21
Assheton Smith, Thomas, M.F.H.: 54, 87; attacked for fostering idleness: 137–138; biography and career: 85–86
Astley, Sir Jacob: 147
Atherstone Hunt: see hunts
Atherstone Hunt Club: 132

Badsworth Hunt: see hunts
Bagot, A. G.: 118
Baily's Magazine: 56, 122, 162; founding of: 60; on hunting and rinderpest: 128; on wire: 125
Baker, George, M.F.H.: 76, 88
balls: see hunt balls
Bathurst, Lord, M.F.H.: 172
Beaufort, Dukes of, M.F.H.: 24, 26, 38, 74, 76, 120, 156

Beckford, Peter: 7, 12, 13, 14, 18; denounced for flogging hounds: 139–140; on hunting law: 71
Bedford, Dukes of: 159
Bell family, M.F.H.: 93
Bell's Life in London: 24, 40, 59, 62, 162
Belvoir Hunt: see hunts
Berkeley, fifth Earl, M.F.H.: 70
Berkeley, Grantley, on cruelty to animals: 141–142
Bicester Hunt: see hunts
Billesdon Hunt: see hunts
Bilsdale Hunt: see hunts
Birmingham Hunt Club: 59
Birmingham sportsmen: 59
Blaine, Delabere: 21
Blane, William: 18, 20
blooding: 4
Boodle's Club: 73
"Borderer" (pseud.): 166
Braes of Derwent Hunt: see hunts
Bramham Moor Hunt: see hunts
Brassey, Albert, M.F.H.: 158
Brocklesby Hunt: see hunts
"Brooksby" (E. Pennell-Elmhirst): 56, 169
bull-baiting, considered more cruel than hunting: 140
Burdett, Sir Francis: 23
Burton Hunt: see hunts

Cambridgeshire Hounds: see hunts
canals, attitude of foxhunters toward: 50
Capel, Hon. & Rev. William: 69

capping: 161, 164, 169
Cardigan, Lord, a Meltonian: 21
cattle-plague: see rinderpest
"Cecil" (pseud.): 73, 92
Chaplin, Henry, M.F.H.: 48, 52, 54
charity events: 104
Chartism: 23
Cheltenham, hunting centre: 55
Cheshire Difficulty: 56, 89–90
Chesterfield, Lord: 135, 136
chimney-sweep, hunting: 24, 26, 38, 102
Christ Church College, Oxford: 48
Christian, Dick: 38, 97
cities, attitudes towards city sportsmen: 41; growth of: 20, 23, 178; railways aid city dwellers: 52; sportsmen: 39–42, 58–60, 159, 164
clergy, as M.F.H.: 36; hunting: 22, 35–38; hunting, attitudes toward: 36–38, 65–66; opposition to hunting clergy: 136
Cleveland Hunt: see hunts
Clowes, S. W., M.F.H.: 109–112
Cobbett, William: 23, 25, 100, 101
cockney sportsman stories: 40–42
Combe, Harvey, M.F.H.: 92
committees: see hunt committees
Conyers, Henry John, M.F.H.: 41, 89, 132
Cook, Colonel John, M.F.H.: 7, 13, 84, 91; on costs of keeping hounds: 78; on farmers: 114
Corbet, John, M.F.H.: 84
Cotswold Hunt: see hunts
Cottesmore Hunt: see hunts
country life: 22; benefits of: 18–20
Coupland, J. R., M.F.H.: 170–172
Coupland-Cunard controversy: 170–172
covert owners: 67, 76, 89–90; choose new M.F.H.: 78; rights: 71–72
covert rent: 119
Cowper, William: 135; hatred of cruelty: 139
Craven Hunt: see hunts
Crimea: 20
Croydon, hunting centre: 40
cruelty to animals: 139–146; Cowper on: 135; not a major factor in opposition: 135
cubhunting: 122
Cunard, Sir Bache, M.F.H.: 170–172
Curnock, Sam, foot follower: 102

Dale, T. F.: 167
damage, claims soar: 156; compensation: 117–118; crops and fences: 60, 114, 115, 154, 156, 169–170; farmers attitude toward: 121–128
damage and poultry fund: 118, 162; voluntary by law: 118
damage fund: 61, 169
Daniel, Rev. William: 36–37
Darlington, Lord, M.F.H.: 19
Davenport, William Bromley: 146
deer hunting: 39–40
deference: 89, 119, 177, 178, 179
depression: see agricultural depression
Derbyshire Hunt: see hunts
dinners: see hunt dinners
disputes, among hunts: 72–73
Dorset Hounds: see hunts
Drake, T. T., M.F.H.: 83
"Druid, The," (pseud.): 97
DuCane, Charles: 107–109, 111
Durham County Hunt: see hunts

earthstopper: 97
East Essex Hunt: see hunts
East Sussex Hunt: see hunts
Ellenborough, Lord: 69
Ellis, C. D. B.: 46
Empson, Rev. J.: 46
enclosure: 44
Essex, Earl of: 68–69
Essex Hunt: see hunts
Essex Union Hunt: see hunts
Essex v. Capel: 41, 68–69, 121, 130–131, 162
Exmoor Hunt: see hunts

farmers, allow land to be ridden over: 28; as M.F.H.: 33, 93; attitudes of foxhunters toward: 114–115, 149; attitudes toward damage: 121–128; at-

Index

titudes toward foxes: 114; attitudes toward hunting: 114–116, 126, 129–134, 152–175, 179; attitudes toward university undergraduates: 48; benefit from hunting: 115, 132–134; consulted on M.F.H. choice: 78; conflict with landlords: 171–173; dissatisfied with hunting in Leics.: 111–112; do not subscribe to hounds: 35, 165; foxhunters' attitudes toward: 159–160, 167–168; foxhunting their special sport: 64; gain voice in management of hunting: 169–175; hunt in shires: 47; hunting: 25, 26, 31, 33, 65; hunting expenses: 32; hunting opposed by moralists: 34; image for foxhunters: 113–114; in Yorkshire known as avid sportsmen: 34; little say in hunt management: 35; must be conciliated: 82; natural hunting men: 32; on hunt committees: 174; opposition to hunting: 129–134, 146, 152; preserve foxes; 116, 119; pressure from landlords: 116–117; relations with foxhunting: 41, 113–134; sell produce to foxhunters: 166; serve on hunt committee: 119; served by foxhunting: 18; subscribe to hunt: 64; vulpicide: 116–117; walk pups: 119–121
farmer's hunt: 64
farming, scientific, 152–153
Farquharson, J. J., M.F.H.: 92; fiftieth anniversary celebration: 104; resignation: 105–106
fences: 55, 123; barbed wire: 155, 168; wire: 123–125, 155, 167, 168
Field, The: 28, 29, 124; attitudes to railways: 51; founding of: 59; on hunting and rinderpest: 128; on wire: 125
Field Sports Protection and Encouragement Association: 145–146
finance: see hunt finance
Firr, Tom, huntsman: 95, 96
Fitzhardinge, Earls, M.F.H.: 120
Fitzwilliam, Hon. T. W., M.F.H.: 83
Fitzwilliam Hunt: see hunts
foot followers: 101–102, 165–166

Fortnightly Review, publishes Freeman's attack on hunting: 143
fox killing: see vulpicide
foxes, can cause damage: 114; controlled by hunting: 117–118; vermin: 25
foxhunters, social background: 26, 31–49, 50–66
foxhunting, anachronistic in 1850: 138; avenue of social advancement: 29; committees: see hunt committees; conservative force: 177; costs: 32; emerges as national sport: 15–16; fashionable: 12, 53–54, 136; finance; see hunt finance; fosters aristrocratic values: 27; healthful exercise: 19; influence on local economy: 104–105; institutionalization: 67–80; justification: 17–30, 47; law: 70, 71–74; means of social advancement: 58; mirrors values of society: 178; mystique of: 116; myth and ideal: 17–30; national institution: 16; not considered cruel: 139–140; open to all: 23, 25, 161, 177; organized to do little damage: 122; origins: 6–8; part of rural society: 99; political impact: see politics; popular entertainment: 65; popular image of: 176; popularity: 10–13, 72, 77, 84, 99, 100; public entertainment: 100–101; social benefits of: 176; social bond in rural society: 120; social *cachet* of: 29; social consequences: 1, 12, 19; social exclusiveness: 62; social prestige: 12; sport of boors: 18; sport of country gentlemen: 29; symbol of local pride: 105–106; techniques: 2–4; unifies all classes: 24–29, 33, 61, 63, 176; uniquely British: 122; values: 27–28
Freeman, E. A.: 143–145
Freeman-Trollope controversy: 143–145
Frewen, C. H.: 109–112

game laws: 25, 64, 114; prevent farmers from shooting: 32
game preservers: 82; oppose hunting: 146–150
gates hunting: 55

gentry, predominate in hunting field: 31
Gifford, Lord, M.F.H.: 72
Gillard, Frank, huntsman: 95
Gilpin, Rev. William: 37; opposition to hunting: 136
Goodall family, huntsmen: 94
Goodall, Will: 20
Goodricke, Sir Harry, M.F.H.: 131; popularity: 102–103
Gosling, Robert, M.F.H.: 157
Graham, Sir Bellingham, M.F.H.: 77, 79, 131
Graham, Sir Reginald, M.F.H.: 104
Grey de Wilton, Lady: 56
Grogan, Edward, M.P.: 149
Grosvenor, Lady Theodora: 56
Gundry v. Feltham: 68–69

Halford, Sir Henry: 170
Hambledon Hunt: see hunts
Hampshire Hunt: see hunts
Hare, The: 140
hare hunting, losing ground to foxhunting: 11–13
harriers: 11
'Harry Hieover" (pseud.): 28, 62
Hatfield Hunt: see hunts
Hawkes, John: 24
Hazlerigg, Sir Arthur: 172
Hertfordshire Hounds: see hunts
Heythrop Hunt: see hunts
Hill family, huntsmen: 94
Hoare, C. A. R., M.F.H.: 156, 172–174
Holderness Hunt: see hunts
horse breeding: 34–35, 115; does not pay: 135; in Leicestershire: 47–48
horse racing: 35, 103, 104
horse shows: 104
horsedealers: 38
horses, costs and expenses: 31–32, 44, 45, 46, 83; foxhunting promotes breeding: 23; hired: 42; number needed to hunt: 31; second horse system: 43
hospitality, valued by foxhunters: 27
hound poisoning: 148
hound shows: 103, 104
hounds, costs: 82; 18th century: 7; speed: 10; speed of Meynell's: 8
Humanitarian League, does not attack foxhunting: 145
Hunt, Henry: 23
hunt balls: 103; social status of guests: 103–104
hunt club: 103
hunt committee: 77–78, 87, 88, 90; includes farmers: 119
hunt dinners: 103; social status of guests: 104
hunt finance: 61, 78–80, 83, 156–158
hunt servants: 94–97; fired during depression: 158; salary and perquisites: 95–96
Hunts Servants Benefit Society: 96–97, 162
hunt service, family tradition: 94
hunting: see foxhunting, harehunting, deerhunting
hunting people: see foxhunters
hunts,
  Albrighton: 77
  Atherstone: 79, 83, 168
  Badsworth: 86
  Belvoir: 9, 33, 43, 74
  Bicester: 83
  Billesdon: 57, 169–172
  Bilsdale: 33, 64, 93
  Braes of Derwent: 79, 83
  Bramham Moor: 59
  Brocklesby: 33, 64, 74
  Burton: 52, 86, 118, 121, 157
  Cambridgeshire: 11
  Cleveland: 78, 93
  Cotswold: 104
  Cottesmore: 9, 43, 46, 169
  Craven: 47, 64, 78, 157
  Derbyshire: 86
  Dorset: 104, 105
  Durham County: 76, 88
  East Essex: 64
  East Sussex: 80
  Essex: 41, 88, 89, 159
  Essex Union: 79
  Exmoor: 83
  Fitzwilliam: 83

Index

Hambledon: 86
Hampshire: 35, 79, 83
Hatfield: 49
Hertfordshire: 82
Heythrop: 79, 83, 87, 158
Holderness: 51, 53
Hurworth Hounds: 93
Lamerton: 93
Meynell: 79, 156, 158, 159, 174
New Forest: 88, 89, 90
Newmarket and Thurlow: 93
North Cotswold: 79, 154
North Devon: 121
North Staffs: 60, 159
North Warwickshire: 101, 164
Northumberland: 78
Oakley, 75, 79, 90, 127, 159
Old Berkeley: 68–69, 162
Old Berkshire Hounds: 24, 36, 71, 72
Old Surrey: 84
Puckeridge: 157
Pytchley: 75, 83, 84, 86, 101
Quarley Hounds: 75, 77
Quorn: 21, 43, 46, 51, 57, 79, 86, 102, 103, 119, 124, 162, 167, 169, 174
Rufford Hounds: 28
Sinnington: 33, 93
South Berkshire: 174
South Down: 52
South Durham: 64
South Essex: 64
South Notts: 86
South Staffs: 164
Southwold: 86
Suffolk: 104
Surrey: 58
Surrey Subscription: 42
Taunton Vale: 119, 174
Tedworth: 86
Thurlow: 84, 86
V.W.H.: 72, 169, 172
Warwickshire: 78, 84
West Somerset: 78
Whaddon Chase: 164
Worcestershire: 79, 174
huntsman: 2–3; duties: 81, 94; social position: 95
Hurworth Hounds: see hunts

industrialization: 23
Innkeepers: 38
Ireland, opposition to hunting as symbol of England: 138, 150

"Jorrocks, Mr.": 15, 41, 51
journalism, sporting: 10, 40, 59–60; changes as result of railways: 54; growth of: 13–15

kennel rent: 89
Kingsley, Rev. Charles: 22, 65, 137

Lambton, Ralph John, M.F.H.: 76
Lamerton Hunt: see hunts
landlords, dispute with farmers: 172–173; pressure on farmers: 116–117; tension between and tenants: 152
landowners, accept M.F.H.: 84; oppose hunting: 146; rights: 67–69, 171; sporting rights: 121–122; welcome Meynell to Leics.: 8
Lang, Cosmo Gordon, Archbishop of York: 65–66
largesse: 119; ideal: 61; valued by foxhunters: 27
Lawrence, John: 140
League Against Cruel Sports: 107
Leamington Spa, hunting centre: 55
Leicester, social centre for sportsmen: 9; best hunting ground in England: 8
Leicestershire, best hunting ground in England: 8; hunting centre: 12–13
Littleton, Sir Edward, M.F.H.: 74
Liverpool sportsmen: 59
Lloyd, Rev. Griff: 37
Lockhart, J. G.: 15, 137
Londoners, hunt in Essex: 159, hunting expenses: 32, hunt using railways: 52; also see, cities, sportsmen
Long family, M.F.H.: 88
Lonsdale, Lord, M.F.H.: 21, 166, 167, 169
Loughborough: 111; social centre for

sportsmen: 9
Lowth, Rev. Robert: 36
Lowther, Sir William, M.F.H.: 9
Luttrell, George: 158

M.F.H.: 81–94; above all reproach: 58; advertise for new: 87–88; agent of subscribers: 90; as huntsman: 87; choice of new: 77–78; 87–89; duties: 81–82; expenses: 82–83; family traditions: 88; independence eroded: 89; independent gentleman: 89; itinerant: 85–87; local men: 88; morality of: 172; non-gentry: 91–94; popularity with local people: 101–103; power: 90–91; private ownership: 74; a public figure: 90; qualifications: 81; should not get involved in politics: 106; social background: 84–94; standards expected of M.F.H.: 56; status: 84
Mainwaring, Arthur, M.F.H.: 89
Maldon, Lord, M.F.H.: 162
Mark Lane Express, on wire: 125
Manchester sportsmen: 59
manliness, foxhunting promotes: 21–22
Manners, Lord John: 109–112
Manners, Sir William: 106
Marriott, Richard, M.F.H.: 108
Marsh, Thomas, alias Walker: 141
Master of foxhounds: see M.F.H.
Masters of Foxhounds Association: 73
Masters of Foxhounds Committee: 73, 90, 171
Melton Mowbray: 9, 42–48, 111; expenses: 45, 46; a masculine society: 45; social attitudes at: 47
Meltonians: 9–10, 31, 42–48, 123; "birds of passage": 46; changing character of: 55
merchants, serve foxhunters: 126
Meynell, Hugo: 43, 176; attitude toward farmers: 33; career of: 7–10; increases popularity of hunting: 11–12
Meynell Hunt: see hunts
Middleton, Lord: 157
Military: see War, Army Officers
Monson, Lord, M.F.H.: 121

Monthly Review, attacks Peter Beckford: 139–140
Moreton, Hon Henry, M.F.H.: 72
Morland, T. T., M.F.H.: 72
Morrell, James, M.F.H.: 92
muscular Christianity: 65
Musters, John, M.F.H.: 85, 87, 147; biography and career: 86
Musters family, M.F.H.: 88

National Sports Protection and Defence Association: see Field Sports Protection and Encouragement Association
New Forest Hunt: see hunts
Newmarket and Thurlow Hunt: see hunts
Nimrod: 13, 23, 32, 33, 45, 46, 47, 87, 123, 132; attitude toward city sportsmen: 42; attitude toward farmers: 35, 114–115; career: 14–15; on refinement of foxhunters: 136; popularity: 15; reaction to railway: 50
North Cotswold Hunt: see hunts
North Devon Hunt: see hunts
North Staffs Hunt: see hunts
North Warwickshire Hunt: see hunts
Northumberland Hunt: see hunts
Notitia Venatica (Vyner): 20

Oakeley, W. E., M.F.H.: 167, 168
Oakley Hunt: see hunts
Observations on Fox-Hunting: 13
Old Berkeley Hunt: see hunts
Old Berkshire Hounds: see hunts
Old Surrey Hunt, see hunts
opposition to hunting: 129–150; by farmers and landlords: 146; by shooters and game preservers: 146–150; cruelty not a major factor: 135; cruelty to animals: see cruelty to animals; farmers: 152; foxhunters as country bumpkins: 135; hunting a waste of time: 137–138; hunting causes neglect of duty: 137–138; hunting leads to immorality: 136; political grounds: 138; also see vulpicide.
Osbaldeston, George, M.F.H.: 45, 46,

48, 54, 55, 85, 102; biography and career: 86
outsiders, resentment toward: 160

Paget, E. A.: 124
Pall Mall Gazette: 152–153
Parker, John, M.F.H.: 93
Parrington, Thomas, M.F.H.: 93
parsons: see clergy
Partridge, Robert: 107–108
patriotism, inspired by foxhunting: 23
Peel, Sir Robert (son of the statesman): 106–107
Pennell-Elmhirst, E.: see "Brooksby"
Penrhyn, Lord, M.F.H.: 132
Petre, Lord, M.F.H., on duties of M.F.H.: 82
Phillpotts, Henry, Bishop of Exeter: 36
politics: 106–112; North Essex Election, 1865: 107–109; North Leicestershire Election, 1868: 109–112; opposition to hunting: 138
poultry fund: 158, 169
Price, Bob, huntsman: 96
private packs: 74
property rights: 67–69
Puckeridge Hunt: see hunts
Punch, pro-hunting: 137
puppy walking: 119–121, 132
Pytchley Hunt: see hunts

Quarley Hounds: see hunts
Quarterly Review: 47; publishes Nimrod: 15
Quorn Hall: 8–9
Quorn Hunt: see hunts

R.S.P.C.A., never attacks hunting: 142
radicals, attitudes toward hunting: 23, 109, 138
railway boom: 48
railways, aid to foxhunting: 51–53; attitudes of foxhunters toward: 50; break down distinctions between town and country: 53; cost: 52; effects on foxhunting: 50–66, 176, 177–178; hunting tickets: 52; increase popularity of foxhunting: 53
resort cities as hunting centres: 48
Ricardo, G. C., M.F.H., on costs of keeping hounds: 78
riding, fashion in shires: 43–44
rinderpest, epidemic of 1865–66: 128–129
Rolle, Hon. Mark, M.F.H.: 121
roughriders: 38, 97
Rounding brothers: 84
Royal Agricultural Benevolent Institution: 167
Rufford Hounds: see hunts
Rugby, hunting centre: 55
rural community, breakup during agricultural depression: 154
rural life: 99–112
Rural Sports: 36–37
Russell, Rev. John (Jack Russell): 36
Rutland, Dukes of, M.F.H.: 9, 74, 106, 109–112, 120, 157; on wire: 124

S.P.C.A.: see R.S.P.C.A.
Salisbury, Marchioness of, M.F.H.: 49
Sandford and Merton: 140
Saturday Review, attitudes toward hunting clergy: 65; on cruelty to animals: 145
Scrutator (pseud.): 26; on Skittles case: 57
Sefton, Lord, M.F.H.: 43, 44, 77, 84
Selby Lowndes, W., M.F.H.: 161, 162
sexual morality: 56–57
Shenstone, William: 135
shires: 10, 39, 55
shooters: 28; oppose hunting: 146–150
shooting, conflicts with foxhunting: 28
Sinnington Hunt: see hunts
Skittles: 57–58
Smith, Will, huntsman: 122
Smith family, huntsmen: 94
snobbery: 62
social pretentions: 62
South Berkshire Hunt: see hunts
South Down Hunt: see hunts
South Durham Hunt: see hunts
South Essex Hunt: see hunts
South Notts Hunt: see hunts
South Staffs Hunt: see hunts

Southwold Hunt: see hunts
Spectator, on cruelty to animals: 144–145
sporting journalism: see journalism, sporting
Sporting Magazine, The: 7, 10, 12, 13, 24, 39, 41, 45, 75; founding and early history: 14; growth of: 15; on wire: 125; railway map: 51
Stamford, Lady: 57
Stamford, Lord, M.F.H.: 130
stockingers: 102
Styles, John: 142
Sutherland, Duke of, M.F.H.: 168
Sykes, Sir Tatton, M.F.H.: 92
subscribers: 88, 89–90; choose new M.F.H.: 77–78; influence: 82
subscription packs: 76–77; financial problems: 80; origins: 74–75
subscriptions: 27, 32, 60, 76, 79, 82, 157, 158; amount: 80; minimum, opposition to: 164; required or minimum: 161–165; voluntary: 61
Suffield, Lord. M.F.H.: 88
Suffolk Hunt: see hunts
Sumner, Arther Holme: 172
Sumner, Beatrice Holme: 172
Surrey, hunting in: 40
Surrey Hunt: see hunts
Surrey Subscription Hunt: see hunts
Surtees, Robert Smith: 15, 33, 38, 41, 53, 62, 93; attitude toward railways: 50–51; on farmers: 121; on qualifications of M.F.H.: 81

Tailby, W. W., M.F.H.: 57–58, 112, 170
Taunton Vale Foxhounds: see hunts
Tavistock, Marquis of, M.F.H.: 75
Tedworth Hunt: see hunts
Thoughts on Hunting: 13
Thurlow Hunt: see hunts
Tilbury, John: 42
Times, The: 26; on hunting and rinderpest: 128; publishes attack on Assheton Smith: 137
Torrington, Lord: 19

Tower, C. T., M.F.H.: 88
Trollope, Anthony: 22, 90, 137; controversy with E. A. Freeman: 143–145

universities, foxhunting at: 48
urbanization: see cities

V. W. H. Hunt: see hunts
"Van Driver" (pseud.): 162, 163
Villebois, John H., M.F.H.: 35
Villebois family: 92
volunteer movement: 105
vulpicide: 107–108, 116–117, 118, 128, 129–130, 148, 149, 150, 154, 155
Vyner, Robert: 20, 73

Wales, Prince of: 12
Walters, Catherine: see Skittles
war, foxhunting as training for: 20–21; Revolutionary and Napoleonic: 12
Warde, John, M.F.H.: 47, 84; career: 85
Warwickshire Hunt: see hunts
West Somerset Hunt: see hunts
Westminster, Marchioness of: 56
Whaddon Chase Hunt: see hunts
Wheble, John: 14
Whipper-in: 3, duties: 95
Whitbread, S. C.: 159
Whyte Melville, George: 54, 60
Williams, Percy: 147
Willoughby de Broke, Lord, M.F.H.: 54; on status of M.F.H.: 84
Wilson, Harriette: 45
Wilson, Wharton, M.F.H.: 132
Wilson, William, M.F.H.: 83
wire fences: see fences, wire
women; at Melton Mowbray: 45; attitudes toward women foxhunters: 56; do not hunt in early 19th century: 48; hunt: 136; hunting in increasing numbers: 55–56
Worcestershire Hunt: see hunts

Yarborough, Countess of: 56
Yarborough, Earls of, M.F.H.: 33, 74; sell hounds during depression: 158

www.ingramcontent.com/pod-product-compliance
Lightning Source LLC
Chambersburg PA
CBHW060947230426
43665CB00015B/2089